Bipolar Kids

Bipolar Kids

Helping Your Child
Find Calm in the Mood Storm

ROSALIE GREENBERG, MD

Da Capo
LIFE
LONG
A Member of the Perseus Books Group

Many of the designations used by manufacturers and sellers to distinguish their products are
claimed as trademarks. Where those designations appear in this book and Da Capo Press was
aware of a trademark claim, those designations have been printed with initial capital letters.

Grateful acknowledgment is made for the following previously published material:
Churchill Papers at the Churchill Archives Centre, Cambridge University, www.winstonchurchill.org
Diagnostic and Statistical Manual of Mental Disorders,
fourth edition text revision (2000), excerpts reprinted with
permission from the American Psychiatric Association
Physicians' Desk Reference, 60th ed. (2006), Thomson PDR, Montvale, New Jersey.

Designed by Trish Wilkinson
Set in 11.5-point Goudy by the Perseus Books Group

Library of Congress Cataloging-in-Publication Data

Greenberg, Rosalie.
    Bipolar kids : helping your child find calm in the storm / Rosalie Greenberg. — 1st Da Capo press ed.
        p.   cm.
    Includes bibliographical references.
    ISBN 0-7382-1080-3 (hardcover : alk. paper) 1. Manic-depressive illness in children. I. Title.
RJ506.D4G74 2007
618.92'895—dc22   2006101127

First Da Capo Press edition 2007

Published by Da Capo Press
A Member of the Perseus Books Group
www.dacapopress.com

Note: The information in this book is true and complete to the best of our knowledge.
This book is intended only as an informative guide for those wishing to know more about health issues.
In no way is this book intended to replace, countermand, or conflict with the advice given
to you by your own physician. The ultimate decision concerning care should be made between you
and your doctor. We strongly recommend you follow his or her advice. Information in this
book is general and is offered with no guarantees on the part of the authors of Da Capo Press.
The authors and publisher disclaim all liability in connection with the use of this book.
The names and identifying details of people associated with events described in
this book have been changed. Any similarity to actual persons is coincidental.

Da Capo Press books are available at special discounts for bulk purchases in the U.S. by corporations,
institutions, and other organizations. For more information, please contact the Special Markets
Department at the Perseus Books Group, 11 Cambridge Center, Cambridge, MA 02142,
or call (800) 255-1514 or (617) 252-5298, or email special.markets@perseusbooks.com.

10 9 8 7 6 5 4 3 2 1

To my parents, Molly and Sam,
who taught me the importance of
helping those who speak with none to hear,
and lending a heart to those who cry with none to listen.

Contents

Acknowledgments

This book may have my name as the author but as anyone who has spent any time with me over the last several months knows, it has really been the work of seemingly countless people and hours.

Most important, this book could not have been written without the patients and their families in my practice who have generously allowed me to share their stories in the pages of this book, in the hope of helping others. To you, I send a heartfelt "thank-you."

My agent Molly Lyons introduced me to the world of publishing and helped this book become a reality. Thanks for your vision and your encouragement. Wendy Holt, my editor at Da Capo Press, has been amazing; planning a wedding would be enough of a task for anyone, but to work so hard to review, change, and try to perfect a manuscript at the same time is an unbelievable feat. I am very grateful. Thank you to Lissa Warren, my publicist for increasing the mass media's awareness of pediatric bipolar disorder. I would like to thank Annetta K. Miller for her help with the manuscript. Her sensitivity, facility with words, love of these children, and her great sense of humor were invaluable in writing this book.

I am also truly grateful for the support, encouragement, late night sessions, and exceptional writing talents of Shawn Ortiz. Thanks to Carlos and Andres for sharing her with me. I have also been very lucky to have my close friends and colleagues offer to read, add input, and reread the manuscript, during these past several months: Faye

Brady, LCW; Michael Osit, PhD; Regina Peter, EdD; Lois Tigay, MSW; Robin Shimel, LCSW; and the Davis and Pyne families. I hope you know how much I appreciate all that you have done to help in this endeavor.

To Faye Cunningham, the woman who made sure my deadlines got met and that my office runs efficiently, thank you. A special thanks as well to Lynne Weisberg, MD; Mary Fristad, PhD; and Stefanie A. Hlastala, PhD for their help with the manuscript.

A warm thank-you to my sister-in-law Claudette Spano for her creative input.

There are not enough words to say thank you to Jackie Tull, a very special woman who helps make daily life run smoothly for my entire family. I am also grateful for the help my brother-in-law, Amos Gern, provided during this whole process. My sister, Evelyn Gern, has been more than anyone could ask for in a sister. I thank her for her unflagging faith in me throughout our lives together. Her support, encouragement, and love, would have made our parents proud.

I thank the major men in my world—my husband Soly Baredes, MD, and my sons, Ryan and Matthew, for putting up with me being unavailable for so many months. Their support, both mental and physical (including doing the laundry), continually teaches me about life's riches. I am truly blessed to have the three of you as the center in my life. And last but not least, "Thanks" to Sunny, my special four-legged friend, for making sure I didn't get too much sleep.

Introduction

My mood swings like a pendulum. Sometimes it swings in one direction and I'm way too happy, and sometimes it swings to the other side and I'm way too sad. But why can't I be right in the middle—and just normal?   —JORDAN, 11

When I'm angry, the bad side of my brain that's red takes over the good side of my brain that's white.   —JOANNA, 10

I know more about math than the teacher. She should let me teach the class.   —BILLY, 12

I want to die because I feel so lonely even with people around.
                                                          —CARLOS, 9

Why doesn't God care about me?   —SOPHIE, 11

My mind is too busy . . . racing. I think about different parts of a book I read . . . about school the next day, things like that, and then I end up thinking about fifty things at once.   —HARRY, 8

Mom, I made you a museum to cheer you up. See, I drew five paintings on the wall.   —NATALIE, 5

The voices of children with bipolar disorder can be brimming with sweetness, creativity, empathy, and humor. But too often, they are overflowing with pain, anger, opposition, and despair—unwelcome by-products of an illness that until recently was not even believed to exist in children.

As a child and adolescent psychiatrist specializing in juvenile onset bipolar disorder, I have treated children with mood disorders for twenty-five years, and I learn something new from my patients every day. "My kids," as I call them, are a wonderful bunch. They face tremendous challenges in their lives; just getting out of bed in the morning can be a monumental effort for many of them. Yet time after time, they are blessed with spirit, imagination, and an amazing ability to think outside the box. They never cease to surprise me with the things they say, be they tremendously precocious, deeply introspective, or simply outrageous.

Many of my kids have spent years being misunderstood by family members, teachers, neighbors, peers, and even therapists and doctors. And the kids aren't the only ones whose behavior is misinterpreted. Parents of bipolar kids get their fair share of misunderstanding, too. When a child acts out in the classroom, throws a baseball through the neighbor's window, or has trouble getting to school in the morning, at whom do the fingers point? At the people who raised him, of course. I can't tell you how many of my kids' mothers and fathers have been sent to parenting classes. Some have been to so many of these classes that they could probably teach the subject themselves.

In reality, the vast majority of the troublesome behaviors bipolar children display are not driven by willful disobedience or by inadequate parenting. Instead, these behaviors are the result of an unforgiving biology that affects kids' developing brains.

Bipolar disorder, previously known as manic depression, is commonly defined as alternating periods of mania and depression. Until the 1990s, doctors thought the condition affected only adults. It's now known, however, that children can and do have bipolar disorder. But in the majority of cases, they experience it much differently than grown-ups. A child may be overly active, giddy, bossy, and oppositional in the afternoon and by bedtime become tearful and afraid to sleep alone because she's thinking about her hamster that died three years ago. Another child may one minute be making grand plans for the Halloween costume he'll wear months later and the next be devastated because he's told he can't have pizza for dinner (which he had the night before).

In many youngsters, bipolar disorder goes unrecognized for years. A recent study by the National Depressive and Manic-Depressive Association (NDMDA) shows that many adults struggle with symptoms of bipolar disorder for an average of ten years before the illness is even discovered and labeled.[1] In children, who are harder to assess, the diagnostic interval may be even longer. That said, an estimated half a million to a million children in the United States are thought to have the condition.[2]

My goal in writing this book is to help you, whether you're a parent, caregiver, teacher, therapist, doctor, or other concerned adult, to get the proper diagnosis for your child and then learn to see bipolar youngsters in a new way—to celebrate the brilliance, the kindness, and the gusto for life that these kids invariably possess. So often, it seems to me that no one is actually *listening* to what these kids are saying. Over the years, I have learned that children, even very young ones, can be much more aware of how they feel than grown-ups realize. Careful attention to their words can give the listener an invaluable glimpse into these kids' inner emotional world—the pain, the anger, the joy—that helps explain the unusual behavior they often exhibit.

One of the things that makes helping a bipolar child so difficult is that the disorder's symptoms are routinely mistaken for more familiar and better-studied neurobiological disorders. What's more, for the majority of children who suffer from it, bipolar disorder doesn't occur in isolation.[3] It often rides sidesaddle with these other conditions, which include attention-deficit/hyperactivity disorder (ADHD); autistic spectrum disorder (ASD), including autism and asperger's syndrome; obsessive-compulsive disorder (OCD); oppositional defiant disorder (ODD); and separation anxiety disorder. Even child psychiatrists concede that teasing out the subtle nuances that distinguish these conditions can be confounding.

This diagnostic morass is more than just baffling. It can be devastating and sometimes even life-threatening for children. That's because bipolar disorder is too often treated with antidepressants and/or stimulants, medications that not only have the potential to cause mania and/or depression in children with bipolar disorder but also may activate bipolar genes in those who previously did not show evidence of the disorder. Imagine, for instance, a bipolar child who is diagnosed with ADHD and put on a stimulant such as Ritalin to calm him, then on an antidepressant for apparent depression. Instead of getting better, he may begin to develop severe mood swings. The improper diagnosis, followed by treatment with the wrong medications, may well have a significant detrimental effect on his social, emotional, and cognitive development, and in the most extreme case, it might even lead to suicidal thoughts or behavior. Depending on a therapist's experience and how carefully he or she investigates and interprets the symptoms, a youngster can easily be headed down a road of inadequate or harmful treatment.

My hope is to allay some of the diagnostic confusion surrounding childhood bipolar disorder and to provide parents with these words of comfort: You are not alone. The truth is that plenty of caregivers are confronting this disorder day in and day out. On the following pages, you'll hear chronicles of how they came to know this condition and how they deal with it successfully or at the very least cope with it one day at a time.

I also want to help absolve parents of some of the tremendous guilt they often feel when raising a child with bipolar disorder. I'm a psychiatrist, but I'm a mother first. And as a mother, I know that almost any parent who has a child with a problem (whether it involves learning, social skills, or behavioral issues) in some way feels guilty. Society has a way of telling us that all of our children are supposed to be perfect, so if they have a problem, it must be our fault. The guilt is compounded if a child behaves inappropriately in the outside world. When you take your youngster to the grocery store and he hits you, throws temper tantrums, and shouts bad names, it's a mortifying experience. The stares from other people seem to say, "What a spoiled brat! What's the matter with that mother! Doesn't she know how to control her own child?"

But in the case of bipolar children, this kind of episode is rarely touched off by incompetent parenting. Instead, it's generally the outgrowth of biology gone awry. The parents of the kids I see in my practice deserve awards for the way in which they handle what they live through each day. And yet, they are the constant targets of criticism— by unsympathetic spouses, relatives, other parents, teachers, physicians, and even mental health professionals. The situation is made even worse by the isolation that they experience. To suffer alone is unnecessary and cruel when there are so many other parents struggling with the same problems and misunderstandings. Education and support are crucial elements in successfully raising a bipolar child.

Throughout this book, I'll offer you a peek into the windows of bipolar children's inner lives, sharing stories from dozens of parents and children that will provide a detailed picture of how bipolar disorder plays out in the day-to-day activities of families.

I can't stress enough that how a person feels about himself at seven years of age plays a big role in how he feels about himself at thirty-seven. Therefore, controlling or at least doing the best you can to manage the disorder in your child's early years can set the stage for a better life for him than if the illness is left unaddressed and allowed to wreak havoc on his development. Early intervention is critical. I firmly believe that by taming bipolar disorder early on, you're helping to give your youngster a childhood he might otherwise be denied.

To that end, I'll explore the medications and therapies currently available as well as new treatments on the horizon and share tips for helping your child at home and in school. In addition, I'll share insights about the lives of some of the great leaders, musicians, artists, entertainers, and scientists who showed signs of being bipolar children themselves, among them Winston Churchill and Sir Isaac Newton. Most important, I'll acquaint you with some of the techniques I use in my practice that you can learn too, including one I like to call "professional listening." The goal is to help you, the parent or care-giver, to better understand your child's moods and steer him on the road to wellness.

1

Listen to the Words, Not Just the Music

The first day he came into my office, I immediately liked eight-year-old Danny. A charming boy with blond hair and brown eyes, he hugged his mom in the waiting room and proclaimed, "I love you, Mommy; you're the best mommy in the world."

When I spoke with Danny's mom alone, she painted a fuller picture of her son. Danny was the family comedian and loved to do goofy imitations of his favorite cartoon characters. He was unusually bright and creative. When he was still a preschooler, he could name all the planets and discuss in great detail the debate over whether Pluto belonged on the list. On many occasions, he was a compassionate, caring youngster. For instance, when his sister went to the emergency room for stitches in her finger, it was Danny who comforted her. "It's OK, Katie," he had said. "I get lots of needles, and it's not so bad."

At other times, however, Danny could make Dennis the Menace look like a choirboy. At age three, he had been sent home from nursery school for throwing jelly beans and calling other kids "doodyheads." When he was four, he was kicked out of the school permanently for throwing a chair at the teacher's aide and for trying to bite another student.

Danny had an up-and-down relationship with his sister, who was two years older than he was. On some occasions, the two played nicely and he was interested in what she wanted to do. But on others, he was provocative and purposely tried to irritate her. When reprimanded by his parents, he often said things such as "OK, why don't you just kill me? You hate me and you love Katie more. I know it." He would then burst into tears and say, "I don't know what's wrong with me, I have a bad brain." His excessive guilt at these times made it difficult for his parents to discipline him, as he was so hard on himself.

The transition to elementary school had been a difficult one for Danny. He had trouble separating from his family, and he was often late because it could take twenty-five minutes or more for his mother just to get him out of bed in the morning. Danny insisted on wearing the same pair of shorts every day, and he refused to leave the house at all until the seams on his socks felt exactly right. Once he was in first grade, it was hard for him to stay seated on the rug long enough to participate in the daily storytime activities. For the first few hours of the day, he was often grumpy and refused to interact with the other children or go to the playground for soccer practice. But by afternoon, he usually brightened considerably and sometimes volunteered to lead storytime, where he would regale the group with his cartoon imitations. The kids thought it was hysterical, and frankly, so did the staff.

But Danny's antics weren't always laughing matters. In first grade, he had tried to push a classmate off a moving swing. In second, he called the teacher a witch when she took away his drawing paper and said it was time to move on to the next assignment. Still, his mom reported, Danny was always sad and remorseful after such incidents. "I'm no good," he would say tearfully. The teacher said she had never taught a child quite like Danny and told his mother that something had to be done.

Danny's parents were as confused as his teacher by his unpredictable behavior. By second grade, they had been through a revolving door of doctors' offices to figure out how best to help him. At first, his dad had thought Danny simply needed more structure and limit-setting. His mom thought, and hoped, that he would grow out of some of these bad behaviors. Both parents wished they knew how to do more for their son. But they could never be sure which Danny they would be dealing with on any given day: Dr. Jekyll or Mr. Hyde.

It's not uncommon for parents to share concerns similar to those of Danny's parents if a child has been "acting up" in school or at home. But how is a parent to know if this is just typical kid behavior? How does a parent know if the child is just having a few bad weeks, if he is just a spunky kid, or if there is something more serious behind his ups and downs? Some parents, like Danny's, arrive at my door armed with a laundry list of various diagnoses, none of which seems to have been quite the right fit for their son or daughter. Parents may worry that they've done something wrong: Maybe it's all their fault, or then again, maybe they're just overreacting and have a lower tolerance level than most parents for a child's poor behavior. Many feel as if they've been on a roller-coaster ride for years, both emotionally and physically, with their child, and they are desperate for answers.

Although the term *bipolar disorder* is bandied about in popular dialogue much more frequently today than it was in the 1990s, there's still a fair amount of confusion among both parents and practitioners over what bipolar disorder looks like and how it exhibits itself in a child. Danny's parents had been struggling with the correct diagnosis for their child. By the time they came to my office, they were, needless to say, distressed and disillusioned. Danny had gotten so many different diagnoses over the years—attention-deficit/hyperactivity disorder (ADHD), major depressive disorder (MDD), oppositional defiant disorder (ODD), pervasive developmental disorder (PDD)—that his parents couldn't even remember all the acronyms anymore. The medications they had tried either hadn't worked or had worked for a period of time but then seemed only to make matters worse.

When I met with Danny, I thought he could be helped but explained to his parents that the process would likely involve some trial and error. By carefully observing Danny and studying his history of diagnoses and his behavior over two weeks, I saw many of the signs that would make me consider a diagnosis of bipolar disorder. First, the stories from Danny's parents indicated that many of their son's symptoms were cyclical rather than constant; that is, they would come and go. When his mood was essentially stable, his ability to pay attention was fine, but when he appeared very depressed or too "up" (manic), concentrating was almost impossible for him. His social behavior also seemed mood-related: Danny could be irritable and isolated in the morning but charming and gregarious in the afternoon and then unable to settle down at bedtime.

He also displayed many of what I call the hidden symptoms of bipolar disorder (these will be discussed in more detail in Chapter 3), including a significant problem with waking up in the morning. When he experienced extremes in moods, either at the height of his mania or the depths of his depression, his parents described him as especially distractible and restless. On these occasions, his behavior sometimes resembled that of a child with ADHD.

Initially, Danny's parents reported, his attention problems had responded to the stimulant medications that are typically used to treat ADHD, but after a few months, his problems began to increase significantly. The same was true when he was treated with an antidepressant for his depression: There was clear improvement within a few days, but this, too, was followed by a period of marked decline (into intense depression and irritability). This pattern is something I often see in kids with a bipolar predisposition who are treated with stimulants and/or antidepressants. The medicines seem to help for a time, but then, for many, the medication either seems to stop working or the problems dramatically intensify.

In Danny's case, his depression manifested itself as a lack of interest in interacting with his peers and an inability to enjoy most things he had previously liked, including playing soccer. He also had great difficulty switching from one activity to another in the classroom, as evidenced by his verbal altercation with the teacher during art class.

I like to tell parents that the first rule of thumb I use to treat any child who I strongly suspect has bipolar disorder is this: Treat the mood disorder first, and see what's left behind. And that rule applied to Danny. By treating his mood shifts first (and seeing if his moods evened out at all), we could begin to determine which symptoms seemed related to mood and which might be related to other problems, such as ADHD. In about two weeks, Danny began his first mood-stabilizing medication (see Chapter 7).

I wish I could say that it worked beautifully and that everyone lived happily ever after, but in fact, treating bipolar disorder in kids is seldom so simple. As with many children, it took a number of weeks and trials of a few different medications before we began to notice a positive change in Danny. After a couple of false starts, we finally hit on a combination of medications—a mood stabilizer and an antipsychotic—that worked well together to even out his moods. At the same time, Danny and his parents started seeing a therapist skilled in treating families with bipolar kids to help them better understand his illness.

Within a few days after starting the new medication combination, Danny's mood swings began to decrease in frequency and intensity. Over a period of weeks, his interaction with peers and adults began to improve, and his teachers reported that he was more attentive in the classroom; he was also more cooperative at home. Although he still had difficulty waking up in the morning, his teachers reported that he performed well in school once he arrived. He eventually began to make friends and wanted to invite other kids over for playdates. Granted, the medications and therapy didn't eliminate every one of Danny's symptoms. He continues to be somewhat slow to get going in the morning. But overall, he is far more able to cope with the demands placed on him at school, and, most important, he is more able to feel positive about himself and have a good relationship with his parents and siblings.

Defining Bipolar Disorder

Danny's story illustrates the complex and sometimes baffling ways in which bipolar disorder presents itself in young children, but many parents are equally baffled when it comes to explaining what could be going on inside their child that might cause such behavior. What exactly is bipolar disorder? And what explains it? These are often the first questions parents ask me when we discuss bipolar disorder as a possible diagnosis for their child. Without going into an involved scientific discussion, it's worth taking a look at the basics of bipolar disorder and some of its possible causes, as identified by the psychiatric community today.

First, the term *bipolar* refers to the predominant mood states—mania and depression—that are the hallmarks of the condition. I'll discuss these states in greater detail in Chapter 2, but in general, mania refers to an elevated, expansive, or irritable mood, and depression is characterized by a sad or irritable mood and/or the loss of pleasure in nearly all activities. By definition, either of these mood states must be accompanied by changes in energy level and behavior as well. (Bipolar disorder's previous name, manic depression, was changed within the mental health community in the 1970s as part of an attempt to add clarity and uniformity to psychiatric diagnoses. From that point on, mood disorders were divided into two groups: unipolar, those that involve only one end of the affective [emotion] spectrum, and bipolar, those generally characterized by shifts between the two states.)

My young patients never cease to amaze me with the creative analogies they come up with for describing their swings between mania and depression. Some say they feel like a ping-pong ball bouncing back and forth between their different mood states. Others describe it as having an angel on one shoulder and a devil on the other. Their vivid language reflects their often daily struggles with the abrupt and unanticipated shifts they experience when bouncing between their highs and lows.

These mood states are also associated with a variety of symptoms, including sleep and appetite disturbances, concentration difficulties, major unexplained changes in energy levels, and distractibility. But it's seldom that I see a youngster with all of the possible characteristics. One child might have significant sadness and low energy, whereas another may be highly energetic and bossy. One may be predominantly irritable, and another may be very silly with rapid speech and in an "up" mood most of the time. Still others may exhibit a grab bag of bipolar symptoms. To further confuse matters, bipolar kids' moods tend to shift much more rapidly than those of grown-ups with this disorder. Adults most commonly experience weeks or months in a single mood state—either manic or depressive—but youngsters often have ups and downs in the course of just one or a few days. (This pattern of frequent mood shifts is also seen in adults but much less often.)

Like many conditions, bipolar disorder exhibits itself in different ways and in varying degrees from child to child. Thus, one youngster may be incapacitated by the illness and unable to participate in school or extracurricular activities, and another may function quite well outside the home but struggle significantly with family life. And even if the child is not one of the extreme cases featured in the media, she may still benefit from treatment.

The truth is that diagnosing a bipolar child is more like making a movie than taking a snapshot. Sometimes, the diagnosis is clear fairly quickly, but in other cases, it's necessary for a psychiatrist to observe a child's behaviors and moods over weeks or even months.

As for the question of what causes this disorder, I like to tell parents that if I could answer that, I'd win the Nobel Prize. But we do have some information to point us in the right direction. Scientists believe that a variety of factors, including genetics, chemical and/or physical changes in the brain, and environmental influences, all play a role.

It is generally accepted in the mental health community that the cause of bipolar disorder is largely biologic, whether rooted in the genes or in particular changes in the brain. Recently, researchers have focused much of their efforts on locating the specific genetic underpinnings of bipolar disorder. It appears that more than one gene is probably responsible, and the quest to determine which genes are aberrant and how they interact with each other continues. The hope is that a better understanding of the genetics of bipolar disorder will eventually lead to better treatment.

Scientists have long suspected a genetic role in bipolar disorder because, as with many other biologically based disorders, this condition often runs in families. According to studies on children with bipolar parents, if one parent has bipolar disorder, a child has up to a 27 percent risk of developing it; if both parents have bipolar disorder, the risk increases to 60 percent. These figures are compared with a 0.5 to 1.5 percent risk in the general population.[1]

The concept of a chemical mechanism in the brain also contributing to the development of bipolar disorder is still being investigated. But researchers are studying the connections between mood disorders and the chemical messengers in the brain known as neurotransmitters. These substances, which include norepinephrine, serotonin, and dopamine, allow the brain's nerve cells to "talk" to one another in order to smoothly perform the tasks of mood regulation and other mental functions.

Although the role that neurotransmitters play in mood changes is still not entirely clear, it appears that too much or too little of a particular neurotransmitter—or perhaps an imbalance among them—can affect how particular nerve cells behave; that is, one cell may be talking too much, while another is saying too little. The result is that the messages being sent along the brain's pathways may be changed in some way, causing differences in an affected person's mood.[2]

Structural or physical differences in the brain are also thought to play a role in bipolar disorder. In recent years, scientists using advanced imaging techniques have discovered a possible relationship between bipolar disorder and the volume of particular areas of the brain. The bipolar adults they studied appeared to show an increase in the volume of the amygdala (the almond-shaped groups of neurons located deep within the medial temporal lobes of the brain) and a decrease in the volume of other parts of the temporal lobe.[3] Both of these areas appear to be involved with mood and emotions.

In some cases, symptoms of bipolar disorder can be caused by certain medical illnesses or conditions. People with temporal lobe epilepsy, hyperthyroidism (overactive thyroid), or a stroke in particular areas of the brain, for example, can exhibit signs of mania. Those with hypothyroidism (underactive thyroid), multiple sclerosis, or stroke in other select areas of the brain may experience depression.[4]

But biologic factors don't tell the whole story. Identical twins will both have bipolar disorder only 70 percent of the time at most,[5] which tells us that some other factors are at work. Research studies lend support to the idea that environmental factors, such as head trauma and life-threatening events, are also occasionally associated with the onset of bipolar episodes.[6]

Despite the fact that scientists are learning more and more every day about what causes bipolar disorder, many kids like Danny still aren't getting the treatment they need. Why? Because many mental health professionals are either skeptical that bipolar disorder exists in children or unsure of how to make the diagnosis in this population. Their skepticism is due, in part, to the guidelines traditionally used by the mental health community to diagnose the disorder. Unlike specialists in internal medicine, who can order blood tests, X-rays, computerized axial tomography (CAT) scans, magnetic resonance imaging (MRI) studies, and so forth, psychiatrists must diagnosis illnesses by listening to a person's symptoms and determining how those symptoms fit into a specific pattern. In diagnosing most psychiatric illnesses, clinicians use the *Diagnostic and Statistical Manual of Mental Disorders,* fourth edition, text revision (the DSM-IV-TR), a manual that lists the standards a person's symptoms must meet before a particular diagnosis can be given.

Determining whether a symptom is present and to what degree can involve some level of subjectivity, of course. But for children with bipolar disorder, there's an even bigger complication: The DSM-IV-TR still lists only adult criteria for bipolar disorder, and children are not just mini grown-ups. We also know that bipolar children often don't show symptoms in the same ways as adults who struggle with the disorder, presenting another difficulty in diagnosis.

Some doctors believe that if the symptoms of bipolar disorder don't follow the DSM-IV-TR criteria, then we shouldn't call the child's illness bipolar disorder. Given what we know now, however, I believe the label itself is not the crucial issue; we can call it bipolar disorder or polar bear disorder as far as I'm concerned. The important thing is ensuring that these children get the help they need.

Yet when health professionals don't even have pediatric bipolar disorder on their radar screens (something that I hear from frustrated parents time and again), the chances of a child getting the best available care when she needs it is greatly reduced. It reminds me of the old malapropism sometimes attributed to baseball great Yogi Berra: "If I didn't believe it, I wouldn't see it." Because many therapists, pediatricians, and psychiatrists are still not sure if they believe in pediatric bipolar disorder, they don't see it as a possibility. The result is that some children end up losing vital periods of their childhoods.

How do we prevent this from happening to kids such as Danny? In my mind, one of the critical but often forgotten words is *listening*. In this age of insurance-driven office visits, the time clinicians have available for just sitting and listening to kids is often limited. But I'm always astonished by how clearly young children can articulate the way they feel and what their problems are if they are simply given a chance to be heard.

One of the best instructors I ever had in the art of listening was a seven-year-old boy named Ben. I had been treating Ben for only a few weeks with a medication I had used with success in a number of other children with bipolar disorder, and I was fairly confident that it would help him feel calmer and even out his moods. But when his mom brought him for his scheduled appointment, she was worried: Ben had been tearful and despondent in the early part of the day, and by late afternoon, he was pounding on the wall and trying to hit his younger brother with a plastic baseball bat.

My first instinct was to adjust the dosage on Ben's prescription. Then he sat down, squared his shoulders, and cut right to the chase. "I think this medicine is makin' me nuts," he said. "I'm the only one who knows how I really feel." Although no one in medical school ever mentioned anything about seven-year-olds participating in their treatment plans, Ben seemed to be on to something. I told him I agreed that he was an expert on his own body: "You know how you feel better than anybody else."

I asked him if we could just try to increase the medication one more time to see for sure whether a higher dose might help him. "You and I are detectives trying to solve a case," I explained, "and we have to weigh all the evidence; each clue is important. If we increase the medicine and you feel worse, then it will be clear to the two of us that this medicine is not for you (just as you say). If it helps, then we'll know that the dose was probably just too low."

His next appointment was scheduled for three days later, so that if he didn't feel well, we could stop the medication quickly (although he knew he could always ask his mother to call me if he couldn't wait). He reluctantly agreed to the trial.

When we met later that week, Ben said, "I feel so angry. I know I'm right. This medicine makes me sick." I weaned him off that medication and cautiously started a different mood stabilizer, another anticonvulsant. During his next visit the following week, I was surprised at the gains Ben had made. He still had difficult days, but his mood shifts had become less extreme and of shorter duration. The crying had lessened, and his mother reported that he was getting back to playing baseball, his favorite activity.

Sometimes, it takes a Ben to remind us that a major part of our job as doctors, therapists, or parents often boils down to "professional listening." Do a child's words indicate that he's more angry than usual? That nothing seems to please him? That things that once made him happy no longer do? Typically, parents will come into the office and explain that their child has been incredibly irritable or that he is giddy and revved up, especially at bedtime. In the case of children with bipolar disorder, that doesn't tell me enough. Most children are irritable at one time or another, and many kids get overly active at nighttime. What's especially important to know, in addition to the broad clinical overview, is the "small change," that is, the details of a child's day-to-day existence. The small change of daily life is what determines one's repository of psychological wealth—and what gives me significant clues to a child's state of mind.

Collecting the Small Change

Did Katie laugh during her beloved *SpongeBob SquarePants* episode yesterday? Was Corey able to finish his essay on Thomas Jefferson? I want to know not only what a child is doing but also what he is saying and how he is saying it. Does he get all wound up over his Christmas list and make elaborate plans for winter vacation even though it's still August? Pester you for a taco even when told you'll be picking up dinner from the Italian restaurant? Complain that the thermostat is turned up too high even though it's set at sixty-eight degrees?

Why bother to remember such seemingly mundane remarks? Because these and other conversational snippets can yield important clues as to whether your child is exhibiting signs of a bipolar disorder. Careful attention to a child's words may also help you discover whether a prescribed medication is effective or if another treatment option needs to explored. If you want to get a good read on what a bipolar child is feeling and where his mood is at any given time, the first step is to listen to him.

Most parents, of course, *listen* to their child, and some might think they listen to the point of sheer exhaustion, till they can't possibly listen anymore! But we all have different ways of listening. In our society today, where everything is supposed to be fast and concise, we communicate in sound bites: Skip the details—what's the bottom line? The problem is that in our rush to communicate effectively and what we think is efficiently, we lose a lot of important information.

The diagnostic confusion that surrounds pediatric bipolar disorder is partly due to the pressure to convey information rapidly, with a lack of focus on details. Let's say a young girl, Shirley, comes home from school and asks her mother to take her to the toy store to buy the newest, hottest doll that her girlfriend Marta just got for her birthday. Her mother first explains that Marta got the doll for a special day, her birthday, and then says, "The doll costs a lot of money, and maybe Santa Claus will bring it on Christmas. We are not going to get it to-day. You'll have to wait." After repeatedly being told "no," Shirley starts screaming and stomping her feet; she throw pillows off the couch and has a major temper tantrum. Then Shirley starts yelling.

On the one hand, she might say, "You're mean, stupid and very ugly. You never listen to me—no matter what I say. You hate me, just go ahead and kill me!" On the other hand, Shirley might say, "I hate you, I wish you were dead. I wish a car would run over you and kill you." In both situations, the child is out of control and verbally abu-sive. There is no question that this is an irritable, demanding, and out-of-control child. But if we "listen to the words" (the language) closely and not just "the music" (the noisy refrain), we begin to see things differently. In the first scenario, Shirley feels that she is a vic-tim and that her mother doesn't care about her. In the second situa-tion, Shirley feels that her mother is the problem, and her rage is externally directed.

Let's look at another situation; whether or not the child is bipolar is irrelevant. Suppose a boy throws a rock at a window to break it. Obviously, this seems to be a bad thing. But what if he did this be-cause his house was on fire, he didn't have a key, and his sister and brother were still inside? He knew time was of the essence, and he had a chance of saving them. Alternatively, imagine that the boy's neighbors kicked him out of their house because of his aggressive behavior toward their children. He came back when he knew they wouldn't be home and decided to break into their house to steal some things. He didn't have a key, so the only way to get in was by breaking the window with a rock. In the first scenario, the boy is a hero. In the second, he is a strong candidate for juvenile court.

What does this scenario have to do with bipolar kids? On its surface, many may think that the bipolar child's behavior is driven by simple willfulness or defiance. But as you see in this example, careful attention to the details of a situation is paramount if one really wants to understand a youngster's emotions and behavior.

"People Hear What They See"

In my practice, I've found that children with bipolar disorder are often especially bright, self-aware, and adept at revealing their emotional and physical states, in either a direct or an indirect fashion. For example, you might think your child is kidding when he tells you, "If I don't wake up in time for cartoons in the morning, throw a bag of ice on me." But, in fact, parents of bipolar children report an uncanny similarity in the way in which their bipolar kids talk about the extreme measures necessary to awaken them in time for school. The reason is that these kids often have changes in their sleep/wake pattern that make it difficult, if not seemingly impossible, for parents to rouse them when it's time to get up (for more on sleep problems, see Chapter 3). Many parents report that when their kids really want to make certain that they'll get up in time for a special activity, they'll beg for a wake-up call that involves either ice or cold water or multiple alarm clocks.

Bipolar kids are also frequently great planners and list makers. Six months before her birthday, a bipolar child in an "up" mood may regale you with detailed plans for her party, obsessing over the smallest details of what present Grandma may buy her. Of course, childhood enthusiasm might account for some of this behavior, but it may also be indicative of an elevated mood in a bipolar child who carries it to extreme lengths. Kids who are "up" are busy, driven, and thinking of grandiose things.

When this kind of energy interferes with a child's functioning, it can play havoc with daily life. But sometimes, it can also be channeled—with proper treatment and the caring guidance of a parent—into academic or creative activities such as artwork, musical presentations, and science or literary projects. One of my patients, a six-year-old boy named Henry, wrote and illustrated an entire book, all while sitting in my office waiting room. It was about a superhero he called Shirt Man. After he read it to me, he described his plans for the sequel, "Beyond Shirt Man," as well as a movie version. I was convinced that with the proper treatment, he could wind up as the next Steven Spielberg.

It's fairly easy to listen to your child when he's in a creative, expansive mood like Henry was. But in difficult times when a bipolar child is irritable or acting up, parents often block out the child's words and remember only the turmoil. I'm reminded of a phrase I heard in the movie *Beyond the Sea*, the story of the late Bobby Darin. At one point in the film, his wife, Sandra Dee, tries to comfort him after a failed comeback performance at the Copacabana nightclub. Unlike his previous shows, which included a visual feast of spotlights, a full orchestra, and dancers, this one consisted of Darin alone singing folk songs and playing his guitar. The songs were beautiful and well performed, but the nightclub audience, accustomed to glitz and fanfare, uncharacteristically booed his performance. "People hear what they see," his wife told him. The same is true regarding parents and children. When a child is having a mood swing that results in rage, what you hear is tremendous hate and anger. It is only when you carefully focus on the words that it becomes clearer just which feelings the child is struggling with.

At the same time, parents tend to sanitize episodes that seem too painful, too embarrassing, or simply too bizarre to share with a stranger or even the treating doctor. For example, instead of saying, "Ricardo mooned his teacher yesterday and then told her 'I know how to do math better than you,'" they might say only that "Ricardo was really out of control in school yesterday." But hearing the details is crucial in helping a doctor come up with the proper diagnosis, prescribe the appropriate pharmacological treatments, and devise day-to-day plans for getting the support the child needs at home and in school. In this case, for instance, Ricardo's language clued me in to the fact that he was exhibiting inappropriate social behavior and an I-know-better-than-the-grown-ups attitude, common in bipolar children in the "up" phase.

Even when it seems that a child is simply being annoying and oppositional, there may be clues in his language that he is, in fact, despairing. The child who pestered his mom for a taco at the Italian restaurant, for example, may really be crying out for help with his depression. He's saying, "I might just as well ask for the impossible because I know that no matter what anybody does, nothing is going to help me feel better."

Partners in Treatment

Many young patients talk about having "bad brains" or "two brains"—one that says to do "good things" and one that tells them to do "bad things." They're struggling with trying to explain to *themselves* why they do the things they do and act the way they act. These kids know something is not right; they want to please their parents and teachers and do the right thing, but somehow, they end up acting inappropriately and getting themselves into hot water.

Such was the case with William, a nine-year-old boy who, above all else, loved his dog, Marshmallow, a gentle Maltese. When William's mood was stable, he would make a special bed for Marshmallow out of pillows. He liked to hold his pet on his lap, sometimes for half an hour at a time, and dress him up in his baseball hat or his sister's sweater. "I love you, Marshmallow, you're the best doggie in the world," he would say. When William's mood was elevated to a worrisome degree, however, he would sometimes handle the dog too roughly and pull at its legs to get the sweater on quickly. Then, when the dog snapped at him, he'd become furious: "You stupid dog; I'm going to bite you back."

William's inconsistent behavior represented his internal tug-of-war with the world and his emotions. When he felt good, he was the kindest, gentlest, most wonderful child imaginable. When his mood was unstable, he could seem insensitive or overly sensitive to everything and everyone. Afterward, when he was calm and more reasonable, he felt horrible about hurting something that he loved so much. "I'm so sorry, Marshmallow," he said with tears in his eyes. "I love you. I didn't ever mean to hurt you. Sometimes, I just act crazy. I don't know why."

Even small bits of conversation can yield important clues to what is going on inside a child's mind. Sunny, a bright eight-year-old, noticed one day that another child was accompanied by a specially trained service dog. Her mother explained that such dogs, similar to seeing-eye dogs, can help kids with lots of different problems. "I need a paying-attention dog," Sunny said matter-of-factly. This remark showed that Sunny not only had a good sense of humor but also that she was highly aware of her distractibility issues.

Spoken language isn't the only thing to pay attention to in a child; observing a child's nonverbal cues is also extremely important. The proverbial sparkle, for instance, is often missing from a depressed child's eyes. A child with an elevated mood can be so distractible and busy that he looks like a whirling dervish—on the go and not thinking too much (the truth is that he may be thinking about too many things). At times, simply observing a child's reactions and facial expressions with the "sound" turned down can be a very helpful tool for assessing his moods.

Yet even after careful listening and observation, it can still be difficult to interpret what's going on in a youngster's mind. If he complains that other children give him strange looks or don't like him, this may be paranoia or a reaction based in reality or a mixture of both. Perhaps the child is acting so strangely that he is pushing other children away: One youngster I know would stare at other people and then complain that they were staring at her. One of the important things to take away from this situation, however puzzling, is that the child is telling you how uncomfortable he feels, no matter where reality lies. I'm convinced that in many cases, listening carefully can make all the difference in the world in a young patient's quality of life, especially if it means helping to tease out symptoms of bipolar disorder early on.

Such was certainly the case with Ben, the pharmacologically savvy seven-year-old. During the months we worked together, he continued to be a partner in his treatment. When he said, "Doc, I think those little pink pills help me more than those big white capsules," I paid attention. There were times that his mother and I looked at each other in disbelief because his assessment of his responses to the pills was so on target.

It took some time and lots of trial and error, but Ben's bipolar disorder is now controlled with medication and therapy. He's becoming successful in school and an eager participant in his treatment plan. He deserves applause for demonstrating a maxim that any child psychiatrist—and anyone else who works with children—should take carefully to heart: "Listen to the words, not just the music."

2

❀

Depression and Mania:
Riding the Mood Pendulum

Nine-year-old Adam tells his mom he's taking the train into the city to see the circus. "I know which one to take," he says, frantically. "If you can't take me today, I'm going all by myself!" Seven-year-old Martin, with a look of annoyance, tells his teacher, "The geography book is wrong. I know I'm right. Philadelphia is the capital of Pennsylvania." Tracey, nine, is inconsolable: "I do all the wrong things. No wonder my family is upset with me. What's wrong with me? Everything's boring. I don't even like playing soccer anymore." And Steven, seven, won't come into my office at all. "You can't help me. No one can," he says.

Expansiveness, grandiosity, sadness, irritability—parents of bipolar children are all too familiar with this broad range of moods, and the swing of the mood pendulum can make many stops along the way. Adam was beyond happy and exhibited the sense of invincibility that mania sometimes inspires. Martin was irritable and knew for sure he was right, despite reality staring him in the face. Tracey was suffering from painful sadness and the guilt of depression. And like many other youngsters, Steven had a depression that caused him to seem angry, oppositional, and just plain mad.

It has only been since the 1990s that mental health professionals have begun to recognize that bipolar disorder exists in children and is not extremely rare. Yet more than one-third of adults with bipolar disorder report that their own mood pendulums started to swing before they were fifteen years old.[1] Many remember feelings of extreme sadness or misery and restless agitation (symptoms of depression) alternating with periods of silliness and giddiness, elation, or bossy irritability (symptoms of mania). Others describe periods of hypomania (similar to mania but not as extreme). Still others remember that their mood disorder began with major depression and that mania and hypomania didn't follow until much later in life. A child, however, may fluctuate between mania and depression several times during one day, going from zero to sixty on the mood speedometer in a matter of hours or even minutes. Let's take a closer look at how five mood patterns—depression, mania, mixed states, hypomania, and cyclothymia—look and feel in children.

Major Depression

Tracey was always a bit shy in school, but more recently, she seemed to have become excessively clingy at home. Her mom reported that for the past few months, Tracey had been getting tearful before bed every night, saying that she was worried that her dog might one day get hit by a car and die. Almost every night, her mom had to stay with her until she fell asleep, which could take up to an hour. Tracey also worried that she'd have one of her terrible nightmares. She was especially fearful of the one in which a monster chased her around a castle, then bit off her arms and legs and left her in a pool of blood.

She complained of feeling tired all the time (despite getting more than eleven hours of sleep since the onset of her mood and behavioral changes). She no longer wanted to go on playdates and preferred to stay home with her parents, where she'd lie on the couch with her dog and watch television. She didn't want to eat much except for junk food—cookies, pizza, soda, and chocolate candy—which her parents

allowed, if only to get her to eat something. Her teacher commented on how the sparkle had left her eyes, and every morning when her mom dropped her off at school, she'd start to cry. The school nurse began to see Tracey as much as her teachers did. She was having a hard time focusing on her schoolwork, and homework was a horror. She had always seemed a little distracted in the classroom, according to her teacher, but now she "couldn't focus for beans," as her teacher put it.

Tracey also began having social difficulties. She felt as though the other girls at school didn't like her and thought they were saying mean things about her. Her teacher told Tracey's mom that she didn't believe the other girls were rejecting Tracey. Instead, it appeared that Tracey was isolating herself from her peers. What's more, she had always gotten along well with her older sister, Kara, but now often seemed to be provoking her. Tracey would tease her sister about eating too much and being fat. (This wasn't really true, but like most early teenagers, Kara was struggling with changes in her body.)

It had always amazed her mom that Tracey, who could be so loving, had the incredible ability to figure out how to really hurt the person she was upset with. Put another way, she was great at "going for the jugular." By contrast, if her mom was sick with a cold, who but Tracey would be sympathetic and bring her orange juice and toast and say, "Just like you always try so hard to help me feel better when I don't feel good, now it's my turn to take care of you, Mommy."

Until the late 1970s, it was believed that young children such as nine-year-old Tracey were not intellectually developed enough to be able to experience depression in the same way that adults do. Therapists talked about "masked depression," a term that indicated children could not express depression directly but rather communicated their sadness through a variety of other signs and symptoms, among them headaches, hyperactivity, and insomnia. Children were thought to be tabulae rasae, or blank slates, who were shaped by the people who raised them. Today, we realize that each child enters the world with

her own biology and her own temperament, which, in turn, is affected by the environment.

Early leading researchers in childhood depression, including Joachim Puig-Antich, Dennis Cantwell, Gabrielle Carlson, and Elizabeth Weller in the 1980s, provided strong evidence that, like adults, children can and do suffer from depression. And today, few would question the idea that a biologic depression can affect youngsters. In fact, at press time, Joan Luby, MD, associate professor of child psychiatry and director of the Early Emotional Development Program at Washington University School of Medicine, was conducting new research that indicates depression can potentially be diagnosed as early as the preschool years in children.[2]

To meet the criteria for major depressive disorder, as the condition is known in the psychological world, a child must have experienced the following: a two-week period of either a depressed mood (or irritable mood) and/or decreased enjoyment of things that used to be pleasurable. In addition, he must exhibit some of the following symptoms: weight loss or weight gain, sleeping problems (too much or too little), excess guilt, decreased ability to concentrate, a change in energy level (being either physically slowed down or very restless and agitated), and possible thoughts of death and/or suicide. The symptoms of depression are not so different between children and adults, but it is necessary to make developmental modifications when assessing kids. For example, depressed kids may deny being sad but say instead that they are bored all the time.

Although youngsters are often poor at communicating the time and the frequency of events (if a young child has been sad for a few months, it wouldn't be unusual for him to report that he's been sad "all my life"), they can provide important information that their parents do not know. When it comes to questions about whether a child has hallucinations (for example, seeing things or hearing things that are not really there), delusions (false beliefs), or suicidal or homicidal thoughts, he knows the answer better than anyone else. He may not

know the adult names for the symptoms, but he often knows enough to realize he's having thoughts or experiences that are so strange that most people don't talk about them.

During the evaluation process with a child, it's not uncommon for me to discover that he has thoughts of killing himself or of not being alive or that he has hallucinations that he has not shared with anyone, including his parents. When I ask children why they have never told anyone such thoughts, more than a handful answer, "Because no one asked." The bottom line is that by talking to children directly, a clinician can potentially obtain a significant amount of information— much more than most grown-ups realize.

Many children I talk with do not agree that they feel sad. Instead, they may notice that they feel angrier than usual. Little things that typically wouldn't bother them now really annoy them. Parents may notice that their child rarely looks very happy. Little seems to excite him for more than a brief period. Although children may not be aware of their sad feelings, they often experience depression more as *the absence of pleasure*: Nothing is right or good enough. The fact that Mom arrived home with cookies rather than cake for dessert can bring them to tears. They may feel that other children and parents are against them or are nicer to other kids. They complain of boredom even though there are plenty of things to do that they would normally find fun. They may feel excessively guilty about inappropriate things they've done or imagine that they've done, recently or in the past. One boy, for example, felt horribly guilty over having taken a pencil from a store some weeks earlier, even though his mother had made him immediately return it and apologize to the store manager.

Depressed children, like depressed adults, also often tend to go over and over in their minds the things that make them sad or that remind them of upsetting things. One seven-year-old told me that he felt sad because he missed his dead grandmother. When we explored this relationship in more detail, I was surprised to discover that his grandmother had died a few months before the child was born! After getting over my initial shock, I asked the little boy why he missed her so much if he never really got to meet her. His answer was that he heard from his mom and other family members how much fun she had been to be around and how much she loved to watch sports with the family. He felt cheated that he had never known her.

Another six-year-old told his mother that he was sad because he was worried that his neighbor might move one day and that he wouldn't see Jinx, the neighbor's cat, ever again. Despite his mother's reassurances that the neighbor had no plans to move, the boy couldn't stop thinking about the possibility of Jinx going away.

In some cases, kids become uncomfortable and perplexed when they can't pinpoint the cause of their pain. One nine-year-old patient, for example, went to his school guidance counselor on his own because he felt upset. He told her, "I feel really sad, but I don't know why. I've tried very hard to figure it out myself, but I can't come up with a good reason for it."

Even children as young as four are able to recognize that they feel unhappy or that something is wrong. When we talk about what types of things make them sad, they sometimes get incredibly serious looks on their faces and appear on the verge of tears. One eight-year-old girl described her sadness to me as feeling nothing, "kind of like being dead": not happy or sad, just "nothing."

Kids with a biologically based depression may report only that they feel much more tired than usual. They'd rather stay in the house than go outside with their friends or family. Twelve-year-old Jeff's mom says that when he was very down, kids from the neighborhood invited him on playdates, but he didn't want to leave his house. After asking him to play a few times, the other kids stopped inviting him, which Jeff took as proof of his suspicion that they didn't like him. He seemed completely unaware that he was giving off vibes that his friends should leave him alone.

Of course, some kids experience depression not as sadness but as extreme grumpiness and agitation. Steven, age seven, the boy who boycotted my office, let me know in the waiting room, in no uncertain terms, that he didn't want to be there and that he wasn't going to talk to me.

"All you doctors are stupid. No one can help me," he said.

When his mom asked him to come into my office, he dug in his heels, "I don't want to and you can't make me."

She told him if he didn't come in, he was not going to get the video game they planned to buy later this afternoon.

"I don't care," he retorted.

His mom said she wasn't kidding and he needed to change his attitude *immediately*. He finally came into my office with his mother and sat on the couch, looking miserable. When I asked him his age, he confirmed that he was seven years old. Then he asked if he could leave if he answered my questions.

"Maybe. Let's wait and see," I said.

I acknowledged his angry feelings and asked if he felt angry like this a lot.

"Yeah, so?"

"What are you so angry about?"

"Everything."

"Well, what do you do for fun?"

"Nothing, I don't have fun!"

"You don't? Well, would you like to?"

"You can't help me."

"Maybe I can."

"The last doctor said that, and his medicines didn't work. Anyway, I don't care. I'm fine. I don't care if I'm angry. I like being angry."

This was basically the tone of our first interaction, which lasted approximately fifteen minutes (but I suspect felt like fifteen hours to both of us). In taking Steven's history from his parents, I learned that although he was very bright, he could at times be oppositional with his teachers. He'd missed thirty days of school in first grade because of a variety of physical complaints: headaches, stomachaches, sore throats, and so on. He was frequently yelling, as well as complaining, about how unfair his parents were. He often appeared impossible to satisfy. He'd ask for something specific for supper one minute and then complain about the way it was cooked. Then he'd complain about another dish the next night. He was mean to his little brother and was shunned by other kids because he always insisted on going first in games and playing unfairly. If he was losing, he would accuse another child of cheating and abruptly stop playing.

Tracey's and Steven's cases illustrate the many ways depression may exhibit itself in children. Every child has rough days, but these youngsters had been unhappy for a number of weeks when their parents finally decided to seek help. Tracey was fearful and clingy and had isolated herself from friends. Steven was irritable, agitated, and oppositional. Both children's needs seemed insatiable, and their problems interfered with life at school, at home, and with their friends. Some of their difficulties might have been mistaken for bad behavior, but actually, these were kids in a great deal of inner distress. And even children who don't exhibit the broad range of depressive symptoms that Tracey and Steven did can still be in pain and may need help. That's why it's important to pay attention to every symptom.

Mania

Unlike the depressed child who wonders what's wrong with himself and why the world is so unfair *to him*, the child in the manic phase acts as though he's the center of the universe and is annoyed if others fail to realize his specialness and follow his lead. The term *mania* refers to the "up" mood phase that characterizes bipolar disorder. During this period, a child may feel abnormally happy, expansive, or irritable. In adults, symptoms of mania must last at least one week. But in a child, mania is not so clear-cut, since kids' moods can swing up and down many times in the course of a day.[3] In the manic state, a child exhibits different combinations of the following symptoms:

- **Grandiosity:** The child may brag that she is a better softball player than anyone else, even before she's taken to the field for the first time. Or she might say, "My swim teacher at camp said I'm a natural and I could be in the Olympics in two years."

- **Decreased need for sleep:** Sleep? Who needs it? When kids are in the manic phase, getting them to sleep at night can seem like a never-ending battle. And they don't stay asleep for long: It's as if they find sleep a waste of their precious time.

- **Pressured speech:** A child may talk more than usual or have speech that sounds nonstop or forced. I describe it as "hyperactivity of the mouth." Trying to get a word or comment into the conversation can be virtually impossible for anyone else. For example, Maurice's mother told him they would go to the supermarket after the cleaners. He became very animated and excited by the plan: "When we go to the store, I want to get vanilla ice cream, chocolate syrup, whipped cream, and rainbow and chocolate sprinkles. I think it'd be great with bananas on top, too. I got it, we'll buy cherries . . . maybe we should get nuts . . . I love almonds." At that point, his mom tried to interrupt to say they didn't have that much time to shop, but Maurice's enthusiasm for his creations wouldn't let her get a word in edgewise. She got as far as "Honey, I don't think . . . " before he chimed in, "I got it! We'll get cones, and fancy cups. Like they do at Supercones. How about caramel syrup? We can't forget the strawberry syrup. I forgot . . . we'll cut up fresh fruit! We'll make little slices of pineapple, peaches, and melon! If we can't get the things there, we can go to Dessert Heaven. I'm sure they've got the stuff there."

- **Flight of ideas:** The child's mind jumps from one idea to another fairly rapidly, and the youngster may feel as if his thoughts are racing, so much so that it's hard to gather them together in a reasonable way. One little boy, Raymond, was talking to his Aunt Evelyn in the kitchen but seemed very restless and couldn't get himself comfortable on his stool, almost falling off multiple times. She told him how she had just flown back from a vacation in Florida on a new jumbo jet. Raymond responded, "I want to fly. If I can't fly, I want to die. My cat died last week. My dog died two years ago. Have you seen the neighbor's new dog? When are my parents going to get me the dog they promised me for my birthday? They also promised me a DVD player for my birthday. They didn't get that for me either!"

- **Increased interest in goal-directed activity:** Kids may make plans for Christmas when the calendar still says July. Or they begin in October to make lists of many possibilities where the family might spend spring vacation. Granted, most children love holidays and vacations. But in bipolar kids, the sense of anticipation takes on an entirely different quality; they are constantly planning and turning things over and over in their minds, sometimes thinking about events that are months in advance.

- **Poor judgment:** A youngster's impulses can have exceedingly negative results. For example, most kids know that punching a schoolmate on the bus can get them in trouble faster than they can say "detention," but when a bipolar child is enraged, he may think of this outcome only after the fact.

All kids can be silly and goofy at times, but the elation and silliness that we're talking about in kids with mania goes far beyond this normal behavior. It is excessive given the situation and often seems inappropriate and out of place. Ten-year-old Tessa could get wild running around with her younger siblings, Kyle, four, and Julia, five. To make fun of them, she'd call her brother "Toilet" and her sister "Toilietta" and run away so they'd have to chase her. When they'd catch her, she'd initiate a "ticklefest." Then the situation would often get out of control. As Tessa was much bigger and stronger than her brother and sister, she frequently ended up overwhelming them and hurting them. She tickled her sister until she cried and had problems catching her breath. Most children would have stopped by then, but not Tessa. She was having so much fun, she didn't recognize the fact that her sister almost couldn't breathe.

Studies indicate, however, that bipolar kids in their manic phase are more apt to be irritable than euphoric. They can have prolonged aggressive temper outbursts, also known as "affective storms,"[4] when they are in this angry state. The angry manic child can be violent, hurting siblings in play, or even go so far as to carve "I hate Dad" with a ballpoint pen into the kitchen table after being told "no" about something minor. Such behavior may sound right out of the horror movies, but these things happen in families with bipolar kids.

Impulsivity is another hallmark of mania. In fact, manic children wrote the book on this behavior. Eleven-year-old James, for instance, told his mother that he was going to call the police and tell them what bad parents he had. Mom told him to go ahead. Of course, James picked up the phone and dialed 911, but he quickly hung up when someone answered. Imagine his surprise when two police officers arrived at his house five minutes later!

The changing energy levels of kids in the manic phase often understandably affect the entire family. Consider the story of ten-year-old Jeremy. Jeremy began asking his younger sister, Hilary, seven, to join him every night for push-ups and sit-ups, since he had decided they both needed to get into shape. But that wasn't enough. He began setting the alarm so that they could get up at 6:15 in the morning to work out again. Sure enough, even though Jeremy and his sister didn't have to rise until 7:15, he had her up and ready to join him in exercise at his proposed time. As some children do when they are hypomanic or manic, he needed less sleep than usual and would wake up full of energy. (When he was depressed, he was impossible to get out of bed in the morning.)

Jeremy's mother explained that she knew Hilary was happy to be getting her brother's attention, but she was concerned that the young girl would be exhausted during the school day if she continued to try to keep up with her brother. After two mornings like this, the mother told both kids that she thought it would be healthier to shift their exercise routine to the afternoon. Jeremy agreed, and his sister went along with the plan. Within a few days, though, Jeremy became depressed, and that was the end of their fitness craze.

It might seem that it would be easy to recognize a child or an adolescent whose mood is up. Indeed, many children appear one step away from swinging from the chandeliers. But in order to *diagnose* someone with mania, a physician must first rule out a medical reason (such as thyroid disorder), a reaction to medication (such as steroids for the treatment of asthma), or the ingestion of illegal drugs.

The Difference Between
Irritable Mania and Irritable Depression

It's important to distinguish irritable mania from irritable depression in a child. Either condition may result in a child becoming violent, intense, or impossible to reason with, and in either case, a child may need to be hospitalized.

In irritable depression, there is tremendous anger, but the child is angry at being rejected by the world and at herself for her own inadequacy. Suppose that a child gets a low mark on her spelling test and that she was depressed even before she got the test back. She becomes angry, and her eyes fill with tears. She then rips up the test paper and throws it to the floor. The teacher tells her to pick it up, but she refuses. She then thinks: "I hate this creepy teacher. I know she never liked me. I can't believe I did so lousy on the test. I'm so stupid. I don't know anything. I always mess up. No wonder everyone is mean to me. My mom tells me I'm smart, but I know she doesn't really mean it. I wish I wasn't born. No one would care if I wasn't here." In irritable depression, the child feels as if she is a powerless victim and the world is against her.

In irritable mania, a youngster's anger is directed at the outside world. The experiences of Monty, age ten, demonstrate how irritability looks on the manic side of the pendulum. One day, Monty came home from school very upset. He told his mother that his teacher was mean and had refused to call on him in class when he had his hand up and knew the answers to some hard questions. The more he discussed the incident with his mother, the more enraged he became. He said that he was sure the teacher didn't choose him on purpose and stated that he was "going to get even with her" by making a bomb in the garage and blowing up the whole school. That would teach her! His mother, obviously alarmed, explained that this was against the law and that many children and other teachers would perish in the explosion.

"I don't care. They deserve it. They won't let me play with them at recess, and all teachers are mean and stupid."

"What about the fact that you'd be in jail for the rest of your life?" his mom pressed.

"It'd be worth it. Anyway, I'll shoot the policemen if they try to get me," he responded.

By listening carefully to Monty's words, you get a fairly good sense of how irritable mania sounds.

Mixed States

To further the diagnostic confusion, children are more likely than adults to experience "mixed states," that is, to have the full symptoms of mania and depression occurring at the same time. This seems to make no sense on the face of it, for how can someone be manic and depressed at the same time? But anyone with a bipolar child who exhibits these symptoms knows just what this looks like. A youngster in a mixed state may say, "I'm a wizard and I'll turn you into a toad, but then you'll hate me like I hate me." The standard diagnostic textbook, the DSM-IV-TR, requires that the mixed state has to be present for at least a week in order for the diagnosis to be made. It has been estimated that only 30 percent of bipolar *adults* present with this picture of mixed symptoms.[5] But studies indicate that mixed states are the most common way in which mania presents in children.[6] In fact, one study conducted at Massachusetts General Hospital by noted bipolar researcher Janet Wozniak, MD, found that 84 percent of forty-three manic children under age twelve presented with mixed episodes rather than discrete periods of mania or depression.[7]

It is the youngster in a mixed state who can be at greatest risk for extremely destructive behavior to himself or others. He may act as if every problem is someone else's fault, but he also feels bad, guilty, and incompetent; the rage is both externally and internally directed. In a mixed state, a child may sleep excessively and be difficult to awaken (as in the depressive phase), or he may require much less sleep than usual (as in the manic phase).

If a youngster has excess energy (mania) but also feels self-loathing (depression) and destructive, the risk of suicide and other difficulties increases dramatically. The mixed state is an extremely uncomfortable one for a child and potentially dangerous for a bipolar child.

Such was the case with nine-year-old Rory, who had been in an unstable mood for a few weeks. Part of the day, he would threaten to cut his sister and brother with a pair of scissors when they wouldn't follow his commands, but at other times, he would ask, "Why did God make me this way? Why does He hate me?" It was a very difficult time for the family, especially for Rory's mother. As their tenth anniversary approached, Rory's parents made plans to have the grandparents watch their two boys so they could share a romantic evening alone, including an overnight stay at a nearby inn. But Rory phoned his parents frequently while they were away, at one point calling to say, "I miss you, Mom. I need you. It's so hard without you." Then he suddenly became giddy on the phone and started singing, "Happy birthday to you" (though it was no one's birthday). This outburst was quickly followed by an exclamation delivered in a voice filled with excitement: "Oops, goodbye, I gotta go!" When he started his conversation, Rory was very sad, missing his mother terribly, but within a few minutes, the sadness had disappeared and he was inappropriately silly and excited.

Malcolm, age nine, was also in a mixed state when he declared, "I'm the best baseball player on my team, but I hate the coach. He's an idiot. He doesn't realize how good I am. He likes Sven better. Just because Sven hit a home run last season. If I did that, the coach would like me better than Sven. No one ever wants to give me a chance. Why are they so mean to me? Why don't they like me? Why does this always happen to me? I know. I'll show them. I'll throw rocks at the kids when they try to run to home base. Boy, will they be surprised. They'll see who is the best, just wait!"

Listening carefully to the language of children who are in mixed states is particularly important because their words may signal the need for professional intervention that addresses both the mania and the depression.

Hypomania

According to the DSM-IV-TR, hypomania refers to "a distinct period of persistently elevated, expansive, or irritable mood, lasting at least four days, that is clearly different from the usual nondepressed mood." A child or adult with hypomania experiences similar symptoms as in manic episodes, except that the symptoms are not as severe. How often hypomania occurs alone in children, without the additional presence of one or more extreme mood shifts, is not known. Unlike children with mania, kids with hypomania generally do not have severe impairment in school or in social functioning. Indeed, hypomanic children who do not go on to have full-blown manic episodes can function relatively well in some environments. If you think about it, this makes perfect sense. A person who is bright and creative, who thinks outside the box and needs little sleep as she pursues her goal, and who is quite charming, fun to be with, and highly persuasive has in her nature the very elements that may lead to incredible success.

Consider nine-year-old Freddie, who walked into my office one day as though he owned the place, took a long whiff of my trademark hazelnut coffee, and declared, "Ah, the sweet smell of Dr. Greenberg's office." We should all be as charming as Freddie is when he is hypomanic. How could I not smile?

Steven, the irritable boy mentioned earlier, also has hypomania from time to time. Although his main issue is depression, his parents say there are regular periods, lasting several hours, when he can be delightful. He has an intensely creative side and loves to draw comic book figures. He makes up the characters, and his plots are fascinating, with multiple twists and turns. He can dictate a story to his mother and draw for hours. He sometimes argues about going to sleep because his ideas are "so good" that he is fearful he won't remember them by the next morning. He often has a hard time sitting down and focusing on homework, but his storytelling ability comes naturally, and when he feels like it, he can write and illustrate amazing tales. During these times of prolific writing, he seems easy to get along with. He and his brother play well together, although they are silly at the kitchen table during dinner, with Steven instigating most of the antics.

If a child is in a hypomanic phase, he may exhibit times of increased energy, heightened busy-ness and creativity, grandiosity, silliness, or excessive irritability (especially when thwarted). But even though a hypomanic child at times can be very pleasant to be around, it's important to remember that for many bipolar youngsters, hypomania is a transient state, one that can unexpectedly shift to full-blown mania or depression.

Cyclothymic Disorder

The term *cyclothymia* is used to describe the state in which an individual has multiple periods of fluctuating hypomanic and depressive symptoms that do not meet the full DSM-IV-TR requirements for a manic episode or a major depressive episode. Cyclothymia is a chronic condition. To meet the criteria for cyclothymia, a child must have no symptom-free period lasting longer than two months over the course of one year (in the case of an adult, the duration is two years). Cyclothymic symptoms may be too brief or too infrequent to be considered mania or depression, and they don't cause major problems in functioning, nor do they create severe difficulties in several areas of a person's life.

Defining the Terms

As you work to find the right help for your child, you may come across other terms that are used to differentiate forms of bipolar disorder.

Bipolar I: This term is used when a person experiences one or more manic episodes or mixed episodes. Often, individuals labeled as Bipolar I also have a history of one or more episodes of major depression. In other words, Bipolar I is defined as mania with or without a depression.

Bipolar II: If an individual experiences one or more major depressive episodes and has at least one hypomanic episode, he is said to suffer from Bipolar II. Put another way, Bipolar II is major depressive disorder with at least one episode of hypomania.

Bipolar disorder not otherwise specified (BPD NOS): According to DSM IV-TR, this classification includes disorders with bipolar features that do not meet the full criteria for mania, depression, or mixed states. A person diagnosed with BPD NOS might experience intermittent mood shifts that last no more than two days and therefore do not meet minimal duration criteria for a manic episode or a major depressive episode or a mixed state and are not frequent enough to be called cyclothymia.

Rapid cycling: This is the name given to the pattern of bipolar disorder in which an individual has had at least four mood episodes (which can be manic, mixed, hypomanic, or major depressive episodes) in the preceding twelve months. If cycling occurs within a span of weeks to several days, the pattern is called ultra-rapid cycling, whereas distinct, abrupt mood shifts of less than twenty-four hours' duration are referred to as ultra–ultra rapid, or ultradian, cycling. This ultra–ultra rapid cycling is the pattern most frequently seen in bipolar children. One of my nine-year-olds calls it "instant moods."

These include Bipolar I, Bipolar II, and bipolar disorder not otherwise specified (BPD NOS).

Not every child with mania or depression looks like Damian the Devil Child. True, when the diagnosis of childhood bipolarity is discussed in books and magazines or on television, it is often only the extreme ends of the mood spectrum that get attention. But it is vital to realize that bipolar disorder is similar to many other biologically based illnesses in that it has different gradations of severity. It's not like being pregnant, where either you are or you aren't. Instead, it more closely resembles hypertension (high blood pressure): You can have mild, moderate, or severely elevated blood pressure. In a mild case, all that may be needed is to watch your weight, increase exercise, decrease stress, and practice relaxation techniques. Severe hypertension, at the other extreme, is a medical emergency, and the use of medication is absolutely necessary.

In the same way, a bipolar child may have mild difficulties or suffer from such severe symptoms that he can't function well at home, at school, or with peers. Most of the kids I see have temper issues, but the majority of my patients are not trying to seriously harm their family members or others, nor do they want to destroy property. They're angry, and they're going to let the world know it. If things aren't done the way they want, there will be an outburst. It's not uncommon for parents to hear such phrases as "I hate you!" or "If you don't do what I say, I'm going to kill you" or "I wish you were dead." Such statements may sound shocking to most people, but they are indicative of the intense emotions youngsters experience when they are in the throes of a mood swing. That they say these things doesn't necessarily mean they're going to do something dangerous or that they really are deeply hateful, but it does show how angry and irrational they feel. Because these children know what is and is not proper behavior, excessive guilt and tears often follow these outbursts.

How does the mood pendulum swing in one particular child in the course of a day? A brief description of a ten-year-old boy named Raul suggests how a child might sound in his different mood states. Raul is a charismatic youngster with a flair for drawing and a passion for basketball. One Saturday morning, he asked his mother to take him to the art-supply store in the mall so that he could buy some new paints. His mother explained that they'd have to do it later because that morning was their time to run errands in town. Besides, he had plenty of paint and paper in his room, she told him, and they'd promised him new art supplies for his half birthday the next week. Instead of being placated by his mom's reassurances, though, Raul grew enraged and began to throw a tantrum.

This, of course, is behavior that all children—those with disabilities and those without—display from time to time. In the case of a child *without* a psychiatric disorder, however, the scenario might unfold like this: The child complains about how unfair this situation is, slams the door to his room, mumbles under his breath about his terrible parents, sulks for fifteen minutes behind closed doors, and then reemerges and asks grudgingly, "So where do we have to go?"

But in Raul's case, the tantrum takes on a far different quality, depending on the time of day and whether he is experiencing the depressive or manic phase of his illness. When he is depressed, often during the morning hours, Raul is apt to cry and accuse his parents of neglect. In the instance just mentioned, his reaction might have been like this:

"That's not fair," he rants. "We could find the time. I want some new paints, and you promised them to me. You never listen to me. Sure, if my brother wanted them, you would get them. I know you'll probably come up with a reason not to get them—even next week. I never get anything I want. You guys don't care how I feel."

He then takes his brother's completed homework, which is lying on the table, and rips it up. When his mother says, "What are you doing? He just finished working on that!" Raul screams, "See, I knew you liked him better than me." He starts throwing pencils and crayons around the room, and his father tries to restrain him. Raul begins to look like a caged animal.

"Let go of me. Let go of me. Stop hurting me."

At this point, his mother tries to intervene and has the father put the child in his room. The boy runs to his bed, puts his pillow over his head, and cries.

"Why don't you just kill me? I know you'd all be happy if I wasn't here," he wails.

After a few seconds of silence as his mother gently rubs his back, he says, "I'm so sorry. I don't know what's wrong with me. I hate myself. I wish I was dead."

And then he cries almost inconsolably. Raul's remorse and self-loathing are quite obvious and painful for his parents, even though they are still angry over his earlier behavior. No matter what alternatives his parents present ("We'll go to the art-supply store tomorrow; we'll order the paints online"), nothing seems to soothe him when he's in this depressed state, or if something does, the positive effects are transient.

By contrast, when Raul is experiencing the kind of irritability associated with the manic phase of bipolar disorder, he might have a tantrum that sounds more outwardly directed:

"Why can't I have the art supplies now? You promised! You always tell me I'm supposed to keep my promises, but what about you? You always lie! You tell me you'll do something, and then you don't."

His mom tries to talk to him, and he puts his hands over his ears and makes a face at her, taunting "Blah, blah, blah, blah!"

His mother says, "That's very disrespectful, and I want it stopped."

"So?" he replies. "You're disrespecting me. If you won't get me what I want, why should I listen to you? I hate you. I wish you both were dead." He then picks up a bag of peanuts on the kitchen table and starts throwing them at his parents.

His mom cries. The father, enraged, uses every ounce of his self-control and says, "Go to your room!"

"Make me!" Raul shoots back.

The father picks up the boy, who is kicking and screaming, puts him on his bed, and says, "Stay there until you are able to control yourself!"

Raul says, "I hate you, you pig! Get out of my room." He throws his stuffed animals at his bedroom door.

During all tantrums, children appear angry, say mean things to their parents, and can be disrespectful. They struggle with accepting the word *no*. But the non-mood-disordered-child, though angry, is able to take a break and then be reasonable (not happy, perhaps, but accepting that he can't get his way). Raul's case shows a child who is much more enraged, one who lashes out at his parents. In both the depressive and the "up" phases of his illness, he behaves irrationally, and his tantrums may or may not be short-lived. In both instances, his outbursts could appropriately be termed "rage attacks" or "mood storms." Again, these behaviors are driven not by willful disobedience but by biology.

We need to listen to Raul's words to understand better what is happening and not just the "music" of his rages. In the first instance, he expresses feeling less loved than his brother and less cared for by his family. He feels as though they hate him, and he sees his cup as half empty. He feels powerless in the interaction. The child feels bad about himself, thus the tears and despondency. He lashes out with anger and then feels guilty about his behavior. Underneath his anger is tremendous pain and misery. If you listen to Raul's words, there's no question that he's depressed and that the frustration of a simple "no" was enough to bring his depressive feelings to the surface.

The second scenario reflects a child who is thinking of himself as an adult, his parents' equal. There is a sense of power and entitlement in his behavior. How dare his parents not listen to him! His anger is much more apt to be directed outwardly rather than inwardly. He is a child in the manic phase of his illness.

The detailed descriptions that Raul's parents provided, together with his medical history, made it clear to me that he needed to be put on a mood stabilizer. Now, several months later, his parents report that his reactions to their limit-setting are more like those of the child without a psychiatric disorder. He's interested in basketball once more, and his drawings have taken on renewed verve and richness.

Although certain phases of childhood bipolar disorder can be more challenging than others, learning to recognize and manage a child's particular pattern of experiencing the illness is key for every bipolar kid—and his parents. When youngsters can learn to deal with their own mood pendulums early on (even young children can begin to do this with the help of the adults in their lives) and at the same time harness their creativity, the likelihood that they will become happier and better-functioning adults is significantly increased. I have no doubt that a number of my kids will be quite successful and do some very exciting things when they grow up. They just have to make it through childhood first.

As most parents with bipolar kids already know, all this is easier said than done. Childhood is probably one of the few times in life when bipolar kids are forced to do the things they are worst at— waking up early, going to bed on time, and concentrating on challenging subjects such as handwriting and math in a busy classroom. But that doesn't mean things can't or won't get better. Parenting, educating, befriending, and treating these children is a challenging but potentially fascinating journey. I'm reminded of the New York lottery slogan: "You've got to be in it, to win it." Parents have to be willing to put in the necessary hard work to help their child, but this can result in an incredible outcome. The odds of winning the lottery are low, but the odds of your hard work paying off when your child is older are exponentially higher.

3

✿

The Hidden
Aspects of Bipolar Disorder

No set list of symptoms definitively identifies bipolar disorder in children, but the condition is marked by a number of signs that often go undetected by parents and mental health professionals alike. These are the hidden (or at least not always recognized) aspects of bipolar disorder. Keep in mind that none of these features makes or breaks the diagnosis of bipolarity. But if several of the traits discussed in this chapter sound familiar in regard to your child, it may be time for further investigation.

Skip the Surprises

Surprises—even happy ones—can send certain bipolar kids into a tailspin. For instance, one mother remarked that her nine-year-old son sometimes came unglued when she arrived home from work with his favorite ice cream cone for a surprise treat. Over time, she learned to "head off a tantrum by calling him ahead of time to assess his mood and let him know what to expect."

How could a pleasant surprise be so upsetting? After all, wouldn't any kid would want an ice cream cone or a surprise birthday party or an unexpected gift? In the case of kids with bipolar disorder and other disabilities, the answer is often "no." To my mind, a key reason is that bipolar children often experience such excessive internal anxiety in their everyday lives that merely navigating along the rocky road of daily events can be a major challenge. Negotiating the noise and commotion of a crowded school bus, for instance, can be hard in itself, and getting through math class without an outburst or a meltdown may require every bit of mental energy a bipolar child can muster. Throw in a surprise, and it may be all the youngster can do to hold things together.

When kids are at the mercy of their mood shifts, unspoken questions such as "What will I get as a reward?" "Will I like it?" "Will I be disappointed?" may be enough to send them over the edge. If they at least know what's coming and when, they can feel more in control of their lives and their emotions.

In addition to surprise-filled events, clowns, the embodiment of surprises, are another source of distress for some bipolar children. Over the years, I have noticed that a number of my patients are unusually afraid of clowns. When taking a patient history, I wouldn't ordinarily ask a child, "Are you afraid of clowns?" It's not a standard question on any child psychological symptom checklist, and the patients in my practice are not, for the most part, preschoolers. Indeed, many of them are eight, nine, ten, or older—ages when you'd expect kids either to think clowns are silly or fun or to be bored by them. But for some bipolar kids, this just isn't the case.

Why is this? When you think about it, the pieces seem to fit. I suspect the most disturbing part of a clown to these youngsters is the look of his face. What do children see in a clown's face? It's hard to say, but the asymmetry and strange colors may be unusually frightening to a bipolar child. In addition, clowns are unpredictable; they pull things such as bouquets of flowers or handkerchiefs out of their pockets with no advance warning. In short, it may be that to a bipolar kid, a clown is a surprise on legs—not to mention a walking assault on the senses.

Holidays can also be particularly upsetting for a bipolar child. One mother of a seven-year-old mentioned that each year, she has to tell her son weeks in advance what gifts will be waiting for him under the Christmas tree. If he isn't sure what he will find on Christmas morning, he cries hysterically when he opens the presents. So, his mother has learned to give him a list ahead of time. "Several of my relatives have hinted that they think that he's just spoiled," she told me. On the contrary, her youngster's behavior isn't the result of being spoiled; rather, he is trying hard to structure his world so as not to make a scene on Christmas morning, and he knows himself well enough to understand what he needs in this situation. I give this kid a lot of credit: He knows what he can and cannot tolerate at this stage in his life. And he wants to do the right thing—he just needs the right people to listen to him.

"Don't Shift My Gears"

Clinicians sometimes refer to a child's emotional rigidity as the inability to "shift set." This rigidity often comes into play when getting a child ready to transition to a different activity or begin a new routine. For example, every week, Mark and his mother went to karate class. And every week, getting out of the house was an ordeal. Mark's mom often spent at least half an hour begging and cajoling him to go to class. Yet once there, he consistently had a great time. Nonetheless, the memory of the previous week's positive experience didn't carry over to the next time he had to go to lessons, and his mother's begging and arguing would begin anew.

Over the years, I've found that a definite correlation exists between a child's rigidity and his mood. When a bipolar child is depressed, everything becomes more difficult. Certainly, it's true that all children, even those without disabilities, can sometimes have trouble transitioning from one activity to another. Any child may protest being called to dinner when he's playing a video game or watching television. He probably doesn't like being interrupted while he's having fun, and he might say, "Just one more minute. I've got to do it. I'm about to get to the fifth level on the game." But once his mom restates the rules—"I told you five minutes ago that it's going to be time to stop. You got the warning. Enough is enough. If you don't come to the table right now, you won't be able to watch that program you like on Animal Planet"—the nonbiopolar child might seem annoyed but will eventually go to the table for dinner.

The same scenario with a bipolar child might look much different. His mom gives him the same warning, "Look, Joseph, this is the last time I'm telling you this. If you don't come to the dinner table, you won't be able to watch that show on Animal Planet before bedtime."

"I don't care. You're mean. You probably weren't going to let me watch it anyway. You always promise things and then change your mind. You don't listen to me, so why should I listen to you?"

With that, Dad walks in. "What is going on here? Joseph, why were you yelling at your mother?"

"She won't let me just finish my game. She wants me to go eat now. I can't. She's mean. I know she hates me!"

"You know your mother doesn't hate you. You know she loves you. But it's dinnertime. So let's go."

Joseph doesn't move. His father then proceeds to turn off the video game. Joseph gets angry and pushes him backward, and Dad lands on the couch.

"That's enough!" Dad says and holds Joseph securely, to restrain him. In doing so, he accidentally taps the boy's chin, ever so slightly. Then Joseph starts screaming, "That's child abuse! I'm calling the police."

Many people who don't have a bipolar child find such a situation incredible. They assume that the parent handled the situation in the wrong way. But parenting techniques that are good enough for most kids simply don't work with many bipolar kids. Here, you have two reasonable people attempting to reason with an unreasonable one. There is little room for progress.

This kind of rigidity plays a role in any number of situations in which a transition is required for a bipolar child. It may be the teacher saying, "OK, let's move on to the next subject" or "Gym is over; it's time to go back to class."

Transitions can be hard enough for bipolar kids in the best of times. But an onset of depression can make their rigidity even worse, or it can cause them to *think* that a change has occurred even when *nothing* has changed. Mom can make the same tuna sandwich every day for lunch (with the crusts taken off and the sandwich cut diagonally), then one day, the child becomes depressed and starts screaming, "This isn't the same tuna, it tastes different. I can't eat this! Why did you change it?" Nothing the mother does is different, but the child is more depressed, so to her, it's as if nothing is right.

Dealing with these situations is understandably difficult. I often suggest to parents that they should give *themselves* a time-out to re- coup their sanity and impulse control before attempting any kind of intervention.

Dr. Jekyll at School, Mr. Hyde at Home

A surprising number of bipolar children are able to hold themselves together long enough to meet the considerable demands and pres- sures of the school day but then dissolve into tantrums or tears once they reach the safety of home, where they're finally able to let their feelings show. This particular pattern of behavior (and it's not one that all bipolar children display, by any means) typically invites a lot of criticism and advice from relatives, teachers, and even therapists. If a child has problems at home but not at school or during social ac- tivities, others think, "Aha! It must be the parents who are doing something wrong." After all, if Ninette *really* had a biologic illness, wouldn't it be evident everywhere? And particularly in school, where the pressures would seem to be greater?

On the surface, this attitude makes a lot of sense. Look at kids with ADHD. Their symptoms of overactivity, inattention, and impulsivity are present in many different settings. In the case of bipolar kids, however, the Dr. Jekyll-at-School/Mr. Hyde-at-Home behavior pattern is far more likely to be the result of very good or excellent parenting than it is of some kind of neglect or overindulgence. The parents have somehow impressed on their child that it is not acceptable to behave poorly in the outside world. Kids get this message and use all their strength to hold things together during the day.

But by the time they get off the school bus, they are ready to explode. Kids know that if they act out of control in the outside world, they will surely be rejected and singled out as different. If they let their feelings loose at home, it's safer. They trust that their parents love them and will not abandon them no matter what. I remember asking Barry, a nine-year-old, why he thought he had a tantrum everyday when he got home from school. He looked at me as if I'd asked an absurd question. "I feel so angry," he answered. "I can't let it out in school. I'll get in trouble with the teacher."

Parents who don't understand this phenomenon can have incredible feelings of guilt. They search their souls for what they have done wrong. They think: "If he's so good at my parents' house and his friends' homes, the problem must be me"; "Everyone in my family tells me I give in to him too much and spoil him"; "I let him get away with things I should never allow"; "Maybe they're right. I am not so lenient with his sister."

What the outside world doesn't see is the tremendous patience and creativity these kids require. Most caring parents realize early on that they have to pick and choose their battles. If not, they could be fighting with their bipolar youngster all day, every day.

It's amusing to listen to parents of bipolar kids with this pattern describe their first parent-teacher conference of the year. The parents brace themselves for the worst. Instead, the teacher reports that their son or daughter is a star student; has excellent manners; and is kind, polite, sweet, thoughtful, and considerate. On the way out the door, the parents begin to speculate about whether their youngster might have been sent away to the witness-protection program and replaced by a stand-in. "Are you sure she was talking about our Chester?" one parent asks the other.

Of course, not all bipolar kids are able to keep it together at school. If it hasn't happened already, the time may come when your child loses the battle to control his behavior at school as well as at home. A mother or father may think, "I guess I'm a failure as a parent. I haven't even been able to teach my child boundaries like some other parents of bipolar kids can."

But all parents of bipolar children need to recognize that the illness is *not the fault of either the parent or the child*; further, how the youngster *deals* with his actions and behavior is his responsibility. Understanding this is one of the major tasks of parenting and participating in therapy with a bipolar child. A parent needs to learn how to tell when a child's problems are the result of learned behaviors and when they are the result of out-of-control biology. The child, in turn, needs to learn to recognize and control the types of behaviors that cause him problems. Thus, I tell my patients, "Yes, I know you feel extra angry lately. But being angry is no excuse for you to hit another child. Everyone gets angry, and sometimes it's very hard to control these feelings. But if you were a grown-up and hit someone like that, you'd go to jail."

Sometimes, I'll also give them an example from my own life to better illustrate the point. I might explain how the parking lot outside my favorite grocery store is often overcrowded. Then I tell them about the day I drove around for ten minutes to find a spot until I finally saw one car being backed out of a space; I was patiently waiting for the car to leave when someone else cut my car off and took the spot. Then I explain that I felt so angry, I wished that I could take all the air out of that mean person's tires. But I knew I couldn't. Just because they were doing something wrong didn't mean that I should, too. And if I did what I thought about, I could get in trouble. What I really did was continue to circle the parking lot until I found another spot. Then, feeling very angry, I called my husband on the phone. I told him how annoyed I felt because this person was so mean and unfair. For a few minutes, we talked about how people can be very rude at times—and I started feeling better. I tell the child the point is that we all get angry at times. It's how we deal with our anger that's important. Why get ourselves into trouble when someone else did something wrong?

"I Know Better Than You"

As mentioned in Chapter 2, when a manic or hypomanic bipolar person has wildly unrealistic ideas about his power or abilities, we in the medical community call this grandiosity. But because grandiosity looks different in kids than in adults, it often goes unrecognized by parents and professionals alike. When a grown-up experiences grandiosity, he may believe that the speed limit on the highway does not apply to him, or he might declare that he will run for president and win, even without conducting a campaign. In short, the person elevates himself to a higher level than the rest of the world.

A youngster with grandiosity believes that he is on a higher level, too. And who is at a higher level than a child? An adult, of course. If a bipolar child's mood is elevated, he may well think of adults as his equals or believe that he is superior to other kids. A child may ask the principal, "Are you done yet?" while being scolded for inappropriate behavior. Or he may declare that his science project was the best in the class, even though it was a bare-bones model of Saturn that he threw together at the last minute.

Nor is it uncommon for bipolar children to insist they are intellectually superior to the grown-ups in their world. Jan, a first-grader, came home from school one day and excitedly told his mother, "I learned how to spell 'bottle' today, like what my baby brother Maddox uses to drink milk." His mom enthusiastically said, "Ok, tell me how." Full of self-confidence, Jan spelled "B-O-T-T-L." Her mother gently told her, "That's great! But there's an 'e' at the end." Janet looked her straight in the eye and said, "No there isn't. You're wrong! Even my teacher said that's how you spell it."

His mother said, "Gee, are you sure? I'm kind of surprised. You know what? Let's look it up in the children's dictionary." Jan thought this was a good idea, and so his mom went to get the book. When they found the word, his mother said, "Here it is. You were so close, but 'bottle' does have an 'e' at the end. It's a silent 'e', so I can see why you didn't know it." Jan got outraged and began throwing a tantrum. "The dictionary is wrong! Wrong! Wrong! Wrong!" He felt he knew better than his mother, the dictionary, and probably the teacher as well.

It's also not uncommon for kids in a grandiose state to feel they are free to say anything they want to an adult. When nine-year-old Mitchell's mom wouldn't let him buy the video game he wanted, he launched into a major temper tantrum. "You always lie," he yelled. "You're the worst mother in the world. You meany. You're meaner than the wicked witch in that story we read! And you're uglier, too!" In this case, it's clear that Mitchell felt he was entitled to get his video game, and he spoke to his mother in a way that indicated tremendous disrespect.

Of course, children sometimes also include me on the list of people to whom they feel superior. One seven-year-old, who often told me he was "the best" at many things, walked around my office and noticed my collection of some 150 Beanie Babies and declared that he had many more at home (even though his mother was shaking her head to the contrary in the background). Then he checked out the medical textbooks on the shelf and pulled out one that was more than a thousand pages long. "I read books like this all the time," he declared. He went on to say that his class at school was practicing for the Christmas concert but added, "I am the only one in my class who knows all the words to the songs."

Grandiosity also makes for some creative storytelling. Sure, all kids say things that they know aren't true. But in bipolar children, it's different, in part because they do it more frequently and in part because these kids sometimes have a hard time telling fantasy from reality, especially as their mood gets more manic. It's not unusual for teachers of bipolar kids to tell parents that they were so surprised (or happy, sad, relieved, proud—pick one) about what happened in the family recently. Whatever the event was that the student related to the teacher, it's usually news to the mom or dad.

One mother, for instance, recounted the story of the day that she met her son's first-grade teacher in the grocery store. They engaged in a bit of small talk, and then the teacher asked, "Is your husband back from Africa yet? Robbie told me he was so excited because he had asked his dad to bring home an elephant tusk from the trip." Robbie's mom looked at his teacher quizzically. Then she realized what had occurred. She gently discussed how Robbie's dad had gone to Chicago last week, adding, "But you know what an active imagination Robbie has. He does exaggerate sometimes!" She put a smile on her face and pretended to chuckle over her embarrassment.

Or consider Maynard, who missed one Sunday of religious school and knew the teacher was going to be unhappy about his absence. When asked why he missed class, Maynard explained that his grand-father had passed away and the family had gone to Pennsylvania for the funeral. You can imagine his mother's shock when she got the condolence call!

In the extreme, grandiosity reflects the fact that the boundaries between reality and fantasy truly are blurred or crossed for a child. One young man, Kenny, stated that he had special powers and could read other people's minds. When I asked him what I was thinking, he said I was considering what I was going to ask him—which, in a way, was true but not hard to guess. Then I asked him to try it again, and he refused. I had his mother come in. We discussed Kenny's mind-reading abilities, and his mom said he had mentioned it earlier but that she hadn't taken it seriously. After much intense discussion, Kenny said that "maybe" he couldn't really read minds, but he wasn't completely sure. I explained to him that he might wish that he had special powers but that no one really does. I told him I also believed that his medication needed adjustment, as his boundaries between reality and fantasy were weak. I was concerned that if he was left untreated, he could have a true break with reality.

It's important to remember that if the child's mood is elevated, the information he conveys may be distorted and his "factual" stories more colorful. Depressed kids see the world through dark-tinted glasses, but hypomanic or manic youngsters see it through rose-colored glasses. A mood disordered child's perceptions of the world around him may be off in any number of ways.

Impulsivity

Samantha was a five-year-old patient of mine who decided she would find out whether she could swim *after* she jumped into the deep end of the pool. (She was fortunate to have others nearby to rescue her.) Such impulsivity can get bipolar kids into hot water. Their motto seems to be: Act first, think later. I've had parents tell me that their children have gotten upset and tried to run away from them at the mall or tried to run away from home. It's not as though these kids knew where to go; they were simply angry and decided to leave. Other kids threaten to open a car door while riding down the highway. (I recommend child locks in general but especially in such cases and, if necessary, pulling off the road until the mood storm has passed.)

Impulsivity may also be seen in other forms of risk-taking behavior. An impulsive child may steal something from a friend or a store simply because the opportunity arises. When seven-year-old Joan was asked why she took a doll from her friend's house, she responded, "Because I wanted it." By the same token, kids may decide to satisfy their sexual curiosity by suddenly taking off their clothes and talking a friend into playing doctor and patient.

Spurred by a bad mood, an impulsive child may become angry enough to pick up a kitchen knife or another sharp object and threaten to harm himself or someone else. A parent should not—I repeat, *should not*—say anything such as, "Go ahead, if that's what you want to do." These are children who can act impulsively and irrationally. The parent has to be the rational one in these situations. Parents often say they feel that their child is being manipulative and trying to get attention. This may or may not be the case, but it's critical to be extremely cautious before assuming any outburst is the child's way to control the situation. Even if this is the case, a child may be foolish or stubborn enough to rise to a parent's dare or challenge. It's necessary for the parent to try to remain calm and defuse the situation by gently but clearly telling the child to put down the object. As the parent, you may need to explain that you know he is very upset but that he is a good kid, and waving around something heavy or sharp can accidentally result in someone's getting hurt: "Even if you feel mad right now, you know that you'd be so upset if you hurt someone in our family. So put it that back in the drawer, and let's talk."

Of course, if you really feel that the child may do something dangerous, carefully taking the object away is the right move. In extreme circumstances, you may need to get the other parent to assist you, or you may need to call the police. Your response depends on the circumstances at hand. But not taking the child seriously is seldom the best approach.

Indeed, the most effective remedy for a situation of this type is prevention. If you worry about your child doing something dangerous, put away anything he might use to carry this out—kitchen knives, medications, guns, and so forth. If a youngster seems to be in a volatile mood (and granted, this is sometimes hard to predict) and has threatened to open the car doors while the car is moving, don't venture out on the highway. If there are weapons in the house, lock them up or, better yet, banish them from the house altogether. Accidents can happen—and they do.

"I Can't Wake Up"

Many bipolar kids have difficulty waking up in the morning, even if they've had a reasonable amount of sleep the night before. When their moods are unstable, they can be especially difficult to rouse in time for school, and when they do wake up, it may take quite a while before they are fully alert. Trying to get a bipolar kid up in the morning can be like trying to wake a polar bear when it's hibernating. The problem is compounded when the child also has a hard time falling asleep the night before (because of an elevated mood, anxiety, family events, and so forth). If a child is depressed, he's often extra tired, so he may go to bed early and still be very tired and hard to wake up the next day.

Some mothers have tried setting three alarms in their child's room, set to go off a few minutes apart so that (in theory anyway) the child will wake up by the time the third alarm sounds. Some kids get up, turn off the alarms while they're not fully conscious, and then go back to sleep. I've heard of parents sounding big dinner bells, pulling the sheets off the bed, and having the family dog lick the child on the face in hopes of awakening him, all to no avail.

In many cases, the kids would *like* to get up, but they just can't manage to do so even if they go to sleep at a reasonable time. And after spending a couple of hours every morning doing everything short of hiring a drum and bugle corps to play in their child's bedroom, many parents finally give up. The child continues to sleep until he wakes up naturally at 10 or 11 a.m.—too late to make it to school on time.

This is how one mother and her eleven-year-old son described their daily quest to begin the morning:

MOM'S STORY:
At about 7:00 a.m., I begin to try to wake him up. The two alarm clocks I've set for him begin to ring. I shake his arm, tell him what time it is, pull off his covers, and turn up the TV so loud that I'm sure the neighbors can hear it. I repeat these methods for around fifteen minutes, but Greg seems completely oblivious to all this activity, as if this was ER and he was the person in the coma. I look at the clock, and panic overtakes me. I begin to yell. Loudly. "You have to get up now. You're sleeping away the school year. You're going to miss the science test again, and you know that Mr. Thompson will give you a zero. If you keep this up, you're going to end up failing the class altogether. This is inexcusable. Get up NOW or your TV privileges are HISTORY for the rest of the month."

Greg grunts and bats me away with his hand, as if in a trance, then falls back to sleep. I begin to feel guilty about yelling and soften my approach a bit. "Look, I know it's really hard for you to wake up. The problem is that if you don't get up in fifteen minutes, you're not going to make it to school on time. Please, please. Just try. Here, I'll help you. Hold my hands, and I'll give you a tow. Sitting up is the hardest part. After that, things will get easier. You'll see."

Greg sleeps on. Frustrated, I call in the big guns: my husband, Joe.

Greg responds to his father's attempts to wake him by pulling the covers over his head and elbowing him if he gets too close. There have been some mornings when my husband has actually lifted Greg out of bed and stood him up. We thought for a minute this might work. Greg walked down the hall as if headed for the bathroom, but he didn't make it beyond his brother's bedroom, where he lay down on the bed and fell back asleep. By then, it was time for my husband to head off to work and for the other kids to be in school, and we all finally gave up. Greg usually wakes up on his own around 10 or 11 a.m., but he's extremely grumpy and out of it. It takes him at least an hour to wake up, start functioning, and get dressed.

Since the school year began three weeks ago, Greg has already been late eight times. I can't make up any more excuses about dental appointments, and the guidance counselor at the school is growing less understanding by the day. He says we have to think about putting a behavioral plan in place. "Have you tried getting an alarm clock for him?" he asks.

GREG'S STORY:
At nighttime, I feel good. It's like I could do anything. Morning is bad. No matter how hard I try, no matter how early I go to bed the night before, I can't get myself awake. It's like I'm in a dream and I'm trying real hard to come out of the dream but I can't. If somebody said, "I'll give you a million dollars if you just wake up," I don't know for sure if I could. All I want to do is sleep. I hate it when my family starts yelling at me. I wish they'd just go away and leave me alone for about two hours—and then I could wake up. They don't understand what it's like. Neither do my teachers. I feel bad in the morning. It's like I'm in a fog.

I wish I could get up and go to school on time like the rest of the kids. I always miss computer class and gym first thing in the morning. I hate that 'cuz computers is my favorite subject. I get there just in time for the hard stuff, like math and writing.

What's behind these stressful mornings? Why do bipolar kids have so much trouble waking up? The answers are still murky, but we do have some clues. For one thing, the medications bipolar kids take for their mood disorders (often before bedtime) can cause sedation, making them feel tired in the morning. Another factor, scientists believe, is a little-understood disruption in the sleep/wake cycle in bipolar kids. Just as we use a clock to help us know what time to get up for work, when to have lunch, and when it's time to get ready for sleep, the human body has its own internal clock. This biologic clock controls a person's twenty-four-hour patterns of sleep, temperature regulation, hormone secretion, and a variety of other body functions. These inborn daily cycles are called circadian rhythms.

In bipolar kids such as Greg, the biologic clock may not be ticking along in the way it should. Interestingly, unlike other children, bipolar kids seem to experience their deepest sleep just when it is time to get up in the morning. When other kids' brains are telling them it's morning and time to wake up, bipolar kids' brains may be sending them strong signals to roll over and go back to sleep. When awakened abruptly, these kids may feel only half conscious, as though in a dream state. Some researchers suspect that bipolar patients may have a genetic predisposition to instability in their sleep/wake cycle and that this is what contributes to irregular sleep habits.[1]

Melatonin, a peptide secreted by the brain, helps induce sleep. At night, the presence of darkness typically triggers the release of melatonin in the brain, causing sleepiness. The morning light, by contrast, inhibits melatonin, telling the body, "Time to wake up now." In bipolar kids, it may be that changes in melatonin levels are different from the regular cycling pattern, causing the brain to send mixed signals about when it's time to wake up or fall asleep.

Melatonin also plays a role in the regulation of body temperature, and this, too, affects sleep. Ordinarily, individuals produce less melatonin in the morning, signaling the body that it's time to warm up and wake up. In bipolar kids, this pattern may, once again, be off.

As noted earlier, almost every aspect of bipolar disorder worsens with depression. And sleep is no exception. In fact, a sleep disturbance can be one sign that a child's mood is beginning to change. Sleep deprivation can also *cause* a shift in mood—from depression to mania. Severe sleep deprivation can even result in psychosis (a break with reality).

How do these sleep problems play out in everyday life? To understand this, consider the situation Barbara, age nine, found herself in after a sleepover one Saturday night at a girlfriend's house. The girls had so much fun that they didn't sleep all night. Of course, when Barbara came home, she wasn't very pleasant, but then, what child would be after a night like that? She slept a few hours in the afternoon, but that was it. It took her an extra hour to fall asleep that night. The next morning, she had a problem getting up for school and had to sleep an extra two hours before rising. Again, the next night, it was harder than usual to fall asleep. By the time I saw her on Thursday, she was having temper tantrums and crying fits a few times a day.

One of the key things to do to help stabilize a child's mood is to get him back into a regular sleep pattern. Fixed regimens before going to bed as well as fixed bedtimes and waking times help decrease mood instability. And though sleepovers are fun, parents need to make sure that the bipolar child gets a reasonable amount of sleep; if the child's mood is unstable, sleepovers may need to be postponed for a while.

"Open the Window and Turn Down the Thermostat"

Any parent of a bipolar child will tell you that there is something different about the relationship between his or her child and the temperature in the environment. Demitri Papolos, MD, a specialist in pediatric bipolar disorder, was among the first to describe the abnormality—known as "thermoregulatory dysfunction"—in this population.[2] In general, bipolar kids seem to experience the environment as warmer than the rest of us. In the winter, they don't mind going out in very cold weather without many clothes on, and they may want to sleep with their bedroom windows open or their ceiling fans on. Indoors, they can look for all the world like menopausal women in the middle of a hot flash.

Hot weather makes many bipolar kids suffer. If the child is in a very warm classroom, he feels miserable. I know parents who have kept their bipolar child home from school on extremely hot days because he felt physically ill.

Even when it's not hot outside, bipolar children can look overheated. Papolos has also noted that bipolar youngsters have times when their ears turn red for no obvious reason.[3] Is this a marker of active bipolar disorder? Does it indicate a predisposition to this illness? Many parents have confirmed to me that they've observed this phenomenon in their bipolar kids. Although it may appear that red ears would be related to a state of rage (and there's no question that an enraged person's face can become red), here we're talking only about flushed ears, not faces, and the kids are not necessarily angry.

Initially, I was a bit skeptical about the correlation between red ears and bipolar disorder, but then I remembered Charlie, a nine-year-old boy I had treated for depression almost twenty years earlier. Occasionally, Charlie's ears would become bright red. At the time, I thought this was unusual, but I wasn't sure whether it was specific to his condition. Time passed, and his family moved to another part of the country. Then, a few years ago, Charlie's mom sent me a Christmas card saying he'd been diagnosed with bipolar disorder. Now, I frequently ask parents if their child sometimes gets red ears for no apparent reason, and I'm surprised by how many times I hear, "How did you know?"

"Mom, the Monster Is After Me"

A lot of my bipolar patients have violent nightmares, and in some cases, they have a preoccupation with thoughts of death and violence. (The phenomenon of gory, frightening dreams in bipolar children was first described by Charles Popper, MD, a psychiatrist at Massachusetts General Hospital.[4])

Unlike most of us, who wake up at the end of a nightmare just before we fall off the cliff, get eaten by the monster, or are caught by the bad guy, my kids often report that they don't wake up before something bad happens. Instead, they remain haunted by their bad dreams. Take the case of Wyatt, a handsome five-year-old who came into my office one day looking very sad. His mother explained that he had had an upsetting, scary dream the night before. She described (while Wyatt clung to her side) how he had awakened at 3 a.m. and gone into his parents' bedroom, terrified.

Wyatt said that in his dream, he saw his house and his neighborhood, but there were no people around. When I asked him if there was any blood in the dream, he said "yes." When I asked where, he pointed to the center of his forehead. He explained that there were people in his dream who got killed and had blood coming out of their foreheads. Why, then, had he said there were no people in the dream? I asked. Wyatt explained that there were no *live* people and that after they had been dead for a while, their bodies had disappeared. Obviously a very bright and verbal five-year-old, he had endured a horrible dream that would upset anyone, let alone a very young child. After his mom held him and reasured him that it was just a dream, he finally calmed down as long as he was able to sleep next to his mother.

"Don't Leave Me!"

Many parents of bipolar kids report that their children are still having difficulties separating from them—even at ages seven, eight, nine, and older. Separation anxiety refers to the excessive anxiety that occurs when a child has to leave the home or the person to whom she is very attached. We all know that having problems separating from parents is normal at certain developmental stages. But these children have heightened anxiety at a time when it is no longer age appropriate.

Unlike in other children, this separation anxiety extends well beyond the first few weeks of school. It can go on for weeks, months, or even years. Some children, though they may not seem upset over being away from their parents, may not want to be away from home. They refuse to go on sleepovers and may not even want to go to different parts of their own house alone. They dream and worry about separation from their families and are often extremely fearful that something bad will happen to a family member. Eight-year-old James, for instance, regularly refused to go to bed by himself and demanded a parent be with him as he fell asleep. Around three or four in the morning, he would go into his parents' room and say he had had a bad nightmare and was afraid to be alone.

Some kids sleep in sleeping bags, on sofas, on the bedroom floor, or even in the hallway outside their parents' bedroom door because they cannot separate. At times, the child is so scared and hysterical (an indication of being genuinely terrified) that he becomes physically violent if the parents try to get him to stay alone in his room.

If you think about it, this makes more than a little sense. If you had scary, violent dreams (say, a monster burned down your house and killed your whole family), would you look forward to going to sleep alone? As with other facets of bipolar disorder, separation anxiety is also somewhat mood dependent. Kids who are more depressed experience much more anxiety. Getting a child to sleep in his own bed when he's depressed may be an uphill battle (remember, think terrified). It will be much easier to work with the child when his mood is more stable or mildly elevated. At these times, he can be more flexible and approachable. Keep in mind that it's not that the child doesn't want to stay in his own bed, it's that he may feel that he simply *can't*.

"I'm Anxious"

Signs of generalized anxiety and other anxiety disorders (such as Obsessive-Compulsive Disorder) are often present in bipolar kids. But treating the mood disorder first may make the anxiety symptoms disappear or at least lessen. Jenny, who was eight years old when I first saw her, was a prime example of this. A red-haired, blue-eyed cherub, Jenny could have moments of being a very cranky child. She had different signs of anxiety, but the most striking was her fear of elevators. In fact, I was able to get a sense of her mood just by asking her whether she walked or took the elevator to my fourth-floor offices. When she was depressed, she became elevator phobic and always took the stairs. When her mood was fairly even or a bit elevated, she had no problem at all in using the elevator. On one occasion when she was full of excess energy, I saw her coming out of the elevator smiling while doing a dance. I knew exactly where her mood was that day. The lesson is this: If anxiety intensifies, a depressed mood may also be present. If the anxiety remains after a child's moods have been stabilized, then there's a good chance that the anxiety disorder needs to be specifically addressed.

"Hi Poopyhead, or Should I Say Sexy?"

It's not uncommon for parents to report that, much to their embarrassment, their adorable six-year-old son is fond of kissing Grandma on the lips or pulling down his pants when people come to visit. Now, this doesn't mean that your young bipolar child is interested in having sex with others, the way we might interpret this behavior in an adult who is overly preoccupied with sex. But it may mean that he is experiencing hypersexuality, a symptom of bipolar disorder in some kids. Hypersexuality means that the child is displaying an excessive interest in and awareness of sexuality. In youngsters, this can take a variety of forms, for example, saying "potty words" at inappropriate times, looking at others' private parts, or excessive masturbation. I have heard many reports from parents of young kids who love to dance naked around the house. The common thread is that these children have inappropriate sexual interests for their age. The proper response by a parent is to address the issue calmly and explain that the behavior is not acceptable.

"Get That Off of Me Now!"

As we all learned in elementary school, we have five senses—touch, taste, hearing, vision, and smell. In some children with bipolar disorder, one or a few of these senses may be amplified, that is, the person is extremely sensitive to what affects these senses. Sensory hypersensitivity, as this phenomenon is called, is sometimes seen in children without mental or emotional issues, of course, but it is especially common in bipolar children. For instance, Ellie, a very sweet six-year-old, is almost impossible to buy clothes for. She will only wear a certain brand of socks because other socks have seams that are "too scratchy." Her mother has to take all the tags off her new clothes; if she doesn't, Ellie will not wear them, or she'll try to rip the tag out herself (and destroy the shirt in the process). Even with the labels off, she still rejects some shirts. Marcy, seven, also has tactile hypersensitivity. When she was in kindergarten, she refused to wear underwear beneath her clothes or socks on her feet because she didn't like the way they felt.

Then there's Harvey, who had to leave a trip to the circus because he couldn't tolerate the loud noise. And Terrell, who says he feels nauseated whenever someone even talks about eating fish. The first time his mother made baked swordfish, Terrell ran through the house yelling, "This house smells. It's disgusting. I'm going to puke. Get rid of it. Now!" Jessica's mother says that as a baby and toddler, she'd spit out food if she didn't like the texture. Even today, at age six, she refuses to eat chunky peanut butter or anything with a rough texture. Like many other problems we see in kids with bipolar disorder, sensory dysfunction is somewhat mood dependent: When the child's mood is stable, the dysfunction may lessen or go away completely; when she is depressed, it will likely be intensified.

"Out of the Way! That Chocolate Cake Is All Mine!"

Talk to a bipolar kid about what he wants for supper, and you'll likely hear a list something like this: pizza, pasta, candy, bread, and ice cream. Not only do bipolar kids crave high-carbohydrate and salty foods, some seem to eat them nonstop. For instance, Ian's mom had to stop bringing cookies into the house. If his mood was off, her son could go through a whole box of thirty cookies in one sitting. (I can't tell you how many mothers say they've resorted to hiding candy, boxes of cereal, and other high-carb foods.)

Of course, craving carbohydrates is not exclusive to kids with bipolar disorder. It is seen in other mood disorders, including seasonal affective disorder, the mood shift associated with certain changes in the seasons, and hysteroid dysphoria (a diagnostic label no longer in use) that refers to depression often precipitated by rejection or loss of a romantic relationship. Whatever the diagnosis, evidence exists that there is a distinct correlation between craving carbohydrate-rich foods and mood. Studies indicate that the neurotransmitters serotonin, norepinephrine, and dopamine play a role in determining how much individuals eat as well as the types of food they prefer.[5]

In a 2001 study, researchers Larry Christensen and L. Pettijohn surveyed 113 male and 138 female college students concerning the relationship between their moods and eating behavior. They found that carbohydrate cravers felt distress during their cravings but were happier and relaxed after they ate enough to feel satisfied. By contrast, protein cravers felt anxious or hungry before their cravings and happy, normal, bored, and energetic after eating a lot of protein.[6] Interestingly, scientific analysis of all the data from this study indicated that there was a significant association between carb craving and mood but not between protein craving and mood. We also know that low serotonin levels have been associated with depressive disorders and that some antidepressants as well as carbohydrates increase serotonin levels.

There's less in the medical literature about salt cravings, but I see a predilection for salty foods in a fair number of patients as well. The bottom line is that a bipolar child's food preferences are not primarily driven by chance or boredom but by basic biology. A parent should see these cravings as clues that the child's mood may be changing. As much as possible, the parent should encourage healthier eating choices, but this effort may be difficult when a child's mood is off.

"My Sinuses Are Killing Me"

I've also observed that many of the bipolar kids I treat get frequent sinus infections, more than I've seen in other psychiatrically ill groups. It isn't known why this occurs and whether it is truly more common in bipolar children (although this is what I observe in my practice, it doesn't mean it's true for other groups of bipolar kids). It is an area open to future study.

"I Feel So Good When It's Spring"

Since the 1980s, an unmistakable relationship between the different seasons and some individuals' moods has been established. Of course, most people might agree that everyone feels better in spring and summer, with the warm weather and nature in full bloom. Winter is just too dark, and even in late fall as the daylight hours decrease, the world seems more dull and boring. Lying in bed watching TV seems like the kind of activity these days are meant for.

Yet there are individuals who are unusually sensitive to these seasonal changes. They have significant mood swings that affect their behavior and functioning in a variety of ways at different times of the year. They are, if you will, slaves to the seasons. The term for what these individuals are experiencing is seasonal affective disorder.[7] It's unclear how many bipolar children experience seasonal affective disorder, but I see it frequently in the bipolar kids in my practice. The typical pattern of a child with this seasonal disorder is to be depressed in the fall/winter and stable or hypomanic in the spring/summer. In a minority of individuals, the pattern is reversed: They are happy in winter and depressed in summer. Some researchers and clinicians believe that seasonal affective disorder is actually part of the bipolar spectrum.

Treatment of kids with this disorder involves using therapy based on increasing the amount of light they are exposed to each day and, in turn, causing changes in brain chemistry related to mood. (For more on light treatment for seasonal affective disorder, see Chapter 7.)

All of these stories show that pediatric bipolar disorder can be associated with a variety of symptoms that you typically won't find in any medical textbook. Whether it's carb cravings, gory nightmares, or Jekyll-and-Hyde behavior, these symptoms can provide important diagnostic clues. Don't forget to take these symptoms into account—and bring them up with your child's doctor—as you seek answers in helping your youngster find his inner calm.

4

How Bipolar Kids Shine

Much of the information parents hear about bipolar kids focuses on the negatives. But thankfully, there is also plenty of good news to be trumpeted when it comes to the things that set these kids apart. Whether it's an exceptional creative talent, a remarkable sensitivity, or simply an uncanny ability to think outside the box, bipolar children can be special in a whole host of ways. These kids present decided challenges, to be sure, but they also enrich the lives of those around them day after day. Perhaps Kevin, the father of a bipolar son, said it best as he described the joys of raising Matthew, age eight:

So much time is spent focusing on the problems, worrying, wondering how he is inside, it is important for me to step back and remind myself of the joy.

My son is such an extraordinary person. I often wish I were more like him. He is so bright, and his intelligence is both intellectual and emotional.

Intellectually, he is deeply curious, but because of his learning disability, he has had to find other ways to absorb, assimilate, and understand. His ability to connect different pieces of information into a cohesive whole always amazes me. He seems to learn in three dimensions, not in a straight line. His vocabulary will often stop adults in their tracks. One of my forty-year-old friends told me he loves talking to my eight-year-old son because they watch many of the same programs on the History Channel, and he can't find any adults to discuss the shows with. I feel the same connection with my son's intelligence; he is fun to talk with, I learn from him, I seek his opinion. The same mind that can be so tortured by bipolarity also has such extraordinary depth and breadth. Bipolarity seems to create some of our most beautiful minds.

His emotional intelligence is equally deep. His ability to understand feelings and emotions is unique amongst his peers. His compassion for those in need is a constant. He can't stand to see another person cry, another person suffer. He cannot look at a statue of Jesus on the crucifix; he doesn't understand why anyone would do that to another person. He worries about the animals that are pushed from their homes by a new housing development.

His feelings are so often hurt. He cries easily; he doesn't understand peers who are mean. Perhaps his emotional intelligence comes from somewhere else, but I believe it is inexorably intertwined with his bipolarity. He knows sadness, he knows darkness, and he doesn't wish it upon another. That same emotional intelligence will serve him well throughout his life. He will be sensitive, patient, understanding of others' feelings. He will be a nurturing friend, spouse, and father.

If you were to offer me a way to rid my son of bipolarity, I would do so in a minute—for his sake. But if you were to tell me that in doing so we would also lose the magic of his mind, from a strictly personal sense—I would want to say no, his mind is too precious, his spirit is too unique. For me, it is not the sadness that defines my son, it is the joy. Just as the pain of bipolarity is unique, so is the joy. He is an extraordinary person, and I am proud to be his father.

Anyone who walks into my office and takes a look at the collection of paintings, drawings, and other pieces of artwork my kids have created will begin to sense what parents such as Kevin are talking about when they say many of these kids are extraordinary. One patient sketched an incredibly detailed pirate ship that was so skillfully done it looked as if it could be featured in an art gallery. Another boy drew a picture of a space hero that was so realistic I mistakenly thought he'd traced it from a comic book. Seventeen-year-old Julio, in treatment for nine years, brought in an acoustic guitar painted with an incredible checkerboard design. I liked it so much that I commissioned him to design a guitar for my own son, an aspiring rock star.

Of course, art is far from the only arena in which these creative kids can excel. Many of them show signs of talent in poetry, writing, acting, storytelling, architecture, inventing, and fashion design. One fifteen-year-old girl, who could quite possibly be the next Kate Spade, designed a gorgeous beaded purse in art class. Kyrie, age twelve, developed a space-saving plan for his family's basement and then helped his father (a construction engineer) build it.

Some of these kids are masters of costume design, too. I love to tell people that I have some very famous patients in my practice, among them Batman, Spiderman, Superman, Catwoman, and several wizards. OK, I know, all kids like to play dress up, especially on Halloween. But mine seem to love it 365 days a year. There's something special going on with them that anyone would recognize, if they just took the time to look.

A number of scientists and clinicians have pondered the association between adult bipolar disorder and creativity. Scientists have recently found some support for the idea that this relationship may also be true for bipolar children. A new study conducted at Stanford University School of Medicine and published in the *Journal of Psychiatric Research* explored this association.[1] The study, conducted by Kiki Chang, MD, and a team of Stanford researchers, looked at forty families in which at least one parent was bipolar. From these families, they selected forty offspring (twenty with bipolar disorder and twenty with ADHD) and compared them with twenty healthy adults and their twenty healthy children.

All members of these groups were given a psychiatric evaluation, and then they completed the Barron-Welsh Art Scale, or BWAS, a test that tries to provide an objective measure of creativity. The scoring is based on "like" and "dislike" responses to figures of varying complexity and symmetry; past studies have suggested that creative people tend to dislike the simple and symmetric symbols.

The researchers found that the BWAS "dislike" scores (or creativity scores) of the parents with bipolar disorder were 120 percent higher than those of the healthy parents. Further, the bipolar children scored 107 percent higher and the ADHD youth 91 percent higher than the healthy children on BWAS "dislike" scores. These results appear to provide support for the belief that there is a relationship between bipolar disorder and creativity. "I think it's fascinating," Chang, the study's coauthor, said in a statement to the press. "There is a reason that many people who have bipolar disorder become very successful, and these findings address the positive aspects of having this illness."[2] I agree!

It's important to note, however, that Chang's study also found an inverse relationship between how long a bipolar child has been ill and his creative ability. It appears that the longer a child is sick or manic, the lower the BWAS "dislike" score will be. As Chang noted, it appears that "after a while, you aren't able to function and you can't access your creativity."[3]

Overall, however, Chang's findings add to existing evidence that a link exists between mood disorders and creativity. In 2002, Stanford researchers Connie Strong and Terence Ketter, MD, conducted a study exploring the relationship in individuals with manic depression and separate control groups made up of both healthy creative people and people from the general population.[4] Using personality and temperament tests, they found that healthy artists were more similar in personality to individuals with manic depression than to healthy people in the general population. "My hunch is that emotional range, having an emotional broadband, is the bipolar patient's advantage," Strong said. "It isn't the only thing going on, but something gives people with manic depression an edge, and I think it's emotional range."[5]

This may be especially true in certain professions in which bipolar people seem to be more heavily represented than would occur by chance. In the late 1980s, psychiatrist Nancy C. Andreasen, MD, studied thirty writers (three females, twenty-seven males) attending a writers' workshop and compared them to a control group.[6] Results indicated that 80 percent of these writers reported suffering from a mood disorder, compared to 30 percent of the controls. Even though depression was the most common mood disorder among the writers' group, more than 40 percent of these individuals had bipolar disorder. The frequency of manic depression in the writers' group was more than four times that in the control group.

Another study, published in the *American Journal of Psychiatry* in 1994 by Arnold M. Ludwig, MD, the E. A. Edwards Professor of Psychiatry at the University of Kentucky, also found a higher level of bipolar disorder in writers. Ludwig studied fifty-nine female writers recruited from participants in a women writers' conference and found that these writers had much higher rates of depression and mania, as well as other psychiatric disorders, compared to the fifty-nine matched controls who belonged either to the statewide homemakers' association, the medical auxiliary, or the university women's club. Ludwig wrote: "Anecdotal and research evidence of this sort suggests a definite relationship between creative achievement and madness."[7]

Of course, these modern researchers weren't the first to notice the connection between manic depression and creativity. That connection has been a topic of conversation for centuries. After all, it was Plato who once said that a poet's inspiration comes during "divine madness." And psychiatrists and historians now widely suspect that bipolar disorder has likely played a significant role in the creative pursuits of countless writers, composers, statesmen, artists, actors, and scientists in the world, among them Winston Churchill, Vincent Van Gogh, Abraham Lincoln, Ludwig van Beethoven, Sir Isaac Newton, Charles Dickens, Peter Ilych Tchaikovsky, and Ernest Hemingway. And the list goes on: Virginia Woolf, Patty Duke, Jack London, Sylvia Plath, and Kurt Cobain, to name a few. Each could be described as a true creative spirit with a strong inner drive to be successful, achieve greatness, and think independently.

A look at the early years of some of these famous figures suggests that they may have even exhibited early signs of pediatric bipolar disorder. For a number of them, creative energy seemed to have been the mother of invention. Beethoven was composing and playing his own music in public by the time he was twelve. At boarding school, Newton occupied himself with drawing birds, animals, plants, men, ships, and mathematical formulas on the walls of his room.[8] He spent considerable hours inventing and building such things as miniature mills, carts, and machines.

One characteristic of many bipolar kids is the ability to hyperfocus—to concentrate on their own interests to the exclusion of the outside world. As a result, even the most brilliant of these youngsters can sometimes seem to be in a fog. Take young Isaac Newton, whose extraordinary capacity for concentration was described by his friend and biographer William Stukely:

> On going home from Grantham, 'tis usual at the town end to lead a horse up Spittlegate hill, being very steep. Sir Isaac had been so intent in his mediations that he never thought of remounting, at the top of the hill, so had led the horse home all the way, being five miles. . . . The horse by chance slipt his bridle and went home: but Sir Isaac walked on with the bridle in his hand, never missing the horse.[9]

Not surprisingly, this kind of dreamy behavior, combined with other bipolar symptoms, could make the academic world a difficult place for such creative types. It's known, for example, that Winston Churchill, who is commonly thought to have suffered from bipolar disorder as an adult, ranked thirteenth out of thirteen in his class when he was eight years old. Although we can't know for sure, of course, if Churchill had the condition as a child, there is certainly evidence that he seemed to suffer from many of the symptoms often seen in bipolar children today. Among other things, young Winston may have had trouble waking up in the morning. School records show that between June 8 and July 20, 1883, a period encompassing about thirty school days, he was late for classes nineteen times. Though he did very well in some subjects, especially history, he was barely getting by in others, such as composition and writing.[10]

Winston Churchill's Report Card from St. George's School, Ascot, dated June 8 through July 20, 1883.

Composition: "Very feeble"
Translation: "Good"
Grammar: "Improving"
Diligence: "Does not quite understand the meaning of hard work—must make up his mind to do so next term."
Mathematics: "Could do better than he does"
French: "Fair"
History: "Very good"
Geography: "Very fair"
Writing and Spelling: "Good but so terribly slow; spelling about as bad as it well can be."

Source: The Churchill Papers at the Churchill Archives Center, Cambridge University Reference: CHAR 28/44/04.

If academics were a problem for these future superstars, imagine how much trouble their behavior might have gotten them into outside the classroom. Newton may have been the original poster child for early-onset bipolar disorder. He was never officially diagnosed with bipolar disorder as a child or an adult when he was alive, but manuscripts archived by the Newton Project of the Imperial College of London, in addition to other biographical sources, show that he displayed probable signs of the illness early on. His violent temper made him a challenging child, to say the least, a problem that even he recognized. During his first year at Cambridge University, Newton wrote a list of his "childhood sins." He reported: "Striking many," "Peevishness with my mother," "With my sister," "Falling out with the servants," "Punching my sister," "Threatening my father and mother Smith to burne them and the house over them," and "Wishing death and hoping it to some." He had such an unpleasant manner that when he left to study at the university, the servants in his parents' house reportedly were delighted and rejoiced.[11]

Impulsivity and unpredictability were other sore spots for some of these youthful geniuses. The young Winston, for instance, whom his own grandmother referred to as a "naughty, sandy-haired little bulldog," could be as hotheaded as he was loud. As a schoolboy, he was disciplined for stealing sugar from the school pantry. His response to his punishment was to sneak into the headmaster's study and kick the man's straw hat to pieces.[12]

A classmate of Churchill's described the future statesman and Nobel Prize winner this way:

Winston Churchill, a grandson of the Duke of Marlborough, at that time a red-haired and restless boy, rather small for his age, who through his exhibitionism and quarrelsome attitude got on everyone's nerves. As a result of the time he had spent in the stables at Blenheim, Winston had learned words which were highly unsuitable for a young man. Mr. Kynnersley, the headmaster, reacted with shock and apprehension against the not unlikely possibility that the entire school might adopt the spicy expressions of stable lads. When Winston, who was quite tiny—he was only just eight years old—leapt around a classroom table and recited to an attentive group of boys a little song from the stables, Mr. Kynnersley threatened the use of the birch.[13]

At the Harrow School, where Winston attended the upper grades, the assistant master wrote Lady Randolph Churchill, his mother, that though young Winston was not "willfully troublesome," his "forgetfulness, carelessness, unpunctuality, and irregularity in every way, have really been serious." The letter requested that the matter be discussed at home. Even then, Winston was displaying a trait that many bipolar kids demonstrate—being, according to a family member, "regular in his irregularity."[14]

In their book *Manic Depression and Creativity*, D. Jablow Hershman and Julian Lieb, MD, describe how neither the young Newton nor Beethoven, another genius suspected of suffering from adult bipolar disorder, was wildly successful in his attempt to have a social life. In fact, both had periods of intense despair and isolated themselves from the world around them. A family friend wrote that Newton "was a sober, silent, thinking lad, and was never known to play with the boys abroad, at their silly amusements; but would rather choose to be at home, even among the girls," his half sisters.[15]

Perhaps not surprisingly, grandiosity often marked their childhoods as well. Thus, when Winston left Brighton, the second school he attended, his grandmother speculated that he had been "too clever and too much the Boss" there. When he was admitted to the Harrow School, Winston credited the headmaster, Dr. Welldon, for having exercised extremely good judgment in selecting him. He wrote that Welldon was a man "capable of looking beneath the surface of things: a man not dependent on paper manifestations."[16] In other words, Welldon was smart to have recognized the young Churchill's high intelligence and ignored his not-so-terrific academic performance.

Ironically, this sense of grandiosity may have helped drive the greatness of Churchill, Newton, Dickens, and others. As children, they seem to have known inside that they were destined for great things, despite the feedback they were getting from the world around them. When a neighbor complained about Beethoven's sloppy dress, for example, he is said to have replied, "When I'm famous no one will notice."[17]

Of course, we know the conclusions of these life stories. Newton moved beyond his troubled childhood to define the law of gravity and become one the most influential scientists in history. And Winston Churchill, whose writing and composition skills were called "feeble," went on to become not only Britain's most famous and beloved prime minister but also the winner of the Nobel Prize for Literature. As for Beethoven, his words have proven true: No one these days seems to care much that he was a sloppy dresser.

It's helpful to keep the stories of these incredible individuals in mind when we work with bipolar kids. We don't want to make light of their illness, nor do we want to imply that every bipolar child will grow up to be an Isaac Newton or a Winston Churchill. But we do want to recognize and help bipolar kids capitalize on the considerable gifts that lie within them.

For some children, these gifts are apparent from a very early age. For example, Merry provided a glimpse into her acute sensitivity to the world around her when she was just two and a half years old. One day, Merry's mother, then pregnant, took her to the pediatrician's office for a checkup. The pediatrician was also pregnant. She saw that Merry had a piece of paper and a crayon in her hand and asked her to draw a picture for the office. "OK!" said Merry, and she sat down and drew a pregnant woman with a baby visible inside her belly.

When Merry's mother told me the story, I thought it sounded adorable but that she must have had the girl's age wrong. Two-and-a-half-year-olds aren't developmentally able to draw pictures of people. In fact, kids usually don't start drawing stick-figure people until they're somewhat older, let alone babies inside of pregnant women. But the mother insisted she was right. In fact, she could prove it: She called the pediatrician's office and asked one of the staff there to fax the picture, which was still hanging on the wall. When it arrived, I was stunned; Merry's mother was right. The picture was of a woman with a baby in her belly, as confirmed by the pediatrician who had noted the date of it. Merry had been so acutely aware of her environment that she realized there were pregnant women around her and therefore made sure to include a baby in her drawing.

Even those whose gifts are difficult to pinpoint early in life have talents that may lie deep below the surface, waiting to be discovered. Take the case of thirteen-year-old Theo, who not only has bipolar disorder but also has a co-occurring autistic spectrum disorder. Over the years, Theo's parents have tried to get him involved in a number of activities: team sports, the 4-H Club, and piano lessons. None seemed to hold his interest for long, until, that is, a few months ago when he asked if he could take drum lessons. Here's what happened, according to his dad:

Most of the drum teachers I interviewed talked to me about their Juilliard days and their years with the local orchestra. This is not what I needed. I needed someone who would understand Theo and how his mind works. Finally, I found a retired public school music teacher who had experience with special-needs children. And thank goodness he did because on his second visit, our son threatened to throw our solid oak coffee table at him. He was upset because the teacher had shown up ten minutes early and interrupted his computer time.

Undeterred, the teacher simply walked upstairs and waited. Theo's rage got progressively worse, so we decided to call it a day. Then as fast as it had come, Theo's horrific anger diminished, and he began to sob and express true remorse. "I'm so sorry. I don't want to be a bad boy. I'll pay for my own drum lessons. I don't want to grow up and be a bad man. I'll call the teacher and apologize." At thirteen, Theo's thought processes are that of a much younger child, but his empathy and regret are sincere.

The next week, much to everyone's surprise, back came the drum teacher. He acted as though nothing ever happened. This time, Theo was ready for him. From that moment on, we never had to remind him to practice, and though neither of us is musical, the noise coming from his room soon started to sound like it had a rhythm.

The teacher had begun by teaching our son conventional note reading and then, as a reward, allowed him to play along with a favorite song on a CD or music DVD at the end of the lesson. But he soon discovered that what worked for other kids didn't necessarily work for Theo. "He wasn't catching on to the note reading, and I didn't want to frustrate him," the teacher told me. "But when he played along with the music, I could tell he had almost a natural beat and understood what to do. He learns differently than most other kids. He plays almost by ear. If he wants to learn something and I show him, he picks it up after one or two times, and it's in there. Then he's on to something else. So that's how I decided to teach him. We're doing the note reading slowly at the end of the lessons."

One day, the teacher called me in and asked me to listen to the sounds coming out of the practice room. Theo had mastered a Beatles song—and this was only six weeks after his first drum lesson. The teacher beamed with pride.

Our son, a child who struggles with simple math, could figure out and play quarter rests by ear. Theo's graphomotor skills have always been so poor that he has trouble drawing stick figures and cutting food into bite-size pieces, yet now he could expertly manipulate a pair of drumsticks.

Is this his calling? Who knows? It's only been about two months; but never before has anything else come quite this quickly with this much success. He has the interest, the dedication, the patient teacher, the love and support of his parents, and perhaps the gift. It would be great to be interviewed by Rolling Stone *in a few years and beam when we acknowledge his abilities* as well as *his disabilities.*

The remarkable gifts of bipolar kids extend far beyond the creative arts as well. I've found, for example, that many kids have developed an uncanny ability to persevere in the face of physical illness. One patient, seven-year-old Vivian, has always been full of life, at times tryingly so for her family, but she is also a joy to work with. A few months ago, she began having pain in her legs. After a variety of consultations and tests, she was diagnosed with juvenile rheumatoid arthritis. Medication helps a bit with her pain, but she is still very uncomfortable at times. Even so, her father says she hasn't missed a beat. She continues to be active in her dance class and on her soccer team and has generally continued her whirlwind existence. I was happy to hear this because the best thing Vivian can do for herself right now is to not withdraw from life, as many kids with pain do. Her dad, in turn, said that he thought her being hypomanic was helpful to his daughter—and he wasn't kidding. The more I thought about it, the more I realized he was right. Rather than becoming a couch potato and feeling sorry for herself, Vivian continued to be a dancing star, a force with which to reckon.

Although it may seem like a strange thing to say given their mood issues, many bipolar kids are gifted emotionally, as well as intellectually. Remember Matthew, whose father lovingly described him as extremely emphathetic? Like him, many bipolar kids who are stable or approaching stability seem to exhibit an uncommon sensitivity for others that many children don't possess. Here's how one parent described this trait in her young son:

By all accounts, Eric is extremely empathetic and compassionate, especially for a ten-year-old boy. Maybe because of the challenges he faces in life (and the subsequent support he has received from family and friends along the way), he is unusually sensitive to the struggles and feelings of others.

Eric has a number of characteristics that would ordinarily alienate other kids, particularly in towns like ours, where excellence prevails and the atmosphere is very competitive. He has difficulty with his schoolwork, is uncoordinated in the playground kickball games, and has frequent public outbursts in school.

But Eric is well regarded by his peers. I am convinced this is because he has supported each one of them when they were struggling, when no one else took the time or energy to console them. Eric notices everything and treats his peers the way he would like to be treated. (Yeah, I know that's the Golden Rule, but how many kids really live by it?) In turn, his peers are supportive of him, perhaps following his lead.

In some cases, what's special about these kids is their ability to think outside the box. For example, a fourteen-year-old girl who was exceptionally strong in mathematics recounted that her precalculus teacher had given the class a hard problem and that she was the only one who had figured it out correctly—using a method she had made up on her own. Though I wasn't surprised that she got the problem right, I was impressed that she hadn't relied on her teacher's approach but had developed her own original method instead, and it worked.

On more than one occasion, parents have come to me for their child's initial appointment and recited a long list of the problems affecting the youngster—temper outbursts, excessive anxiety, fights over next to nothing, unpredictability every day, inability to take "no" for an answer, and so forth. Yet at some point during our first interview, they inevitably have said something along these lines: "Please don't think that my child is always a holy terror. There are times he can be the sweetest, most fantastic kid." He really has a heart of gold. You should see how loving he is with his six-month-old baby sister. I tell them that they shouldn't feel guilty about focusing on the problems. That's why they're seeking help. I also tell them that I'm glad their child has these wonderful traits and that their youngster's positive attributes—such as a unique capacity for empathy and affection or special creativity—may be nature's way of helping us cope with some of his frustrating behaviors.

Just as creativity has its positive side and can bring great success, it can also have a dark side. When bipolar kids are sad and angry, their creative work sometimes reflects these states of inner torment. Their drawings and stories can be full of violence, gore, and death. One teenager, who was very sweet but socially awkward, had struggled with his confused feelings and impulses since early childhood. His mother explained that when he was five, he was intent on drawing pictures of prisons. Was this a way to contain his uncomfortable thoughts and impulses? I don't know. But his mother knew that these were not drawings typical of a five-year-old. Most kids this age would create things such as flowers and suns or even superheroes engaged in battle but not prisons. In some cases, these dark creations prove to be blessings in disguise, as they provide a tip-off to a youngster's internal state.

Consider the case of Jake, a seventeen-year-old songwriter who composed this rap a few days before he was hospitalized for his depression:

I'm an existentialist with a 40 and a fist
One of my only wishes is for life to stop being so vicious
You don't want your name at the top of my hit list
Cause you'll end up dead like all the religious
Who when killed will realize their god doesn't exist
And that their lives were meaningless

I'm living the high life
Smoking 6 blunts every night
The only time I'll ever be sober
Is the day my pathetic life is over
Which should be real soon
I'm drinking whiskey straight everyday before noon
I'm so depressed!
Thinking about living less and less
Suicide might be for the best

Clearly, Jake wrote this when he was in a tremendous amount of pain and experiencing significant rage, at the world and at himself. He is a gifted writer, but his work at that time was incredibly morbid and violent. Fortunately, he was violent only in his words and not in his actions. During the times his mood was under control, his writing was much less depressing and extremely good. He even won a creative writing competition for high school students. In retrospect, judging from his work and his history, I suspect Jake had been hypomanic for years before developing depression.

What's worth noting is that this kind of angry, negative energy, if properly channeled, can be redirected into all kinds of creative pursuits. Few untreated writers are as successful as Edgar Allan Poe, who exhibited many signs of bipolarity, but he's a good example. His mood disorder and his creativity worked together to allow him to develop some of the most frightening but best-written stories and poems ever created, though at an extremely high personal cost. The fact that Poe could harness his genius in a positive way for society offers a lesson for us all about the potential of bipolar kids.

Poe's poem "Alone" may also ring eerily true to bipolar kids. It begins with these lines: "From childhood's hour I have not been / As others were—I have not seen / As others saw—I could not bring / My passions from a common spring— / From the same source I have not taken / My sorrow—I could not awaken / My heart to joy at the same tone—And all I loved—I loved alone."[18]

To be sure, not every patient has overcome his illness in a way that allows him to function as well as he might. I remember in particular one high school student named Paul, who was known to all his teachers as an amazingly gifted writer. He developed an agitated depression associated with his bipolar disorder, his grades dropped from As to Bs and Cs, and his interest in writing went out the window. Once he started on a mood stabilizer, however, all these things began to improve, yet even at this point of his improvement, he continued to deny that medicine was helpful to him. Periodically, Paul would decide to discontinue the medication, and he invariably dropped back to his lower level of functioning.

To many of those knowledgeable about bipolar disorder, it seems almost incredible that untreated people such as Poe, Newton, Lincoln, Beethoven, and Churchill could achieve greatness despite their emotional illness. John McManamy, author of *Living Well with Depression and bipolar disorder: What Your Doctor Doesn't Tell You That You Need to Know*, wonders if a few close calls could have changed the course of human history: As he writes on his Web site, mcmanweb.com, "Suppose Abraham Lincoln had had one of his colossal depressions as Lee was marching on Gettysburg? What if Winston Churchill had decided to stay in bed as the Battle of Britain was being fought? Then I think of all those who never became famous, all those great minds gone to waste, their talents dissipated by their curse. How many Churchills and Van Goghs and Tchaikovskys and Woolfs might there have been had there been no beast to wrestle with?"[19]

As parents, therapists, and caretakers, we all spend hours trying to help our children tame the wild beast that is bipolar disorder. We need to let our kids know that if they can stick it out, take their medication, and work hard in therapy, they'll have a better chance of capitalizing on their creativity and doing what they want in life. And there's plenty of reason to be optimistic. We've reached the dawn of a new era of early intervention and treatment for pediatric bipolar disorder. The continuing goal is to provide a means by which every bipolar child has an opportunity to shine.

5

The Psychiatric Evaluation: Finding a Doctor and Examining Your Child's Symptoms

Perhaps you're at the point where you've decided that you'd like to have a psychiatrist evaluate your child for a possible mood disorder. Maybe he's having trouble in school, sleep problems, bouts of sadness, or any number of other symptoms. Your first question will likely be: "How do I find a good psychiatrist?" It may take some time and sleuthing to locate a board-certified child psychiatrist. In many states where child psychiatrists are rare, adult psychiatrists, pediatricians, family practice physicians, psychologists, and social workers do most preliminary psychological assessments of children. But if you have a child under the age of twelve and if it's possible in your area, do try to find a child psychiatrist to conduct the evaluation. Your child is not a miniature adult, after all, and it's imperative to solicit the help of a doctor who is accustomed to working with children. Ideally, you will find a physician who also has working relationships with local therapists, support groups, and schools and one who is familiar with psychiatric medications and their use in children (should that become necessary).

Though the undertaking may seem overwhelming at first, a number of individuals and resources are available to guide you on your way. A listing of a variety of resources and contact information is available at the back of this book, but you might first seek advice from the following:

- Your pediatrician
- A school counselor
- Friends whose children have been in treatment
- Other health professionals
- The American Psychiatric Association (your state branch)
- The American Academy of Child and Adolescent Psychiatry (your state branch)
- Local branches of the National Alliance on Mental Illness (NAMI)
- The National Alliance for Research on Schizophrenia and Depression (NARSAD)
- County mental health organizations
- Local support groups for families of children with bipolar disorder
- The Child and Adolescent Bipolar Foundation (CABF)

The Child and Adolescent Bipolar Foundation is an especially valuable resource because its Web site (www.bpkids.org) features a state-by-state list of doctors who work with bipolar children. The site also has chat rooms where a parent can trade information and advice online with other moms and dads.

Or maybe your pediatrician can suggest someone he thinks is the best child psychiatrist or diagnostician he has ever met. But keep in mind that even if someone else believes this doctor is the greatest, he or she may not be the greatest for your child. Before you take your child for an evaluation, try to meet the doctor yourself. If you don't feel comfortable, it doesn't matter what anyone else thinks. Finding a good doctor is, in part, a matter of chemistry, and what's right for one person may not be right for another. If you're going to trust someone to work with you and your child over any period of time, you need to feel somewhat comfortable. Trust your instincts. This may be the beginning of a very long relationship, so at least enter it without a lot of concerns about the doctor.

It may take anywhere from a few days to a few months to get an appointment with a psychiatrist, depending on the doctor's availability and the number of practitioners in your area. (If your child needs immediate treatment, it's best to take him to the emergency department of your local hospital or to an emergency intervention center.) Once you've found a time slot with Dr. Right, what should you expect?

Some doctors begin by sending out forms, such as the Child Behavior Checklist (CBCL) or the Parent Connors Rating Form. (The CBCL asks parents to report on the presence and severity of a number of symptoms in their youngster, including sleep difficulties and anxiety and attention issues. The Connors Form is a standard assessment tool that helps clinicians identify symptoms of ADHD in children.) Other doctors prefer to learn about your child mostly by talking with you. Remember that there is no one right way to conduct a psychiatric evaluation. The essential thing is not how the doctor structures the appointment but whether he obtains the significant information he needs to guide him in determining your youngster's diagnosis and treatment.

To give you a better feel for the process, the following passages will describe how a typical evaluation might go. In my practice, the evaluation usually consists of four sessions spread over two to four weeks The first is with the parents alone; the second is an introductory meeting with the child; the third is another interview with the parents to review anything we may have left uncovered in session one; and the fourth is a series of meetings with the child, the parents, and finally the entire family. In the last meeting, I discuss my treatment recommendations and plan for going forward with the parents first, and then everyone meets together one final time.

Just because this is how I conduct an evaluation, though, doesn't mean that this is the only way to evaluate each individual child. Your doctor may, for instance, prefer to meet with everyone together first. Or a child may have particular needs that require more immediate attention.

The Parent Interviews

In the first and third sessions, I make it a point to meet with the mother and/or father without their child. This is to ensure that they have an opportunity to speak freely and share any information they may not be comfortable discussing in front of their youngster. Some would say that this approach is secretive and that there should be no secrets in a family. I don't necessarily agree. Children often don't need to know, for example, that a relative committed suicide, had a psychosis, or was an alcoholic and spent time in a rehab facility. Granted, this may well be information they should learn later in life, but now may not be the right time. Who knows how a child will make sense of this information? A youngster may worry, "Maybe I'm beginning to go crazy just like weird Aunt Helen."

Meeting with the parents alone also ensures that they won't be uncomfortable sharing what they need to share. Moms and dads often have a difficult time discussing the reason for their visit when the child is present; the youngster may get angry, embarrassed, or uncomfortable, and the evaluation can go downhill from there. In time, I'll discuss the important issues with the child, too. But that will come later.

First, I begin by asking for some basic information—the child's name, age, grade and school, who else is in the home, how and why the parents were referred to me, and what made them seek help when they did. I want to make sure that there's not an emergency—a child's suicidal thoughts, dangerous behavior, and so on—that needs to be addressed immediately.

If the problem at hand is not a fairly recent development, the question in my head is: "Why now?" It's often the case that a child has been exhibiting symptoms for a while—a few weeks, a few months, even a few years. What happened to make the parents decide to seek treatment at this time? Is it because the child's school recommended it? Or because the child did something dangerous? Or maybe it is an old behavior that they'd thought he'd outgrow. They may have figured, "OK, maybe the terrible twos could last until age four, but by six, they should have gone away." Answers to the questions "Why are you here?" and "Why now?" gives me a sense of what to look for and what parents are looking for from me.

Then we discuss the history of the child's illness: previous diagnoses, symptoms, when they began, previous treatment, and past responses to intervention. This step can be complicated and may seem tedious, but it often gives vital clues to what's going on with a child. The mother of six-year-old Mandy, for instance, described her daughter as someone who loved to dance like Britney Spears and wear a teenager's clothes. Initially, her mother brought her to see me because she was concerned about Mandy's temperamental, hard-to-please attitude and her inappropriate and sexually suggestive behavior. In the history part of the evaluation, she told me that Mandy had been seeing a psychologist for the previous two years because she had been sexually abused by a female babysitter. Mandy would sometimes inappropriately touch other people's breasts or buttocks, and her mom said she had grown increasingly clingy recently. At other times, Mandy acted just plain silly: She would dance around the house naked or half-dressed, saying, "Poopy doody, poopy doody, pee pee, pee pee."

When Mandy started nursery school, it took months until she was able to separate from her mother without being hysterical for at least fifteen minutes. The teacher said that on some days, she would be very quiet and refrain from engaging with the other children. It seemed as if Mandy was very tired on such days (despite the fact that she had had a normal amount of sleep the night before). On other days, Mandy would become very bossy with the other kids and tell them that they were stupid if they didn't listen to her. Her playdates were carefully monitored after her mother once found her and a little boy taking off their clothes to play a game Mandy had suggested. Mandy's psychologist believed that much of her behavior was related to her prior sexual trauma.

But after a thorough review of her history and conversations with Mandy, her parents, and teachers at her school, I was certain that there was more going on. A maternal uncle and grandmother had previously been diagnosed as having manic-depressive disorder, as had a paternal first cousin. In addition, there was a strong history of depression on Mandy's mother's side and alcoholism on her father's side of the family. These clues and other behaviors Mandy exhibited supported the diagnosis of a bipolar mood disorder and a history of post–traumatic stress disorder (PTSD)(that is, post sexual abuse), and I prescribed Depakote, a mood stabilizer, for her. After four weeks, Mandy responded fairly well to her treatment with medication. She became less moody, less irritable, more flexible, less fearful, and less hypersexual. Once these positive changes occurred, she became much more amenable to psychological intervention.

Mandy's story teaches a valuable lesson: Even though there was a clear history of another problem (sexual abuse), the child's reactions were compounded by her mood disorder, something that might have been missed if we hadn't explored every avenue.

In the next part of the evaluation with parents, I typically turn my attention to the child's developmental history. I ask questions such as: Did the mother have a complicated delivery? Was the child breast-fed or bottle-fed? How long did it take for him to get into a routine for sleeping and eating? When did he sit up? When did he walk, talk, and become toilet trained? The timing of developmental milestones is important because it indicates if there were early signs of any type of physical or emotional difficulties. A child is a work in progress, and any clinician will want to know how he progressed from one stage to another.

Unlike the old television detective Sergeant Friday, however, I don't want "just the facts, Ma'am." I want to get a feel for who the child really is. What is his temperament? What did he like or not like as an infant? Was he slow to get comfortable in certain situations? Hard to care for? If I just asked about the developmental timetable, I'd miss learning about the toddler who could eat only certain textures of food (he'd spit out anything lumpy) or the parents who had an impossible time getting the baby to keep socks on his feet because he'd kick them off. Asking the questions directly rather than merely reading checklists often provides this type of extra information.

As we continue the developmental history, I ask parents for a summary of each year of the child's life. Here again, I'm not just going for the facts; I'm trying to get a feel for who the child is. Did he have problems separating to go to nursery school? What did the teachers say about him during each year of school? What was he like at home during these years, and how was he with peers?

For instance, Danny, the young cartoon impresario in Chapter 1, was, according to his mom, a very busy baby in utero. Even though his mom's pregnancy was uneventful and the delivery routine, both parents reported that Danny came out crying and frowning—and "hasn't stopped since."

Danny was a hard-to-comfort infant who would only stop crying when carried. He seemed to be a fussy eater, and once he was weaned off formula, he often spit out his vegetables. When presented with something he didn't like, he'd frequently bang his face on his mom's shoulder, as if in major protest, while she held him. His parents later realized that this was probably because he hated certain foods and textures. In addition, his motor development seemed precocious. At eleven months, "he didn't walk, he ran."

From that point on, nothing in the house was off limits. Danny could open any kitchen cabinet, remove all the pans from the cupboard, and climb on counters. No matter what his mother did, Danny didn't seem to like it. Not only was he hard to soothe, he also wouldn't look directly at her the way babies are supposed to do.

As he reached toddlerhood, Danny was a handful. He got into the dishwasher powder under the sink and had to have his eyes rinsed to stop the burning sensation. To get him to sleep, his parents put him

in their bed; this at least calmed him for a while. They tried the excellent techniques recommended by noted pediatric sleep expert
Richard Ferber, MD—and decided Ferber didn't know their son.

When Danny was eighteen months old, his mom tried to introduce him to a playgroup, but he never seemed to interact with the
other kids except to take away their toys and make them cry. If his
needs weren't met, he would try to bite his mom. At age three, he
climbed on the bathroom counter and tasted the cat's medicine. His
mother began to feel like a prisoner of her own son. She couldn't
take him to the playground, since he'd bite and hit the other kids
when things didn't go his way. In the grocery store, he refused to stay
in the cart and would scream until she took him out.

Danny also had intense difficulty separating from his mother
when left with a babysitter. He would sometimes cry for more than
an hour before calming down, so his mom didn't leave him unless it
was absolutely necessary. When she did go out without him, she used
only very close friends as babysitters. When this occurred, Danny
was initially angry and oppositional, and this was followed by a tearful protest.

His mother had tried everything she had read in books and online
about dealing with a toddler but to no avail. By the time he was four,
she had read more parenting books than most nursery school teachers, but she felt as if her family, her neighbors, and even strangers in
the grocery all looked at her as if she was the most terrible parent in
the world to be raising such a "spoiled," "undersocialized" youngster,
as he was called by others. Through the grapevine, she heard that
neighbors would say, "Oh that Danny. Do you know that he once
was outside the house in December in only his diaper and T-shirt?
Where was his mom? Too busy with her decorator, I guess." Truth be
told, Danny had sneaked out the back door when the babysitter accidentally left it open while letting the dog out. He had wet himself,
and she went upstairs to get a change of clothes for him. Everyone
else was shaken by the cold that day, but Danny had looked pretty
happy frolicking in the snow, according to a neighbor.

Danny remained a fussy eater into toddlerhood—no meats, no vegetables (except mashed potatoes). He would eat only pasta, pizza, cheese, and bread. Some days, he refused to eat because the food wasn't cut correctly and would yell, "Make it better. Sandwich no good." This rigidity was present in other areas of his life, too. For instance, he *had* to wear his favorite pair of shorts, even in the winter. Danny's mom was clever enough to have bought three pairs, but it didn't matter; he wore them all out by sporting them under his pants when the seasons changed. On days when he was more cranky and irritable, he would complain that they didn't feel right and say he couldn't go to school because he couldn't wear them. He *hated* the labels in the backs of shirts (they came out as soon as the clothing was purchased).

His parents' narrative about Danny's moodiness during the preschool years was immensely useful in helping to narrow down his bipolar diagnosis. His impulsivity, demonstrated in so many of the anecdotes his mom recounted, along with his overactivity, pointed to ADHD. Danny's other symptoms—sensory hypersensitivity relating to food and clothing, as well as his separation anxiety and rigidity—are symptoms applicable to a number of diagnoses, but they, too, offered key information about what made Danny tick.

In interviewing adults, I would ask a number of questions about their functioning at work, and I like to do something similar for children. Children, of course, don't have jobs per se, but they go to school to learn. That's their job. So the natural question is, How are they doing at their job—that is, in school? Here are some of the things I'm interested in:

- Is your child having any change in her performance at school?
- Does she have any problems with classwork or homework, with teachers or peers, or with classroom rules?
- Does she have any trouble getting to school?
- How many times has she been absent so far this year?
- Is her homework getting done? Is it done at the speed of lightning and barely legible? Is this new or old behavior?

I also want to find out the following:

- Is he arguing with the teacher or refusing to do work because he "doesn't feel like it"?
- Does he throw major fits when he comes across something difficult in his homework?
- Does he tell his parents that he thinks the teachers are stupid and don't know what they're doing?
- Does he complain that the principal or other people at school are suddenly just plain mean and "picking" on him?
- Do his accounts of incidents at school differ from those of the teacher?
- Is his behavior different at school than it is at home? In what way?

One other part of a child's life to probe during an evaluation is his relationship with peers. Does he have friends? What type of relationships does he have with kids his age? Does he belong to any after-school activities or religious children's groups?

Next, it's important to explore the details of a child's past illnesses and treatments, including:

- Does the child have any allergies to foods or medicines?
- Has she had any hospitalizations? If so, for what?
- Has she had any head injuries or experienced a loss of consciousness?
- Has she had heart, lung (including asthma), or kidney problems?
- Has she had neurological problems? Seizures?
- Is there a history of tics or Tourette's disorder?
- Has she had any broken bones or injuries requiring stitches?
- At what age did those injuries occur?
- Are there any other medical problem we haven't discussed?

You might be surprised by how these bits of information can provide significant diagnostic clues. For instance, a "yes" answer to the question about broken bones may indicate that a child (1) is accident-prone, (2) is the victim of child abuse, (3) has a vitamin deficiency, or (4) has a problem with bone development.

It's often surprising to me how many times parents will notice a change in their child's behavior and then a few days later discover that the youngster has a medical illness, such as an ear infection or strep throat. Physical and mood symptoms often get confused in adults, so why should we expect children to be any different? The sick child may be very tired and have no interest in doing anything before an illness fully declares itself. Is the exhaustion due to medical illness or depressive biology? It's sometimes difficult to say, but before making any treatment decisions, I like to do whatever possible to rule out physical causes that might contribute to a child's difficulties.

Roberta, age five, is a good example. Her mother described the way Roberta emphatically told her one Saturday that she would not be going to dance class. The mother replied, "But we go every Saturday; come on, you'll have fun once you get there." Roberta started crying: "I don't want to go. No, no, no!" Her mother tried to console her, but Roberta continued to sob. "Look, we'll go to Burger Hut afterward and get a cheeseburger and fries," her mom told her, only to hear, "I don't want to go anywhere!" Roberta's crying jag lasted about twenty minutes. Finally, her mother threw in the towel and allowed her to stay home.

Within a few minutes, Roberta started screaming again, but this time she said, "I *want* to go to dance!" Her mother tried to reason with her but to no avail, and the child started crying hysterically again. As she sobbed, her mom held her and tried to comfort her. Finally, she got Roberta to eat some cookies and sit next to her to watch television. About half an hour later, she became very emotional again, insisting, "I want to go to dance." This time, though, Roberta was able to be consoled after five minutes.

It may appear that this is a child who is depressed and/or suffering from bipolar disorder. But actually, as it turns out, Roberta is not bipolar and does not suffer from any mood disorder. Rather, she was on the verge of coming down with a strep infection.

In fact, according to her mom, Roberta is usually a very happy, outgoing, and easygoing child. She generally goes with the flow and is pretty flexible. But before she becomes physically ill, she exhibits an increased sensitivity to whatever is going on around her. She grows moodier, is harder to satisfy, and is more tearful than usual. Her mother had once taken her to the doctor because of this type of behavioral change (in the absence of a physical complaint or fever), only to discover that Roberta had a real physical illness. The end of the story: After Roberta was put on antibiotics for her strep infection, she became less angry and more like her regular, flexible, fun-loving self. The moral of the story: A good evaluation looks at the whole child, not just on one particular day but over the course of time.

Family Ties

The next step in the evaluation process is to explore a child's family history. This is important because existing scientific evidence suggests there is a positive relationship between childhood-onset bipolar disorder and a child's genetic endowment. One researcher, Janet Egeland, PhD, of the University of Miami, and colleagues studied more than two hundred children affected by bipolar disorder. To learn more about the relationship between family history and the transmission of bipolar disorder, Egeland and her colleagues turned to a group who might be said to be tailor-made for studying the illness: the Old Order Amish families of Pennsylvania. As members of a closed society in which people work and marry within their own culture, the Amish have readily accessible family trees and other genealogical data that make it much easier to study bipolar disorder in families. The Amish also have low rates of alcoholism and substance abuse in their communities, factors that might confound the bipolar diagnosis. In addition, they have little exposure to the outside influences of television and other media.

Egeland and her colleagues looked at data obtained at seven- and ten-year intervals after the beginning of the study. They compared 110 children of parents with Bipolar I (defined as having had mania or a mixed state of mania and depression) to a matched control group of 112 children of well parents at the ten-year follow-up. At that time, children of the Bipolar I parents were two and a half times more likely than those in the control group to show symptoms of bipolar disorder. In addition, the symptoms of the genetically at-risk kids changed over time. Compared to the control group, at the seven-year follow-up, they tended to show more evidence of low energy, out-of-control anger, fear, and sensitivity, and at the ten-year follow-up, they exhibited more symptoms that suggested mania, including hyperalertness, mood swings, problems in thinking and concentration, high energy, decreased sleep, and excessive and loud talking. So far, ongoing studies indicate that children of a bipolar parent have a much higher rate of developing early mood disorder–type symptoms that separate them from the well group. Since all of these children share the same environment, genetics are strongly implicated in the transmission of mood symptoms from one generation to the next.[1]

Family history also correlates with the age of onset of bipolar disorder. One study, in particular, found a relationship between this history and the age when children first showed bipolar symptoms: Researchers compared family histories of mood disorders in bipolar children with those of bipolar adults. They found that children with bipolar disorder were more likely to have more relatives with depression and bipolar disorder than those who didn't develop the disorder until adulthood. Put another way, the early onset of bipolar disorder is associated with a child's having a stronger family history of mood disorders than those whose illness appears later in life.

Some doctors believe that compiling a family history is the single most important factor in reaching a correct diagnosis, but there's another reason for delving deep into family history as well: If a child has psychiatric illnesses in his family, finding out what medication other family members have responded to may be very helpful in the child's treatment. If someone in the family did well on a particular medication, the odds are higher that the child will, too.

It's not uncommon, though, for parents to tell me that they're unsure of all their family history or that they don't know of any family history of bipolar disorder. There can be many reasons why parents aren't able to provide a complete and accurate history. In many families, psychiatric illness has not been talked about openly. Even if someone did have problems, the person may not have gotten help unless the problem was severe. Perhaps family members didn't even realize that an individual had a psychiatric problem. Or maybe they were just too embarrassed to talk about it. Or it could be that the parent isn't aware that bipolar disorder is a newer label for what was once called manic depression. Sometimes, certain questions, such as those listed here, can prompt memories of a family member who wasn't medically diagnosed but still exhibited symptoms of a mood disorder:

- Is there any history of substance abuse, alcoholism, depression, manic-depressive illness, anxiety, schizophrenia, seeing things or hearing things, trouble with the law, violent outbursts, or suicide?
- Did anyone in the family ever see a therapist?
- If yes, why?
- Has anyone been treated with medication for a psychiatric problem?
- If so, what was the problem, what medication was used, and did it help?
- Did anyone in the family spend impulsively, losing far more money than he or she could afford?
- Did anyone have problems being faithful and have multiple affairs?

It's amazing how many times going through these detailed questions can lead to important family history information that neither parent thought was relevant. Someone may recall an uncle who was hysterically funny and the life of the party but then had times when he would withdraw to his bed for a few days. Or a cousin who was very successful, made a ton of money, and then ended up bankrupt because of overspending and poor judgment. To uncover these sorts of familial links, I often ask parents to go back to their relatives on all sides of the family tree and inquire specifically about any possible mental illness.

On occasion, it's the parents themselves whose mood or anxiety disorders are undiagnosed or have gone untreated. One or both of the child's parents may come into the office looking sad and depressed. Given what many of them have been through with their child's illness, this is to be expected. But if they say that they feel like this often and have felt this way for more than a few weeks, I want more details. If it sounds as though they might have an undiagnosed biologic depression (change in weight, sleep problems, excess fatigue, and so forth), it might be that they need to get help, too, by getting a good psychiatric evaluation with an adult psychiatrist. The usual reply is, "I hear what you're saying, but what's most important to me is getting Jason the help he needs. If we get his problems under control, I'm sure I'll feel a lot better. Anyway, he is my first priority. I don't have time to go and see someone for me at this point." Parents often say that they're operating in survival mode most of the time. They are trying to do the best that they can for themselves and their loved ones.

Having a bipolar child can be extremely trying. As a parent, you spend all your time treading carefully, not knowing when the next explosion or crisis will occur. This, in itself, would be enough to make anyone feel battle-scarred. If you have any predisposition to a mood disorder, living with a stressor of this kind can help bring the illness to the surface. To be sure, parents of bipolar children have a long road of child rearing ahead of them, and some parts of that road are bound to be very rocky. Protecting a child, encouraging him, and shielding him from rejection and misunderstanding is a full-time job. When you're struggling with your own mood disorder, this can be especially hard to do well. If a parent seems excessively distressed to me, I recommend that he or she consider getting a psychiatric evaluation; there's nothing to be ashamed of here, especially if it means that parent will be better equipped to help the child. It all comes down to taking care of everyone in the family.

A general medical history of family members is another topic for discussion during parental interviews, for several reasons. Let's say a child's mother and grandmother have a history of hypothyroidism (underfunctioning thyroid). Lithium, one of the drugs often used to treat bipolar disorder, can sometimes cause hypothyroidism. Given that there may be a biologic predisposition to this disorder, lithium would not be a first choice of medication to stabilize the mood of the child. It doesn't mean that it should never be used; it just means I'll try other possibilities first. It's also important to get a family history of diabetes mellitus, high blood pressure, heart disease at a young age, heart attacks—especially in those under the age of forty—heart arrhythmias, strokes, seizures, motor or vocal tics, Tourette's disorder, and so forth.

Such a detailed medical history is necessary because mood disorders can be secondary to medical problems and not asking about them can cause a doctor to miss the diagnostic boat. For example, if a child's thyroid is not working well or she's on certain types of medication for asthma, her mood may be affected. These things need to be looked at before a doctor says for sure that the child has a primary psychiatric disorder. It would be similar to diagnosing a 104-degree fever and giving the person Tylenol but not taking care of the strep throat. You may be trying to control the fever (the mood problem), but even if the symptoms improve, the primary problem is still there.

Here's another example: Let's say a child has a strong family history of heart disease, including two relatives who died suddenly in their thirties. This could mean that the child is at higher risk for hidden heart disease compared to children without this family history, which may affect the appropriate medication choices. This particular child may need to see a cardiologist for an echocardiogram in addition to a baseline electrocardiogram to rule out any structural heart abnormalities before beginning treatment.

As you can see, doing a thorough evaluation can be a very in-depth and time-consuming process. In addition to talking with the doctor and answering her direct questions, it's sometimes useful for parents to supplement the doctor's evaluation with a written "snapshot" of their youngster. This description might include a list of the problems they're most worried about; the past interventions attempted and medications used; and finally, the family history of mental illness. This kind of written document can be especially useful when a doctor needs more information or when the parents have more information to share but the appointment time has run out.

The Child Interview

Generally, it takes about two sessions to obtain the information just outlined. But I don't like to wait until I'm finished gathering it to talk with the child. That's because what the parents tell me sometimes provides only a partial picture of who the child is. One case in particular comes to mind. One day, a mother came to the office and began our conversation by telling me that her child had a pervasive developmental disorder (PDD) or, put another way, an autistic spectrum disorder. (This means the child showed some but not all of the signs of autism.) The mother, a former special-education teacher, told me that her son made poor eye contact, had a preoccupation with certain topics, and had poor social skills, all of which can be indicative of PDD. Both she and her husband were well educated and very caring and involved with their son.

But when I met the boy in person and chatted with him, I was floored. I saw none of the social deficits she had described. Instead, this boy was charming, very sweet, and quite shy. He was eventually diagnosed with attention-deficit/hyperactivity disorder and a general-ized anxiety disorder, both of which can cause intermittent difficulties with social skills. Had I taken the history from the parents and not spoken with the child, I would have come to the wrong conclusion. The parents were not purposefully misleading me, but any event in life is subject to the interpretation of the observer.

The first time a youngster visits, I introduce myself in the waiting room and say, for instance, "You must be Rachel," or I ask her for her name. I believe that children should be treated with respect if that is how I want them to react to me. I may comment about what they're wearing or ask questions about what they're playing in order to help them feel more relaxed. From the moment I see them in the waiting room, I'm observing them. Are they on mom's lap, comfortable enough to play with Legos, or reading quietly on their own? Or are they screaming and crying that they want to leave? Occasionally (thankfully not often), a child will throw a fit, threaten to hit me, or try to throw a toy at me. I explain to him that this is not acceptable behavior in my office and that if he is unable to control himself, then I will be unable to talk with him. My intent is not to be harsh. I just want to let the child know that I'm the captain of the ship and in control. This removes any uncertainty about who's in charge in my office. Then I try to figure out why the youngster might not want to talk to me, which often gives me the clues I need to reach him. Or at least it may help me to know more about who he is.

To begin the session, I first talk to the parents for just a few min-utes (unless the child is too anxious about separating from them, in which case I invite them all in) and ask if anything is new since the last time I saw them. My purpose here is to eliminate any surprises. I don't want to find out at the end of an interview, for instance, that the child threatened to kill himself the night before or had some other serious problem and then have little time to address it.

Once the child is inside my office, I begin by asking why his mother or father told him he was coming to see me. If I'm going to understand him, I have to know what he's expecting from me. If he says, "My parents wanted me to see you because I hit my brother last night, right?" I might say, "From what I hear from your parents, you're a good boy, but sometimes your temper can get out of control, even if you don't want it to. I want to try to help you control your temper because it sounds like it can get you into trouble sometimes."

Initially, I try to discuss neutral subjects to make the child feel more comfortable: What does he do for fun? What does he like and not like about school? What makes him angry? What makes him sad? What would his wishes be if he could have three?

Then I try to get more information about the child's mental state:

- Have there ever been times when he thought his mind was playing tricks on him or making him see or hear things that others didn't experience (hallucinations)?
- Has he ever thought that he had special powers or could do things other kids can't (delusions)?
- Has he felt that he wanted to seriously hurt someone else?
- If yes, has he ever tried to act on any of these feelings?
- If no, what stopped him?
- Has he ever felt so bad that he wished he wasn't alive, that he was dead, or that he had never been born?
- If yes, has he ever hurt himself on purpose or attempted to kill himself?

How I ask these questions depends on the age and characteristics of the child. I once asked an adorable eight-year-old girl if she had these types of thoughts. She looked at me and in sudden alarm said, "You mean suicide?" From her tone and her look, it was clear she thought I was nuts asking her these questions. She told me no, and I told her I was glad because that would be wrong. I explained that I ask every child I see these same kinds of questions because if they feel really badly, I want to know.

Parents sometimes get an earful on the way home from my office when they ask their child about how the session went. Some kids tell their parents, "That doctor was crazy. Do you know she asked me if I see things that aren't there, or if I ever thought about killing myself? She's nuts!" Likewise, some parents are surprised to learn that I asked their child about these feelings, especially suicidal or homicidal feelings. However, on multiple occasions, I've asked a child about these things and discovered to everyone's surprise that he did indeed have such thoughts or had even tried harming himself in the past. Some people are afraid that by asking about suicide, I'll put the idea of it into a child's head. But I've seen kids under five who, with little or no prompting, talk about how they want to get hit by a car and die or be reunited with their dead grandparents. (Generally, I think that probing for detailed information about a child's self-destructive thoughts is best left to a professional. But if a child makes a suicidal statement, the parents should gently ask if he means it. If he says yes, they should ask why but also call a clinician to discuss how to deal with the situation.)

If I don't ask about these things, I may never find out. Of course, it's always important to keep in mind who the patient is—a child and often a young child at that. I remember treating Sidney, a very sad nine-year-old who told his teacher he wanted to be dead. He refused to give anyone in school any more information. When I asked him to share with me if he had thought of how to kill himself, he said yes but refused to tell me how. I tried every way I could to get him to divulge the information but was getting nowhere.

Then it occurred to me to cut a deal with him: If he told me this thing that was so hard for him to share, I would ask his parents to take him to McDonald's for a Big Mac. He agreed and ended up telling me what was going on in his mind—he had thought of jumping off the Empire State Building. I don't believe that Sidney was manipulating me just to get a sandwich. In fact, there was a great deal of additional evidence pointing to the fact that he was in enormous emotional pain. I had to get down to his level, to think the way a nine-year-old boy would think, and in this case, the Big Mac was my ticket in. If only promising a Big Mac would work so well with adults!

I don't regularly offer sandwiches to my young patients, but I do make it a point to offer lots of encouragement and positive reinforcement. All the while, I continue to observe the way a child behaves:

- Is she restless, inattentive, distractible, or shy?
- Does she talk too much and too fast, and is her conversation slightly off target?
- What is her mood like?
- Does she have the light of childhood in her eyes when we talk about what should be fun things?
- Is she too shy to answer questions?
- Does she have a great deal of denial?
- Does she just need more time to get used to me in order to be comfortable and talk?

Even in the best of circumstances, kids can't always verbalize how they feel, but close observation can provide a huge amount of information. I look for a variety of things: the suddenly sad face or upset look in her eyes when I mention a problem, the especially silly response to something that happens in session, a look of annoyance toward her mom for telling me what trouble she got into at school, and so on. For me, I always have to keep in mind that my style in talking to kids is kind of peppy. Does the child get silly as she's imitating my tone (not necessarily on purpose)? If I change my voice modulation, does she? (Some children, especially those with PDD, may have difficulty with spontaneously modulating their voices and instead often imitate the tone of whoever is talking to them.)

What's more, bipolar children, as well as other groups of children, are often suspicious of what I've been talking about with their mothers and fathers. If they ask, I try to explain what we were discussing in a neutral way; for example, I might say, "Your mom told me how hard it's been for you to sleep for the past few days" (as opposed to "You're making your parents crazy by staying up most of the night, and your mom is beginning to feel she's at the end of her rope").

In some cases, I decide it's necessary for kids to see me for a second or even a third session before they'll open up. The more familiar they are with me, the more they usually relax. After I feel that I've gotten to know a child as well as I can, I may talk to his teacher and other school personnel for more input. I also might ask the teachers to fill out checklists to learn more about what they are seeing in the classroom.

Parents may be reluctant for me to talk to their child's current or previous doctor or review their reports because they want an unbiased evaluation. But in my mind, the more information I have, the better. We're all partners in treatment, and the more we all know, the more effectively we can work together to help control the disorder. Even if I disagree with the conclusions of another clinician, it's important for me to know what he or she has observed. Those observations may provide critical clues that may help me work with this child.

At the end of the day, when I'm making the major decision of whether to place a child on medication, it's crucial that I come to my own determination about the diagnosis. After all, the doctor for your child is the one who will be prescribing and taking responsibility for medicating—or not medicating—your youngster. Like any doctor, I want to make sure that any medication I prescribe is truly needed and that it's a good choice for his initial treatment.

Calling Sergeant Friday:
Being a Diagnostic Detective

Many kids come to me because their mood has suddenly shifted or their behavior has changed in some way. Before making assumptions about why this has occurred, however, I need to become a diagnostic detective. Suppose a parent says that his child is having mood swings and that his obsessive-compulsive disorder (OCD) has suddenly gotten worse. Perhaps he's had a sudden rise in obsessions and compulsions—with irrational fears that he'll get rabies or some other disease; maybe he's engaged in repeated hand washing or exhibiting tics (repetitive involuntary movements or vocalizations). OCD symptoms and tics can develop or worsen with mood shifts and stress. But I also know that they can worsen for medical reasons, too. A group of illnesses called pediatric-autoimmune neurologic disorders associated with streptococcus (PANDAS) may be responsible. PANDAS often occurs after strep throat, even if that illness went undiagnosed. Unless I ask the right questions and order the appropriate tests, I won't know what's causing the upswing in OCD symptoms—a PANDAS infection, an unrelated biologic increase in OCD itself, or a worsening of depression.

All the possible causes need to be explored. These may include factors in the child's environment, parental discord, sibling issues, a death in the family, school-related difficulties, or learning problems. In one instance, a parent brought in a child with ADHD whose mood had declined significantly. Had anything changed recently, I wondered? The father explained that the child's grandfather had died a couple of weeks earlier. We agreed to postpone making any decisions until the child's normal grieving process had been allowed to run its course.

In some cases, it's unclear exactly what effect a change will have on a child. When an older sibling goes away to camp or college, for example, this can have both positive and negative effects. On the one hand, it allows the bipolar child to be an only child for a while, and this can be extremely good. On the other, it may cause a youngster to feel annoyed and smothered if it creates a situation in which the parents are overly involved in every aspect of his life. The child may also miss his sibling terribly. The loss of a brother or sister to camp or college clearly changes the balance in the home, and the sibling, whether bipolar or not, can be very affected.

The seasons of the year can also play a major role in diagnosis.[2] Does the child have a history of getting more depressed in winter or hypomanic in spring? I encourage all parents to keep a journal. I ask them to go back to previous years around the same date and see what was going on with their youngster. It's not uncommon to see a child whose mood changes at almost the exact same time every year (typically fall or spring, but this can occur anytime).

When I look at the old notes on a child from the same time in previous years, I'm often astounded to see that what I'm writing is almost word for word what I'd written a year before. Many children with seasonal affective disorder get depressed in September and October. It is very easy to attribute this to the start of school and the difficulties and insecurities that go along with a new school year—including different classmates and harder work. Without a search for multiple explanations, the seasonal component can be missed.

Consider the case of Allen, a fourteen-year-old who seemed to be doing well at his new therapeutic residential school. Suddenly, the teachers reported that he was more agitated and oppositional in class. The therapist and psychiatrist at the school could find no obvious environmental reason for this abrupt change. They wondered if it was because of the upcoming second-semester midterms, but Allen had never seemed unduly nervous about exams before. He had a pervasive developmental disorder (an autistic spectrum disorder that can include problems in social relationships, poor eye contact, rigidity, and communication difficulties), and discussing his issues and feelings was difficult for him at times.

A couple of weeks passed, and Allen's symptoms worsened. He began fighting with other children and threatened to hit a dorm monitor with a telephone (luckily, others were around and grabbed it from him). He was hospitalized for one week, and his medication was adjusted by the inpatient physician. Once out of the hospital, Allen seemed more in control but still was irritated when asked to do simple things, such as to sit up straight in his chair. The school authorities contacted his parents and said they might not be able to keep Allen in the program because his behavior was getting too hard to manage. When Allen came to me, I reviewed his chart and realized that his mood usually shifted at the end of March, and here it was the end of April. (This is one of the advantages of seeing kids for many years and keeping notes.) I was not, by far, Allen's first or only psychiatrist, but I had treated him for the five years before he went off to school. When I saw him during this time of difficulty at school, it was clear that he needed to have his medications adjusted because it was spring and his mood had changed. By the end of the week, he was happier and less angry and was able to return to school in much better shape.

Like Allen, many of the kids who come for help are on some type of medication, and it's necessary to take a careful look at these medications before deciding on a treatment plan. I want to know if there have been any recent changes—even slight adjustments. Kids with bipolar disorder are exquisitely sensitive, and giving them medication or taking medication away can produce remarkable changes in their systems. Decreasing an antipsychotic medication or mood stabilizer or adding a stimulant medication can cause mood instability. So can over-the-counter drugs or prescription medications.

Claire was a precocious bipolar seven-year-old patient who was taking Trileptal (oxcarbazepine), a medication considered to be a potential mood stabilizer. One winter, she came down with a sinus infection, and the pediatrician prescribed Biaxin (clarithromycin), an antibiotic. Within a few days, her mood became significantly more unstable, and her mother brought her in to see me. I knew something was different, but what? Certain prescribed medications can increase the absorption, metabolism, or excretion of other drugs. When I found out that she was taking clarithromycin, Claire took a blood test to measure her Trileptal levels (a measure that helps indicate if a child has a reasonable amount of Trileptal in her system or whether she's getting too much or too little). It turned out that the level of Trileptal in Claire's blood had doubled since going on the antibiotic and was significantly above the recommended range. When the pediatrician switched her to another antibiotic, her Trileptal level returned to normal (and so did her mood and behavior).

Numerous other factors can affect mood as well: missed doses of medication, irregular sleep, and substance abuse, to name a few. Again, your child's doctor-detective has to be thinking about all the possibilities.

The Treatment Plan

One last thing I like to do before laying out my plan is to see the child again alone and then together with the parents, to get more of a sense of their family interaction. A child can act differently with a parent than with me, and at times, things that weren't apparent when the child and I were alone become clear. It's not until we've had this final meeting, with all the clues assembled and everything on the table, that I talk to the parents about my diagnosis and treatment plan. Sometimes, this includes medications; sometimes, it does not. Occasionally, parents are resistant to giving their children any medications whatsoever, despite my recommendations. In some cases, it's fine to wait; at other times, though, the situation is too risky to just sit back and observe (at least to my mind). But they're the parents. As the doctor, I can only say what I see and what I'm concerned about. The decision is ultimately theirs.

In certain instances, I purposely decide to hold off on prescribing any medication until I know more. I may want to order additional tests—such as an echocardiogram to rule out heart disease—or I may want to observe the youngster's behavior for a few more weeks before making a decision. If a diagnosis is unclear, it will often reveal itself with watchful waiting.

If, at the end of the evaluation, I feel comfortable about the diagnosis and think a medication could help the child with his problems,

I explain which medication(s) I recommend and why. If the child is threatening other children and is having a hard time controlling his dangerous impulses, for example, an antipsychotic can be of great help. These drugs work quickly and are usually good for poor impulse control. We then go over the possible side effects and address any questions. I know that the decision to give a child psychotropic (or psychiatric) medications can be a difficult one, and it's important that parents have all the information they need.

Of course, this is only the beginning of our work together. The real test will be in the weeks to come, as we closely monitor the child. I wish that all of the medications I prescribe could work right off the bat and instantly make my patients dramatically better. Unfortunately, this is not the case. Sometimes, it can take several weeks before they begin doing their job. In other cases, a medication may start to work immediately, but in a couple of weeks the dosage needs to be tweaked. In still other instances, a second medication may need to be added. It may be that the first few medications prescribed prove ineffective or even make the child's symptoms worse. Kids are a work in progress, as mentioned earlier, and getting the right treatment often takes time and collaboration by all the key people involved in the child's life. In Chapter 7, we'll look in greater detail at medications commonly used for children—how they're prescribed and how they might help your youngster.

The bottom line is this: Don't be afraid to ask questions if you're confused or feel as if an important part of the evaluation is being overlooked. There is no one right way to conduct an evaluation; every child, every family, and every doctor is different.

6

❀

Comorbidity:
Is This Bipolar
Disorder or Something Else?

If your child is diagnosed with bipolar disorder, chances are good that he will be diagnosed with something else as well. The general rule that applies to childhood mental disorders is that if a child has one, then the odds are high that he may have two or more, and these may occur in any combination. This Chinese-menu style grouping of disorders is referred to in the medical community as "comorbidity." Comorbidity is not an idea exclusive to mental illness; to the contrary, in any area of medicine, it's not uncommon for different illnesses to occur together. For example, Diabetes Mellitus, high blood pressure, and obesity are a common triad.

Conditions most frequently comorbid with, or existing in conjunction with, pediatric bipolar disorder include the following: attention-deficit/hyperactivity disorder (ADHD), separation anxiety disorder (SAD), obsessive-compulsive disorder (OCD), autistic spectrum disorders (ASDs) (also known as pervasive developmental disorders, or PDDs), oppositional defiant disorder (ODD), and sensory hypersensitivity (more on these comorbid disorders later). Understandably, their coexistence can create confusion for both parents and professionals.

The concept of comorbidity reminds me of the story of four blind men who touched an elephant in four different places: ear, leg, trunk, and tail. Each one had a different perspective on the same animal. Given the overlap of symptoms and co-occurrence of different mental disorders, one has to wonder what the relationship is between these disorders in the brain. Is there a bigger picture—the elephant—that we're missing?

Although it would be tremendously helpful if there were laboratory tests or specialized imaging techniques available to give us all the answers, unfortunately that's not yet the case. And though the DSM-IV-TR is the standard psychiatric diagnostic reference used in the mental health field, many bipolar kids' brains don't neatly follow the DSM-IV-TR's guidelines (if only it were that easy!), making it difficult to diagnose clear-cut disorders with clear-cut symptoms.

What further confounds the diagnostic process is that symptoms of various psychiatric illnesses appear to overlap. The symptom of inattention, for example, can be seen in children with ADHD, ASD, and schizophrenia. To complicate matters more, most symptoms are present on a continuum; just as all kids who have bipolar disorder may not experience two-hour rages, all kids with ADHD may not have tremendous difficulty with school work (especially in elementary school if they're bright and the subject matter isn't too complex). And some kids with separation anxiety disorder may be able to sleep comfortably overnight at a cousin's house. Understanding a child's illness is more like cutting into a seedy watermelon than peeling a banana. You have to go through several layers and toss out some extraneous elements to get to the heart of the matter. It's a lot of work, but in the end, it's worth it.

What has been most interesting to me in the course of caring for many bipolar children over the years is how often treating their mood disorder also results in a decrease in the appearance of the symptoms of the comorbid disorders. Put another way, it seems that the different mood states seen in bipolar disorder may be associated with the onset or intensification of symptoms of another disorder. Take a child who has both mood swings and OCD symptoms. Because of the OCD, she may feel the need to tie her shoelaces using exactly the right amount of tension. When the child is depressed, she may have to repeat this action several more times before she can stop focusing on it. But when her mood is stable, she might need to do it only one or two times or perhaps not at all. When treated with a mood stabilizer, the symptoms may get better or seem to disappear.

But it's important to stress that this is not always the case. Sometimes, treatment with a mood stabilizer improves a child's mood but not the symptoms of the other disorder. Therefore, the symptoms of each diagnosis must be approached individually and in the proper order. If the co-occurring disorder is not severely disabling (that is, if it does not prevent a child from sleeping, eating, or going to school), I return to my general rule of thumb, which I mentioned in Chapter 1: Treat the bipolar disorder first, then see what falls away . . . and what remains.

This way of thinking also has a precedent in general medicine. Remember the triad of diabetes, high blood pressure, and obesity? Each of these disorders has a somewhat different treatment, but if you take care of the obesity, the other two may go away. In the same fashion, psychiatric symptoms may materialize or grow more intense with changing mood states. Take away the fluctuating moods, and the co-occurring disorder may diminish or disappear altogether.

What follows is a more detailed look at the conditions that commonly co-occur with bipolar disorder, together with an exploration of their similarities, differences, and the ways a clinician might distinguish them from bipolar disorder.

Does My Child Have ADHD or Bipolar Disorder?

Like children with ADHD, bipolar children can exhibit symptoms of inattention, overactivity, and impulsivity. But unlike kids with

ADHD, they tend to show these symptoms, or a change in their intensity, specifically when their mood is unstable. ADHD is the disorder that most often co-occurs and is confused with bipolar disorder. About 11 to 22 percent of children and adolescents diagnosed with ADHD also meet the criteria for bipolar disorder.[1] Moreover, studies indicate that anywhere from 57 to as high as 98 percent of children diagnosed with pediatric mania, that is, the manic episode in bipolar disorder (which can be marked by inattentiveness, overactivity, and impulsivity), also meet the criteria for ADHD.[2] You can see the way in which the overlap in symptoms can make it quite challenging for a clinician to determine whether your child is suffering from ADHD or bipolar disorder. To tease out the differences, let's look more closely at the symptoms.

How Mood Plays a Role

First, here's how inattention, overactivity, and impulsivity might look in a child with bipolar disorder:

- **Inattention** (this can be seen in either the elevated or depressed mood state)
  In bipolar depression: The depressed bipolar child's mind seems to work more slowly than normal or his thinking is foggier. That's why he has a hard time concentrating.
  In bipolar mania: The manic bipolar child often has a hard time paying attention because his thoughts are moving too fast and are too hard to hold onto. He also is easily distracted.
- **Overactivity** (this can be seen in both extreme mood states but is more likely to occur in mania)
  In bipolar depression: Some children and adolescents have what is called an "agitated depression." These children often appear uncomfortable in their own skins and are quite restless and agitated in the depressed state.

In bipolar mania: Like the ADHD child, a youngster in a hypomanic or manic state can have a hard time sitting still, since he is "wired," full of extra energy, and ready to go!

- **Impulsivity**

    In bipolar depression: This symptom can occur on occasion but is much more typical in the hypomanic or manic state than in the depressed phase.

    In bipolar mania: The bipolar child with an elevated mood can be outrageous in his decision making and choose dangerous activities, such as deciding to give himself a haircut with scissors or climbing a tree without any thought that it might be difficult to get down. He also may be sexually inappropriate (for instance, telling his babysitter he likes her "boobies").

It must be stressed again that all psychiatric and general medical symptoms and disorders vary from child to child and often from setting to setting. Thus, children who are overactive, impulsive, and/or inattentive will typically—regardless of their diagnoses, whether ADHD or bipolar disorder—exhibit these symptoms to different degrees in different settings. Some may look as though they are bouncing off the wall (literally). Others sit in their seats but play with everything on their desks or sit on their hands to prevent themselves from getting into trouble (in other words, they've learned some tricks to compensate for their problem). Some make dangerous or foolish decisions, such as setting off the school fire alarm on a whim, and others will call out answers in class rather than wait for their turn.

You may think that your child seems to be able to pay attention quite well when she's doing something she really likes. Keep in mind, though, that it's not that children with the diagnosis of ADHD can *never* focus; what they are doing has to be interesting enough and reinforcing enough to keep their attention. For most children, it is easier to focus on a video game than on their homework because the game is infinitely more interesting, with immediate and constant gratification.

Similarities

In addition to the possible presence of the three core symptoms of ADHD in children with bipolar disorder, we can say that both groups of youngsters:[3]

- Typically have an onset of the illness that is slow or insidious, not sudden
- Often show their first symptoms in the early years
- Are likely to have a family history of mood disorders and/or alcoholism
- May have temper outbursts
- May exhibit destructive and/or dangerous behavior
- May have problems falling asleep

Differences

With all of these similarities, how can a parent or doctor possibly determine whether their child has ADHD, bipolar disorder, or both? It's a tricky distinction indeed, but generally speaking, children with bipolar disorder do show some characteristics that help differentiate the two disorders. Bipolar children tend to:

- **Have more significant difficulties in various parts of their lives than children with ADHD alone.** Consistent with this observation, one study found that a higher percentage of bipolar youngsters (51 percent) than ADHD children (24 percent) needed combined medication and psychotherapy treatment to improve their overall level of functioning in daily life.[4]

- **Need intervention in a variety of venues**—at home, in school, with peers—**in addition to medication** treatment, and some ADHD kids can do well being treated by medication alone.
- **Have their worst difficulties at home.** Teachers often report, much to the shock of the parents, that bipolar kids are "model students" at school (though this is not true for all bipolar children). This may be because some bipolar children are more anxious at school and don't wish to attract attention. Or it could be that they know how they should behave and can keep their behavior under control away from home with a great deal of effort. By contrast, ADHD kids typically show problems in the school setting. In fact, their problems become much more obvious in the classroom, where the key demands are sitting still, waiting for one's turn, and paying attention. They also often show some of the same symptoms when they're with family members outside the home but the demands for focusing, sitting still, and curbing other troublesome ADHD behaviors are not as intense as in school.

Given the common symptoms, some clinicians believe that what has been called pediatric bipolar disorder is actually "bad ADHD." What this means is that the child has the diagnostically necessary symptoms of ADHD but in a quite severe form that causes major problems in day-to-day functioning. Interestingly, one study found that bipolar kids experiencing mania had more symptoms of attention-deficit/hyperactivity disorder than the ADHD group itself![5]

Why is it so important to recognize and differentiate the two diagnoses? Often, the best medication treatment for ADHD is a stimulant, which can cause significant problems in a child with bipolar disorder. This will be explained in greater detail in Chapter 7, but essentially, a stimulant medication has the potential to destabilize the mood of a child who is bipolar or who may be biologically predisposed to having bipolar disorder. The newest treatment agent for ADHD in both adults and children is Strattera (atomoxetine), a nonstimulant, but some doctors have observed that it appears to be associated with mood shifts in certain individuals. Other medicines that have been used to treat ADHD include antidepressants and antihypertensive medications such as clonidine and guanfacine. But for reasons that are unknown, all of these have the potential to cause mood problems in bipolar youngsters. Specifically, sometimes antidepressants have the potential to destabilize a bipolar child's mood and, it would appear, to bring out manic-depressive-type symptoms in a child with no previous history of the disorder. In addition, antihypertensive medications may induce depressive symptoms in children.

Parents often ask me if their child might just be suffering from ADHD and not bipolar disorder. It's surely possible, and that's why it's crucial to look for and assess any mood symptoms that might be present. Further characteristics that may help to distinguish between bipolar disorder and ADHD are outlined in Table 6.1. Many of these comparisons were first described by Charles Popper, MD, at Massachusetts General Hospital.[6]

Does My Child Have Separation Anxiety Disorder or Bipolar Disorder?

Separation anxiety is the excess anxiety a youngster may feel when separating from an attachment figure (typically the parent) or the home. It is part of a child's normal developmental process and begins between six and twelve months of age. In this age-group, separation anxiety occurs because very young children have not yet developed a sense of object permanence. Unlike older children, they don't realize that the fact that they can't see the parent doesn't mean she is not there or is not coming back. As far as a child of this age is concerned, a parent who is out of sight has disappeared.

Mild separation anxiety can occur later in a child's development as well. It's not uncommon, for instance, for kids to have problems separating from their parents at the beginning of nursery school, after

Table 6.1 Bipolar Disorder versus ADHD

	BD	ADHD
Overactivity, impulsivity, and inattention	Yes	Yes
Insidious onset	Yes	Yes
Presence of symptoms early in life	Yes	Yes
Problems falling asleep	Yes	Yes
Temper outbursts	Yes	Sometimes
Dangerous or destructive behavior	Yes	Yes
Family history of mood disorders and/or alcoholism	Yes	Yes
Morning arousal	Slow	Quick
Time required to fall asleep	1–4 hours	Difficult (but shorter than BD
Sleep symptoms	Severe nightmares	No
Response to clinician's interview	Hostile	Pleasant
Fighting	Looking for a fight	Not looking for a fight
Danger	Seeks and enjoys danger	Unaware
Illness	Continuous but intermittent dramatic symptoms	Continuous
Psychotic symptoms	Sometimes	No
Hypersexuality	Yes	No
Destructiveness	Purposeful	Careless
Duration of outbursts	2–4 hours	20–30 minutes

Note: This table should be used as a general guideline. Remember that there are exceptions to these observations.

a move, after the death of a person or pet, or following some other significant stressful life event. If separation anxiety persists for at least four weeks, however, it is considered a disorder that may require psychological intervention.

Bipolar children, in particular, often show an extreme degree of separation anxiety, which is most common when they are depressed. They may fear being alone in a room without their parents. (One mother told me she has to leave the bathroom door ajar so that her daughter will feel less anxious when she's out of sight.) As we've seen, bipolar children may also resist going to sleep in their own beds by themselves at night due to their intense anxiety and fear of nightmares, being kidnapped, and so forth. These youngsters are often genuinely petrified to be alone. When a bipolar child's mood is stabilized, though, she is often no longer so terrified of being by herself at night, and getting the child to sleep alone is often easier once she is no longer depressed.

School can be an especially difficult area for separation-anxious bipolar kids. Some kids cry and scream and take months to settle into their classrooms. Others are fine until second or third grade or even later, at which point they begin experiencing physical symptoms. In the morning, they may complain of headaches, stomachaches, and sore throats and beg their parents to let them stay home. One strategy that is sometimes helpful is to send the child to school with a picture of the person he misses, so that he can look at it whenever he's upset (though this tactic can backfire for some kids because it only reminds them that the person isn't there).

When bipolar kids' moods are euthymic (meaning even) or a bit "up," their anxiety often decreases, and they are much more comfortable. At this point, they may be able to sleep in their beds by themselves, walk around the house alone, and maybe even go on a sleepover at a friend's house. For some bipolar children, the fear of separation may still be present after medication treatment, but their fear often becomes more amenable to behavioral intervention.

Table 6.2 helps to further distinguish between the symptoms of bipolar disorder and separation anxiety disorder.

Table 6.2 Bipolar Disorder versus Separation Anxiety Disorder

	BD	SAD
Distress on separation from attachment figure (AF)	Yes*	Yes
Child worries about losing AF or about harm that may befall AF	Yes*	Yes
Child worries about an unexpected event causing separation from AF	Yes*	Yes
Reluctance to go to school because of fear of separation	Yes*	Yes
Fearful of being alone without AF	Yes*	Yes
Problems sleeping alone or away from home	Yes*	Yes
Nightmares of separation	Sometimes*	Yes
Physical complaints when separation is anticipated	Sometimes*	Yes
Depressed mood	Yes	Sometimes (if the child becomes demoralized)
Euphoric	Yes	No
Temper outbursts	Yes	Sometimes (if forced to separate against his will)
Appetite change	Yes	Sometimes (may not eat when away from AF)
Concentration change	Yes	Sometimes distracted by his worries
Energy extremes	Yes	No
Impulsive	Yes	No (cautious)

*The symptom is often present when the child is depressed.

continues

Table 6.2 Bipolar Disorder versus Separation Anxiety Disorder

continued	BD	SAD
Grandiosity	Yes	No
More talkative	Yes	Sometimes (when in a very high-anxiety situation)
Sleep change	Yes	Yes (nighttime anxiety, before-school anxiety)
Excessive guilt	Yes	Sometimes (if child feels he's a burden)

Note: This table should be used as a general guideline. Remember that there are exceptions to these observations.

Is This Obsessive-Compulsive Disorder or Bipolar Disorder?

A child with OCD may struggle with obsessions, compulsions, or both. According to the DSM-IV-TR, obsessions are "persistent thoughts, ideas, impulses, or images that are experienced as intrusive and inappropriate and cause marked anxiety or distress to the individual." Examples of obsessions include fear of germs, fear of harming a family member (even though this is not what a child wants to do or will do, he is tortured by the repetitive thought), and repetitive self-doubts (such as "Did I save the file on my computer?").

Compulsions are repetitive acts of seemingly nonpurposeful behavior. Examples include the need to put things in order, repetitive hand washing, and repetitive checking (such as checking again and again to see if the homework is in the book bag).

Though a child may not be consciously aware of it, the goal of these obsessions and compulsions, as outlined in the DSM-IV-TR, is to prevent or reduce anxiety or distress, not to provide pleasure or gratification. Youngsters with OCD also often have other disorders, including major depressive disorder and other anxiety disorders such as specific phobias, social phobias, panic disorders, eating disorders, and Tourette's disorder. Children with bipolar disorder and those with OCD can have symptoms that look somewhat similar. Both bipolar disorder and OCD children can be very rigid and may insist on doing things in a certain way. Many bipolar youngsters show their rigidity by demanding the same foods every day. Eight-year-old Angie, for instance, likes to eat ham and cheese sandwiches for lunch—but only if the cheese is shredded cheddar. If not, a major tantrum will ensue.

As for getting to school, bipolar kids with OCD traits are often late because (in addition to all the other reasons) they need to have their socks and shoes feeling "just right"—equal in height and/or with the shoelaces tied with precise and consistent tension. If they can't adhere to their personal anxiety-driven dress code, they will cry, throw a tantrum, and refuse to keep their shoes or socks on until everything feels right. Of course, routine is comforting for most children. But for bipolar kids with OCD traits, as well as for kids with OCD alone, these repetitive thoughts and behaviors are not comforting; they are all-consuming.

For the bipolar child, these rituals and routines are often somewhat mood related. When depressed, bipolar kids often become more rigid and more resistant to change. They may need to go over their bedtime ritual of having their stuffed animals arranged in a certain way or of having mom say goodnight in a particular manner: "Goodnight, Jamie. Sleep well. Have good dreams." The child can get very upset if mom mixes up the word order, and the bipolar child may insist that her mother repeat the words precisely in the correct order before she can fall asleep.

When the bipolar child is depressed, nothing is right and everything grows more difficult. This is part of the reason why a depressed bipolar kid with OCD traits may have an extra hard time seeing that his socks really *are* even and are therefore OK. Or why he may complain to his mom that she put his school snack in the wrong-size bag, even though it's the same size bag she has used for weeks. Instead of the normal whining, however, the bipolar child will become overwhelmed and collapse into tears. If parents give in to the child's requests (and I'm not saying that they should or shouldn't), that likely won't be the end of it. Within a short while, odds are that the child will find something else that is wrong.

It's natural to get annoyed and frustrated when your child has a meltdown over what seems like nothing—invariably at a time when it's incredibly inconvenient. A parent's first instinct is to reason with the child. But at these times, you might have more success reasoning with the family dog. Instead, it may be better to look at your child, take a deep breath, and imagine that he's having a brain seizure. Then think about how much good it would do if you got frustrated with him and told him, "Stop having that seizure!" Sounds absurd, right?

Though it is easier said than done, it's worth trying to regroup and give yourself time to respond with your new perspective. There are no pat answers for these situations, but many of the parents I see have very good instincts. Just remember: If you act frustrated and overwhelmed, you're mirroring what your child is experiencing, except he's experiencing it with even more intensity. You may want to give your child a break and try to discuss the issue with him later. No matter how you choose to handle the situation, the primary concern must always be the safety of you and your child.

Generally, if after treatment for the mood disorder, a child's OCD symptoms are still interfering with his daily life, then more specific treatment for the OCD, such as cognitive behavior therapy (CBT) (see Chapter 8) can be helpful. The goal is to help a child recognize and control OCD impulses. Sometimes, a low dose of an antidepressant may also be necessary.

Table 6.3 shows how the symptoms of bipolar disorder and OCD compare. Again, the symptoms of OCD may appear or become intensified when a bipolar child is depressed.

Table 6.3 Bipolar Disorder versus OCD

	BD	OCD
Repetitive acts	Sometimes*	Yes
Cognitive or behavioral rigidity	Sometimes*	Yes
Exhibits behavior or mental acts that decrease stress	Sometimes (for example, a child needs certain toys around the bed in a certain order to fall asleep)	Yes
Clear mood shifts	Yes	No
Temper outbursts	Yes	Sometimes
Appetite changes	Yes	No (can be yes if food and eating behavior are part of the OCD)
Sleep problems	Yes	Sometimes
Concentration problems	Yes	Sometimes
Suicidal thoughts or actions	Yes	Sometimes

Note: This table should be used as a general guideline. Remember that there are exceptions to these observations.

*The symptom is often present when the child is depressed.

Autistic Spectrum Disorders and Bipolar Disorder: Why the Confusion?

Autistic spectrum disorders, also known as pervasive developmental disorders, or PDDs in the DSM-IV-TR, are characterized by severe and pervasive impairment in several areas of a child's development. These may include difficulties with social interaction and communication skills as well as repetitive behaviors (hand flapping when excited is a common example in some ASD kids), activities such as having to take

Types of Autistic Spectrum Disorders

Autism is a disorder in which a child is markedly impaired in his verbal and nonverbal communication skills and in his ability to interact socially in a give-and-take manner with others. Children with ASDs also exhibit some particular behaviors, such as rocking when excited or bored.

Asperger's Syndrome is characterized by social impairment and restricted and repetitive behavior patterns but not by significant delays in a child's language, cognitive development, age-appropriate self-help skills, or adaptive behavior.

Pervasive developmental disorder not otherwise specified is the diagnosis that refers to children who do not meet the full criteria for autism or Asperger's Syndrome or certain other very specific disorders but do show some symptoms of an ASD.

the same route to school every day, and special interests (talking about trains, trains, and more trains, to the exclusion of other topics). The disorders under this diagnostic umbrella include autism, Asperger's Syndrome, and pervasive developmental disorder not otherwise specified (PDD NOS).

Kids with ASDs are typically rigid and preoccupied with sameness in their day-to-day living. They can be inflexible when it comes to following specific routines or rituals, such as lining up toy cars in a row or wearing their coats every day regardless of the temperature outside. Research by the U.S. Department of Education and other governmental agencies indicates that ASDs are the fastest-growing developmental disabilities among children and affect 2 to 6 out of every 1,000 individuals, or 1 in 166 births.[7] The number of youngsters who have both bipolar disorder and an ASD is unknown, but I have seen quite a few kids with this combination. At times, the overlap of symptoms and the diagnostic confusion surrounding the two disorders can be quite challenging.

The areas of similarity between an ASD and bipolar disorder are further outlined in the list that follows. Children in both groups may have these symptoms:

- **Onset of symptoms of the disorder prior to age three:** Children in both groups may appear overactive, impulsive, inattentive, and aggressive, and they may begin throwing temper tantrums when very young.
- **Sensory hypersensitivity:** They may have tactile, gustatory (taste), olfactory (smell), auditory, and/or visual hypersensitivity that includes intolerance for everything from tags in clothes to loud noises in a concert hall and smells at the zoo. In bipolar kids, this trait is more prominent during the depressive phase.
- **A tendency to become absorbed in certain topics and be somewhat preoccupied by them:** These kids may learn everything about a subject, such as Star Wars or the Beatles, and want everything related to it. This is different from the typical preoccupations in kids without psychiatric disorders. The fascination of bipolar kids and/or youngsters with an ASD takes on more of an obsessive-compulsive quality. These children might talk on and on about their favorite topics without regard to how people around them are reacting. The difference is that the bipolar child whose mood is stable can move on to other subjects. A child with an ASD is very rigid in his interest—to the exclusion of most other possible interests in life. When the bipolar child is unstable, he may show an increase in the intensity of his preoccupations, which at that point can seem similar to the behavior of a child with an ASD.
- **A difficult time transitioning from one activity to another:** Kids in either group can have major temper tantrums around this issue. Again, this is often much more apparent in bipolar children when they are depressed.

But if you look closely, you'll see a number of differences between the two disorders. Bipolar kids, for example, don't show the marked degree of difficulties in social involvement that ASD kids exhibit. Of course, there is no question that many bipolar children are socially challenged, especially with peers. Their irritability, bossiness, and erratic behavior can cause problems in getting along with others. But they are more aware of what is required of them socially than are children with an ASD. ASD youngsters will often talk *at* you as opposed to *with* you (unless the child is manic).

Many other ASD-like features that bipolar kids display are mood related, too. Bipolar kids often become more flexible once they are treated and less depressed; they may be very intense about certain topics when they are in the manic phase of their illness but can show a significant drop in interest when they are depressed. Likewise, repetitive patterns of behavior, interests, and activities may come and go according to their moods.

But what might these disorders look like in everyday life? Consider the following hypothetical example involving four-year-old Sam and four-year-old Georgio. These children have different primary diagnoses, but both are extreme dinosaur aficionados. In other words, like many boys their age, they have a preoccupation with the creatures. Both of them love to go with their parents to the museum store located in a nearby airport. Heaven forbid if the family is in a hurry to catch a plane! But here's how a similar event, bypassing the store, might play out differently in each family.

Sam had always been a child who marched to his own drummer. He had a hard time remembering to look at people when he spoke to them in his monotone voice. Sometimes, he seemed very intense. While in the airport en route to visit his grandparents, he threw a major temper tantrum when his family, rushing to catch a plane, would not let him stop to look at the dinosaurs in the store. Sam kept saying, "I just want to look. I'll look fast. It'll take just a minute." His mother explained that they would miss their flight if they didn't hurry. He kept repeating, "I don't care. I want to see it!" and then cried hysterically as his mother pulled him away from the store. After ten minutes (and a conciliatory bag of gummy snakes), he finally calmed down when he was reassured that his family would visit the dinosaur museum in Florida. They made it to the plane in time.

This was Sam's first plane ride, and he became very anxious when he got on the jet. He started saying, "I want to go home. I don't like planes. I want to go home." Then he began rocking back and forth, repeating the phrases several times. It took his mother five more minutes to soothe him. When they finally settled into their seats, Sam complained that the seat belt felt too tight. She adjusted it a little. He said it wasn't better and started whining. His mom said that she knew it wasn't great but that she loved him and wanted him to be safe. He said it still didn't feel good. She put a small pillow under the seat belt to make it softer and less tight and asked if it was better. Sam wasn't happy, but he said, "Mommy, it's OK. I can wear it now."

When Georgio had to bypass the dinosaur store in the airport, his mother told him the same thing: They had to move quickly, or they'd miss their flight. He refused to listen to her. He wanted what he wanted, and he was not going to take "no" for an answer. He yelled, "I hate you! You never get me anything I want. You don't really love me; you like Becka better." His mother told him that they would try and get the toy in Florida, but if they didn't run now, they'd miss their flight. Georgio began to shriek at the top of his lungs: "No, no, no. I want it NOW! If I don't get it, I'm not going." People in the airport looked at him and his mother in disbelief. His mom, of course, was mortified. She tried to quiet him, but the more she talked, the angrier Georgio got. He started to hit and kick her; his mom held on to him tightly, trying to seize control of the situation, but he started yelling, "Stop hurting me. Mommy, you're hurting my arm." By this time, his mother wanted to disappear. She was so embarrassed, she would have done almost anything to get out of everyone's sight: "OK, Georgio, if you calm down, we'll go in for a minute and look quickly, and then we'll have to run so we don't miss the plane."

Once inside the store, Georgio instantly found an expensive dinosaur that he had to have. His mom started to say "no," but when he began pulling on her arm, she quickly decided that if there was any more arguing, they'd miss their flight—and she'd break down in tears. She relented and bought the dinosaur for Georgio, who calmed down. As they ran to the gate to catch their plane, though, Georgio had to intermittently stop to straighten his socks; he told his mom that he couldn't move "when they're like this."

Once inside the plane, he saw the flight attendant by the door and excitedly began telling her about his dinosaur. Then he began talking very rapidly about his collection at home. It was hardly an interactive conversation, for Georgio was talking at her, not with her. Next, he had a hard time sitting in his seat. He kept complaining that his seat belt didn't feel right and that he wasn't comfortable. He didn't want to keep his seat belt on. He started crying and saying, "I don't like it. Take it off. Take it off." Now his mom felt as if everyone in the plane was watching them.

The male attendant came by and explained to Georgio that he had to put his seat belt on; it was the law. He also told him that after the plane was in the air, he would let Georgio go to the front of the cabin, where he'd show him some special parts of the plane that other people didn't usually see. "I don't care," Georgio said, sobbing. The attendant said, "Well, Georgio, I have to go check someone's luggage. You think it over and I'll be back." Georgio's mom put her arms around him. She repeatedly told him that she loved him and that he'd feel better in a few minutes if he took some slow, deep breaths. Within five minutes, he had calmed down. By the time the attendant was headed back toward them, Georgio said between tears, "Mommy, what's wrong with my brain! I hate it! Why am I such a bad boy? I wish I wasn't here. I wish I was dead. Maybe the plane will crash. I deserve it. I hate myself." Clearly, a part of Georgio knew something was very wrong.

By now, you may have guessed the two boys' diagnoses. Sam has an ASD; Georgio has bipolar disorder with some features of an ASD. Sam had a temper tantrum when he couldn't go into the store. But after a brief time, he was able to let his anger go and could respond to reason. He wasn't thrilled with what happened but realized it was important, and he was able to delay gratification (and accept gummy snakes as a consolation prize). He had intense anxiety when faced with a new situation (the plane) and began rocking. He didn't like the feel of the seat belt, but again, he didn't completely lose control when it didn't feel comfortable. Sam has problems socially, is obsessed with dinosaurs, and has signs of an ASD with obsessional traits and mild tactile hypersensitivity. But his mood and behavior are not as erratic as Georgio's. You don't get the sense that Sam is sad or manic, just more fussy and sensitive than other kids. I wouldn't diagnose him with a mood disorder.

Georgio, by contrast, showed minimal self-control in a few different situations. He exhibited obsessional traits; for example, his socks had to be even. His behavior outburst when he wanted the dinosaur toy sounded as though it was not an infrequent occurrence. You might think, "Well, of course he had a tantrum—to manipulate his mom—and it worked." But his behavior was not that of a child trying to manipulate. It was that of a child who is miserable. You get the sense that even though Georgio got what he wanted, it still didn't make him happy.

It is easy to criticize others and say a child is out of control because of bad parenting. The reality is that a child as difficult as Georgio makes parenting a much harder job. He loses control more often than most children. He exhibits sensory hypersensitivity like Sam (the seat belt doesn't feel right), but unlike Sam, he cannot be reasoned with. Georgio is aware that something is not right with him, and he feels unable to control himself. He shows some evidence of being depressed. Nothing pleases him. He cries easily and is quickly upset. This child, too, may have some signs of an autistic spectrum disorder. He is excessively obsessed with dinosaurs, and he sometimes seems to talk at people instead of with them. But his occasional fast talking is a sign of his hypomania, and in his case, it is largely the bipolar disorder that is limiting his ability to function in this situation. Table 6.4 further delineates some of the differences between bipolar disorder and an ASD.

Table 6.4 Bipolar Disorder versus ASD

	BD	ASD
Inattention	Yes	Yes
Overactivity	Yes	Yes
Impairment in social interaction	Sometimes	Yes
Impaired age-appropriate peer relationships	Sometimes has interest; lacks appropriate skills	Yes
Restricted, repetitive, and stereotypical patterns	Sometimes	Yes
Preoccupation with restricted interests	Sometimes	Yes
Inflexible adherence to restricted routines or rituals	Sometimes	Yes
Impaired use of multiple nonverbal behaviors	No	Yes
Little spontaneous sharing with others	No	Yes
Lack of social or emotional reciprocity	No	Yes
Impaired communication (such as speech delay, not creative or imaginative, impaired communication with others)	No (creative)	Yes (except for Asperger's)
Stereotyped repetitive motor mannerisms	No	Yes
Preoccupation with parts of objects	No	Yes
Mood symptoms	Yes	No

Note: This table should be used as a general guideline. Remember that there are exceptions to these observations.

But the question remains: What difference does it make if kids have both of the disorders or have one disorder and just elements of the other? The answer is that unless a child's symptoms are carefully explored, vital information that may affect how he should be treated (including any medications) can be missed.

So, if a clinician plans to use medication for a child with an ASD and there is strong evidence of bipolarity, then he should be treated with a mood stabilizer. The use of an antidepressant for the OCD traits and rigidity in an ASD child can cause mood destabilization and other disruptive symptoms if the child has a susceptibility to bipolarity.

Fifteen-year-old Victor is a good example. Victor was being treated for PDD NOS, panic disorder, and ADHD with a stimulant and an antidepressant. But as time went on, he became more agitated and irritable and had frequent outbursts. Though he loved art, he was unable to visit art museums because of his mood instability and panic disorder. The more out of control his behavior got, the more remorse he felt for his actions. "I don't know why I do what I do. I hate myself. I should go to jail for what I do," he would tell his parents. Things got so bad that Victor eventually had to be hospitalized. Before he was discharged, though, he was placed on a mood stabilizer for a previously undiagnosed comorbid bipolar disorder. He began to feel better. For the first time in his life, in fact, he was able to go to an art museum with his parents and siblings. In his case, both the "music and the words" were important in making the correct diagnosis. Victor's distress, his reactions to medications, and his parents' descriptions of how he behaved and his feelings of guilt and helplessness had tipped his doctor off to his bipolar disorder.

The summer after beginning treatment, Victor was able to go to a summer camp for youngsters with special needs. It was the first time in his life that he had been able to participate with peers in a non-school setting. His parents say that getting the proper treatment for his bipolar disorder opened the door to a host of new experiences for their son.

It often requires a great amount of detective work to figure out what's what in a child with a co-occurring ASD. In Trynt, seventeen, the differential diagnosis was especially tricky. Trynt had a history of ADHD, OCD, and an ASD and was diagnosed as neurologically impaired when he was very young. He had been on mood stabilizers for a few months for co-occurring bipolar disorder, but he appeared to become more depressed in the fall and winter and a bit "up" in the spring and summer. One day in late summer, he came to my office with his mother, who said that he was unusually argumentative with his younger brother and was having problems falling asleep. When I asked him why he couldn't sleep, Trynt said, "I can't turn my mind off." Even as I talked with him at greater length, I couldn't see any evidence of an obvious change in energy (he had always been restless) or changes in concentration or speech. He didn't seem extra happy or sad.

But a few things were different. Although Trynt had always had difficulties with rigidity and perseveration, he had suddenly become a comedian. His mom related that he had recently become more obsessed with the DVDs of his favorite television comedies, even though he had owned these DVDs for years. He talked about them frequently and would recount amusing scenes to his family. He was more interested in sharing the show's humor with the world than he had ever been before. Was this an early sign of hypomania? Or did it have to do with his ASD? It was still unclear to me. Then his mother said that he had begun talking about subjects he hadn't brought up in years. "If I were a Power Ranger, which one do you think I would be?" he would ask. "Which one am I most like?" He also talked about wanting to see people from his old school to show them how incredibly well he had done despite their teasing years ago. Could this be grandiosity?

Each symptom alone did not indicate any major new concern, but it was the overall change in Trynt that was significant to my mind. He had been doing so well for a long time, and then in a discrete period, he had become sillier and more irritable and had developed increased self-esteem and grandiosity. He also had a decreased need for sleep, reported racing thoughts, and was more talkative than usual. He seemed perpetually hungry. What Trynt was experiencing was hypomania, but it did not present itself in the classic sense. It just took a lot communication between Trynt's mother and myself (with some input from Trynt) before we discovered that he was having a hypomanic episode.

Is This Oppositional Defiant Disorder?

All children get oppositional from time to time. Especially during the teenage years, youngsters are often argumentative and easily annoyed. According to the DSM-IV-TR, oppositional defiant disorder refers to a "recurrent pattern of negativistic, defiant, disobedient and hostile behavior toward authority figures" that significantly impairs a child's functioning with his family, socially, or in school. The problem has to be present for at least six months to be considered a disorder, and it includes some of the following behaviors:

- Often loses temper
- Often argues with adults
- Often actively defies or refuses to comply with adults' requests or rules
- Often deliberately annoys people
- Often blames others for his or her mistakes or misbehavior
- Is often touchy or easily annoyed by others
- Is often angry and resentful
- Is often spiteful and vindictive

I strongly suspect that many parents reading this checklist will say, "Hey, that's my kid." It's important to note, however, that if these symptoms occur *only* during a psychotic or mood disorder, then the diagnosis of ODD is not supposed to be given.

What most parents of bipolar youngsters will tell you is that when the child's mood disorder is active, his oppositional behavior intensifies; when the mood becomes more even, the negative behaviors lessen. In other words, if a bipolar child's mood is effectively stabilized, his ODD may be minimized or more responsive to psychotherapy (see Chapter 8), or it may disappear completely.

What's Sensory Hypersensitivity?

Everyone likes certain textures, smells, tastes, noises, and sights better than others. For example, my son's best friend likes chicken, can take or leave lamb chops, and has a tough time tolerating the smell of fish cooking. But some kids are more sensitive to sensory stimuli than others.

Sensory hypersensitivity means that a child is extra sensitive in one or more of the five senses—touch, taste, smell, hearing, and vision. Many bipolar children exhibit sensory hypersensitivity early on, but so do large numbers of children who don't suffer from any disorder at all. Take the case of Stanley. His mom described him as always having been very sensitive to what the family calls "the smell of home." When he was eight weeks old, the family visited a cousin in another part of the state. For the entire time, Stanley screamed and cried. His mom was positive it wasn't just colic; this crying was different and even more intense. It got so bad that his parents had to cut their visit short and leave after three days so that the rest of the extended family could have some peace and quiet. Once Stanley returned home, the crying ceased. He also seemed to enjoy breast feeding, and he had some unusual behaviors. "If I didn't know better," his mom said, "I'd swear he was sniffing me while he nursed."

It wasn't until he was six months old that his mom realized that Stanley grew inconsolable every time they left the house. She clearly remembered that when he was twenty-two months, they would visit a friend's house, and after an hour or two, Stanley would want to go home. As he moved into toddlerhood, he also became much more expressive about his extreme sensitivity to the texture of his clothing. He would often try to take off all his clothes when at home. If told to put something on, he'd refuse and say his clothes weren't comfortable. As Stanley got older, his sensory issues became even more apparent. He hated socks because the seams bothered his toes. He would only wear the same two pair of socks, and if they didn't feel exactly right, he'd yell, "I hate these yucky socks" and kick them off his feet.

Stanley made his mom get rid of the labels on his shirts and pants and refused to wear anything that was uncomfortable, which was most clothing. Only two or three outfits were OK. His mother was grateful that he loved superheroes, so wearing Superman or Batman cotton underwear (boxers only) was acceptable. She washed the same clothes so often, she couldn't believe they had held up so well. By the time he was five or six, Stanley became a little less rigid. As long as his socks were put on so that the seams were on the outside, he was fine. He began to wear other pants and shirts, but they were usually different colors of the same item from the same company (without labels, of course).

Stanley didn't like anyone touching him when he didn't initiate the interaction. He felt that any incident with others kids (such as someone bumping into him accidentally) was a hostile, purposeful act. The one person he allowed to touch him was his mother. When he was anxious or overly upset by someone, he would jump on her lap and stay there, as if attached by glue. He would try to put his hand in her shirt and start sniffing her skin. His mother found this incredibly embarrassing in public but realized this was just a continuation of what he had done as an infant. For some reason, the scent of his mother was comforting to him.

Stanley's attachment to home continued during his school years. He'd go to his friend's house for a playdate and after a while would say he wanted to go to home, even though he really was having a good time. Once when he came home, he walked around the kitchen, went to the top of the basement steps, and said, "The basement smells so sublime."

Clearly, Stanley struggled with hypersensitivity of his olfactory and tactile senses. Other aspects of his story may indicate elements of different disorders, but they were not causing significant problems in his ability to function in his daily life. He didn't exhibit abnormal mood swings and therefore was not bipolar.

By contrast, seven-year-old Sandy demonstrated what hypersensitivity looks like in a child with co-occurring bipolar disorder. Sandy had a very limited food repertoire. She ate mostly carbohydrates, but they couldn't be too crunchy. She liked macaroni and cheese and soft inside pieces of bread (no crusts), and she absolutely hated breakfast cereals, nuts, hard cookies, pretzels, and vegetables. Any time she tried to eat broccoli, spinach, squash, or green beans, she would start to gag, and on a few occasions, she even vomited.

Over time, Sandy began to expand her food repertoire, but very slowly. Her mother found that when Sandy was sad, her cravings for macaroni and cheese and ice cream appeared insatiable. Then she would complain that the ice cream had a "funny taste" and was not the same kind her mother usually bought, which would spark an outburst: "Life's no fun!" she'd wail. Then she would bury her head in the couch.

But her mother knew that there were certain windows of time, perhaps never lasting more than a day or two, when Sandy would almost sprint out of bed and beg her mother to take her shopping at the mall. Once there, she wanted to buy anything and everything she saw and had a hard time accepting "no" for an answer. She pleaded with her mom to get her what she wanted. Sometimes, she could handle her mom's limit-setting; at other times, she made nasty faces and said under her breath that she couldn't stand her mother. Her mother knew that she had to seize the moment when Sandy was in these energetic, happy moods, and she also used them to get her to eat more healthy foods. They both felt a major sense of accomplishment when Sandy was able to eat a hamburger. For her, the issues were texture and taste.

Both Stanley and Sandy have sensory hypersensitivity, but because of their primary diagnoses, they required different approaches to treatment. For Stanley, who had some learning issues and sensory hypersensitivity, the pharmacological treatment of choice was a type of antidepressant (a selective serotonin reuptake inhibitor). This type of medication could help him become more flexible and less overwhelmed by stimuli in his environment. But for Sandy, the bipolar child whose sensitivities increased as she became more depressed, treatment with an antidepressant had the potential to worsen her mood disorder. Consequently, she was placed on a mood stabilizer, and when she felt better, she continued to expand her repertoire of foods.

All these stories teach us that it's *the grouping* of symptoms, not the individual symptom, that plays a major role in making a correct diagnosis. If your child has more than one psychiatric disorder and bipolar disorder is one of them, it will likely change the way a doctor approaches medication treatment. You may discover that by treating the bipolar disorder first, many of the other difficult symptoms may lessen or fade away. The child's comorbid illness can also affect the presentation of the bipolar symptoms.

In some cases, even if your child's mood disorder is well controlled, he may still require additional treatment for his comorbid disorders. By addressing the bipolar disorder first, though, you may well be able to decrease your child's need for additional medication. Stabilizing your bipolar youngster's mood disorder is the first step toward discovering his true potential.

7

Medication:
The Art and Science of Treatment

Seven-year-old Wally walked into my office and gave a thumbs-up with both hands. Three weeks after beginning treatment with a mood stabilizer, he announced: "This medicine really works. I'm not sad anymore." Eight-year-old Bruce said, "With my last medication, I had too much stuff in my head, silly stuff. Things I created in my mind. I couldn't think straight. The orange pill makes me feel a lot better." Getting the proper dose of the right medication is not always easy, especially when you're treating bipolar children. But as Wally and Bruce will attest, medication can work, and it can be life-changing when it does.

The comment I hear most frequently in any discussions I have with parents about treatment options is: "I'm concerned about putting my child on psychiatric medication. . . . Why not try talk therapy first?" As a psychiatrist and a mother, I can understand where parents are coming from. Putting a child on medication is never something to be taken lightly. After all, the majority of the medications now used to treat pediatric bipolar disorder have not been approved by the Food and Drug Administration (FDA) for this purpose (although some medications have been approved for use in other childhood illnesses, such as seizure disorders). Yet clinicians frequently observe that many children are helped by psychotropic medications (medicines that affect the mind, emotions, and behavior), and often, they are helped considerably.

There is no question that psychotherapeutic interventions that focus on the child, family, school functioning, and social relationships can make a difference in a youngster's life. But if the biology is significantly out of control, psychotherapy alone can only get so far. The potential for much greater improvement exists with the addition of medication.

Statistics notwithstanding, parents sometimes still ask if it wouldn't be better to take a wait-and-see approach with their child. My recommendation depends on the severity of a child's problems. In some cases, if I'm not yet sure of the diagnosis or if the child isn't exhibiting extremely disruptive or dangerous symptoms, I recommend waiting until it's clear (generally to both myself and the parents) that medication intervention is necessary. But when I see youngsters who are clearly suffering and unable to function in their daily lives, early intervention can make a significant difference. We know that if a child is constantly told that he is a failure, lazy, doesn't fit in, has no self-control, and is dangerous, or when he is repeatedly shunned by peers, the likelihood of his becoming a healthy and productive member of society is significantly decreased. Both biology and environment contribute to who we are and who we will become as we get older. But if the biology is not addressed, the dream of a great future can be lost. I openly discuss with parents the ways in which the risks of waiting to treat a child may outweigh the risks posed by the medications.

Understandably, parents want to know about the side effects of these medications. Psychiatrists acknowledge that psychotropic medications can have many side effects, but so can medications for typical childhood infections and even headaches.

Consider, for example, a medication that, according to the medical literature, may cause any one or more of the following reactions in children: anemia, colitis, gastrointestinal bleeding, liver problems and jaundice, convulsions, or a severe allergic reaction.

Now, what if I told you that there's a very good chance you've already given your child this medication, perhaps on several occasions?

And that your pediatrician likely prescribes this medication many times in the course of a day?

If you read package inserts, you may already know the medication to which I'm alluding: amoxicillin, one of the most frequently prescribed treatments for strep throat and ear infections in children. Amoxicillin is given to a huge number of kids every day, and chances are that you, like most parents, don't question the recommendation of antibiotic treatment for your ill child. You're probably pretty sure that this medication would do more good than harm. You know that the illness it's being used for, if left untreated, can result in serious long-term damage to the child's health and, at the extreme, even death. You're also always careful to watch your child for possible side effects. If any appear, you know to call the doctor and, if necessary, stop the medication immediately or taper it off as directed.

The same is true with psychotropic medications and the illnesses they treat. Although there are no long-term studies following medicated bipolar children into adulthood as of yet, it appears that any disorder that disrupts a youngster's childhood has a strong potential to cause problems even when the child grows up. We know that adults who suffer from bipolar disorder are at significant risk for suicide at some point in their lives. Early intervention may help prevent this from happening. In addition, just as with an antibiotic, we have the power to watch, wait, and, if necessary, discontinue a medication that causes intolerable side effects. Fear shouldn't stand in the way of getting the appropriate treatment for your child.

Getting Started

The best way to ensure a child's safety while on medication is to set up a two-way flow of information between the psychiatrist and the family. This exchange typically includes having the doctor explain the types of testing (such as blood work) that may be necessary prior to and during treatment, the medication he is considering, why he is making that choice, and the potential benefits and possible side effects of this treatment. Parents should discuss with their child's doctor any concerns or questions that they have; you're all part of a treatment team, so you need to be able to work together.

What Blood Tests Will My Child Need?

Before giving a child medication for any mood disorder, it's important to get a few baseline blood tests. They may sound intimidating at first blush, but these are standard tests that many physicians will ask for. They include:

- **A complete blood count with differential and platelet count:** These tests are needed to determine that a child has a normal number of red and white blood cells (the latter to fight infection) and a normal platelet count (which is important for blood clotting).
- **A comprehensive metabolic screen:** This is a detailed test that measures a variety of important elements of health, such as levels of electrolytes and glucose and liver and kidney functioning.
- **Thyroid function tests:** These are necessary to ensure that a child does not have a thyroid disorder that could contribute to his psychiatric difficulties. It also serves as a baseline, as some medications can affect thyroid function.
- **A fasting lipid panel:** This checks the baseline total cholesterol, high-density lipoproteins (HDL) and low-density lipoproteins (LDL), and triglyceride level.
- **Prolactin level:** Prolactin, which is secreted by the anterior pituitary gland, is a natural hormone present in all our bodies. It is involved with lactation, and it can, on occasion, be affected by certain prescribed medications (Zyprexa, Haldol, Geodon, and Risperdal).

Some parents say, "But my son won't get within ten feet of a needle. How's he going to have blood tests?" They are not alone. Many children, as well as adults, hate needles and are fearful of seeing blood (especially their own). When told that blood tests are needed, kids may cry or appear extremely anxious—or say that they "*suddenly*" feel better. I tell the kids that I don't like getting poked by needles either. But I explain to them that there's a "magic" cream that parents can put on their arms before a test, so that it doesn't hurt. There are some wonderful topical anesthetic creams (a combination of prilocaine and lidocaine or lidocaine alone) that can be applied to the area where the blood is drawn. These topical anesthetics are available under several brand names, including EMLA cream (by prescription) or ELA Max. I tell children how I have used these creams for myself and for my own children when we've had to get blood drawn, and they've helped a great deal.

Discovering that there are ways to keep the test from hurting can be very calming to kids (although many have to experience this before they believe it). I also try to make a big deal, in a positive way, about the first set of tests. Since fasting is required prior to the initial blood draw, I suggest that parents take the child out for breakfast afterward at a special place she selects and then stop by the toy store to pick out an inexpensive toy. It may seem like bribery, but this relatively pleasant initial experience often sets the stage for good experiences with future blood work.

Other Useful Tests

A few other tests are often necessary prior to starting a child on medication. These include:

- **Urinalysis:** This test indicates if the kidneys are working well and able to concentrate urine, and it helps confirm that there is no evidence of infection or urinary tract problems.

- **An electrocardiogram (ECG):** Before giving a medication, it's important to make sure as best as possible that there are no obvious heart problems. Any history of previous heart problems in the child or heart disease at a young age in any family member should be discussed. Several of the medications used to treat bipolar disorder, especially the antipsychotics, can affect cardiac conduction. Getting a baseline ECG and knowing that there are no known heart problems including abnormal heart rhythms before beginning medication treatment is very important. If your child is treated with a medication that possibly could affect the heart, it's wise to get ECGs.

- **An electroencephalogram (EEG), preferably a sleep-deprived electroencephalogram:** Although not routine, this test, used to determine the presence or absence of a seizure disorder, can yield important information. In some children, seizures can produce some of the same symptoms that are seen in bipolar disorder, including temper outbursts or spaciness. In addition, some psychotropic medications used to treat bipolar disorder may lower a child's seizure threshold (examples are Clozaril, Risperdal, and Zyprexa). Thus, a baseline EEG is helpful.*

If there are any significant concerns about the results of these tests, your child's doctor may discuss them on the phone with the youngster's pediatrician or a pediatric specialist; sometimes, the doc-

---

*The tough part about this test is keeping your child awake for it. Though different labs have different requirements, your child will likely have to stay awake most of the night in preparation for the test. Renting movies and turning the situation into a party can help pass the time. Many parents dread the thought of sleep depriving themselves and their child—but most don't find it as bad as they initially suspected. Most kids, tired and cranky, do not go to school the next day. Some napping during the day makes sense, but don't overdo it, or else getting them to sleep at night may be impossible. Parents are sometimes concerned that missing a night's sleep will throw their child's mood off. But the child usually catches up on his sleep in the next day or two without lasting effects.

tor may decide to send the child in for a consultation before initiating medication.

Getting Your Child to Take Medicine

One question that frequently comes up in discussing medication for a bipolar child is: "How am I ever going to get it into her? She can't even swallow a mini M&M. And she refuses to take most medications anyway."

In some instances, explaining to the child that the medicine can help control her unwelcome angry outbursts is enough to encourage her to comply with treatment. At other times, you may need to use a behavorial plan: "If you take your medication, there'll be a reward; if not, there'll be a consequence."

Often, once a child begins to feel better, she may recognize that the medication improves her mood, and she may become more cooperative with the treatment plan. However, some kids still argue about taking the medication because they feel better and so believe they no longer need it. They don't realize that they feel better in large part *because* of the medicine.

Sometimes, taste or texture is the problem. Depending on the specific medication used, a few different options are available: chewable tablets; sprinkle capsules, which can be opened and sprinkled on food; orally disintegrating forms, which dissolve in the mouth; regular capsules and tablets; and liquid solutions. Certain pharmacists can change the taste and amount of medication per unit using a process called compounding. Ask your pharmacist about this option.

The Medications

Now comes the tricky part: Although a number of antipsychotics and anticonvulsants are approved by the FDA for use in adults with bipolar disorder, lithium is the only FDA-approved agent for use in children and then only for those twelve years or older. This creates a challenge for psychiatrists who treat young patients. If we believe that children get bipolar disorder and that they are not, biologically, little adults, then what medicine do we use? And how do we pre-scribe it? Doctors live by the rule "First do no harm." But this does not mean "Do nothing." We treat children who are in extreme pain, are rejected by the world around them, and may have thoughts of hurting themselves or others, and yet only one medication in our treatment arsenal is approved for youngsters. And even that medica-tion is only approved for older children.

Given this situation, physicians are often faced with using a med-ication "off label." This refers to the practice of prescribing drugs for a purpose and/or in an age-group outside the scope of the drug's ap-proved use. We know, for example, that some anticonvulsant medica-tions, such as Tegretol and Depakote, are approved for use in young children who have seizures and not specifically for children with bipolar disorder. Because they've been used for another condition, they have a bit of a track record, and since they've been around for a while, doctors are familiar with their major side effects and methods of prescribing them. By the same token, we know that several drugs that fall under the class of atypical antipsychotics (Risperdal and Zyprexa are two examples) are successfully used and approved in the treatment of *adult* bipolar disorder. Lithium has an even longer track record in adults, having been in use as a treatment for bipolar disorder in adults for more than fifty years.

For the most part, it's the off-label use of these drugs—lithium, the anticonvulsants, and atypical antipsychotics—that today's child psy-chiatrists rely on when medication is needed to treat bipolar disorder in kids. What follows is a thumbnail sketch of the most commonly used medications, along with some distinguishing features of each, and a list of the forms in which each is available. This information is derived from the *Physicians' Desk Reference* (PDR), the psychiatric literature, and my own clinical experience. A parent can find more detailed information on specific medications in the PDR, 60th Edition (2006), or on the Web at www.PDR.net.

Lithium

Lithium has long been considered the gold standard in the psychiatric community for the treatment of bipolar disorder. Though the exact mechanism of how it works in bipolar disorder is still unknown, it remains a highly effective mood stabilizer for treating bipolar mania and depression as well as an effective maintenance treatment for patients who have achieved stability. In adults, it has been shown to prevent relapse and decrease the risk of suicide.[1] And further evidence suggests there is a decrease in relapse rate for adolescents who follow a lithium regimen over the long term.[2] Potential benefits of lithium treatment in adults include antimanic effects, a decrease in the frequency of cycling between moods, and an antidepressant effect. From my clinical perspective, lithium is an excellent mood stabilizer in some bipolar youth. The problem is that we still can't predict which children and adolescents make up this lithium-responsive group.

One downside of lithium is that, like many psychotropic medications, its use requires intermittent blood tests to determine the level of the drug in the blood. Although tests to monitor your child's levels of psychiatric medications are normally done in an outpatient setting and are monitored by your child's physician, it's generally a good idea for parents to familiarize themselves with the results. (Just as it's important to have a sense of your cholesterol levels, it's wise to keep a record of your child's lithium levels to note any trends that may emerge over time.) The blood tests may be done weekly, monthly, or a few times per year, depending on whether the blood level is in the therapeutic range and if the child is responding. The potential upper therapeutic level (the highest safe level at which a medication can help) is close to the toxic level for lithium (that is, the danger level).

If a child's lithium level is too low, there's a good chance that the medication won't work. If the level is too high, it can potentially cause significant problems. Therefore, monitoring lithium levels carefully is important. (Generally, the recommended blood levels of lithium should be between 0.6 mmol/L [millimole per liter] and 1.2 mmol/L.) Lithium levels equal to or above 1.6 mmol/L can be toxic and result in serious complications. Early in the course of treatment, levels must be measured frequently, perhaps once a week, as the dose is adjusted. Once the patient is doing well and the blood level is stable and not too high, blood testing may be done once a month or two for a while and then possibly once every three months.

The timing of the testing is also important. It should be done ten to twelve hours after the last dose, at a time when the lithium levels are relatively stable. In some cases, over-the-counter products can alter lithium levels. For example, sodium bicarbonate (found in baking soda and also in antacids) tends to decrease levels of lithium by increasing its excretion. Anti-inflammatory drugs such as ibuprofen (Advil or Motrin) can also raise the levels. What's more, lithium is exchanged for sodium in the body; thus, if a child is losing sodium by vomiting, sweating, or diarrhea, the body holds onto the lithium (instead of sodium), and the levels can rise. It's important that a youngster on lithium drink fluids to replace sodium and fluids lost due to sports activities, sunbathing, or a high fever or during a very hot day in the classroom. If a child is ill and taking in only minimal amounts of food and liquids, it may be necessary to contact the doctor to discuss lowering the lithium dose until the illness is under better control.

If you and your doctor decide lithium is the right choice for your child, you should let school personnel know as well. The excessive thirst and increased urination that lithium often causes makes it necessary for a child to increase his fluid intake. You may want to ask the teacher to allow your youngster to keep a water bottle or a sports drink such as Gatorade, which provides sodium, minerals, and fluids, at his desk.

Lithium, like all medicines, can have a variety of side effects even when the dosage is at acceptable levels (in general, the potential for side effects of lithium increases as blood levels rise). In discussing these side effects, it is not my intent to alarm parents, but I do want to stress that they are certainly something to be mindful of if your child begins lithium treatment. Potential side effects may include hand tremors, gastrointestinal problems such as diarrhea and nausea, excessive thirst, bedwetting, and negative effects on the kidneys or heart. Thyroid problems, especially hypothyroidism (underfunctioning thyroid gland), are not uncommon side effects. If a child appears to have a very good response to lithium but has thyroid problems, the physician and parent may discuss keeping the child on lithium while adding supplemental thyroid replacement medication to the child's treatment regimen.

Lithium is available in liquid, tablet, and capsule forms. Some are immediate-release preparations, and others are slow-release.

The Long Road to Lithium

Occasionally, parents try a number of newer medications before finding that lithium—a name that initially evokes fear in the hearts of many—is the right choice for their child. This proved to be the case with Sharon, as her mother described:

When she was an infant, we nicknamed Sharon "Jake the Snake" after a professional wrestler who was famous for his inability to stay still. Diapering her was always a challenge, as she would never lie comfortably on the changing table. As she became a toddler, it was difficult to keep her safe. She ran into streets and parking lots and could not be contained in stores or in the library. My husband and I attended parenting classes where our parenting skills came under criticism. We were led to believe that Sharon's aberrant behavior was our fault.

After she started school, Sharon was diagnosed with ADHD and put on Ritalin. She did well in school but became agitated after school—so much so that at one point during an argument with another child in the neighbor-hood, she punched through her bedroom window, shattering the glass and requiring emergency medical treatment. She sometimes made up bizarre lies. Once, she began telling people that her family members beat her. Her habitual lying made it hard to keep friends.

In the summer before second grade, the doctor took Sharon off of her meds because she had developed a tic. She also developed school refusal. On the second day of school, she bolted from the classroom into a nearby woods. Once, during a minor dispute while we were in the car, she at-tempted to open the door and jump out. At this point, a pediatric psychia-trist prescribed an antidepressant (SSRI) for her anxiety. For two months, her agitation became more severe and her oppositional behavior more ex-treme, and we requested that the medication be discontinued.

Sharon was off meds from second through fifth grades. We consulted numerous professionals. Personal therapy and behavior modification all failed consistently. During this time, everyone in Sharon's life felt as though they were walking on eggshells, desperate to avoid explosions.

The summer before starting middle school, Sharon developed depression. Often, she refused to get out of bed in the morning. She went on another antidepressant, and sixth grade began successfully, until she began to show signs of mania. She began lighting matches in the classrooms and lunch-room. She began sticking herself with pins.

We switched psychiatrists, and Sharon was finally diagnosed with bipolar disorder. But that didn't end her struggles. We tried a variety of medication through seventh and eighth grades, including three anticoagulants for mood stability, with little success. We were highly skeptical that any medication was going to work, but we were becoming desperate for some solution. Sharon's antisocial behavior was having a major impact on her self-esteem and the quality of life at home.

Our adolescent psychiatrist then recommended reducing medication to a single prescription: lithium. We were hesitant because we'd heard about lithium's side effects. To our surprise, however, Sharon's difficulties seemed to level off. She had fewer temper flare-ups, and for the first time, it was possible to reason with her. By eleventh grade, she had developed a close and loving relationship with a boyfriend and started to drive. She is now in her senior year in high school, she's not getting into any major trouble, and she is starting to think about what to do with her life. We recognize that we still have a way to go in helping her get her life together, but there's no question in our minds that persistence pays off when it comes to treating a bipolar youngster.

The Anticonvulsants

Many anticonvulsants (those medications used to prevent or control seizures) can also act as mood stabilizers and have been approved by the FDA for this use in bipolar adults. At this writing, however, no anticonvulsant has received FDA approval for treatment of bipolar disorder in children. But the various anticonvulsants available have been studied and used for treatment of different types of seizure disorders in both children and adults. Therefore, safe blood-level ranges have been established, and in many cases, the side effects are well documented. In general, a child's blood levels are taken before the morning medication is administered (generally twelve hours after the last dose of medication); levels are then checked as the medication dose is increased (perhaps once every one to two weeks) until there is clinical improvement or the medication is at the highest acceptable level. Thereafter, blood levels can be repeated in two to four weeks and then, if they are clinically stable, once every few months, unless there is a reason to check them sooner. The anticonvulsants discussed in this chapter have all been tried as mood stabilizers in adults, some with very good results.

Depakote (Divalproex Sodium) or
Depakene (Valproic Acid)

Depakote (the enteric-coated form of valproate) has been in use since 1983 in the treatment of epilepsy and has been approved for the treatment of acute mania in adults since the mid-1990s. Studies indicate that it is a good treatment option for mania and more effective than lithium in treating adults with mixed states or rapid cycling (the therapeutic blood level for Depakote in the treatment of seizure disorders is 50 to 100 mg/L [milligrams per liter]). Overall, Depakote appears to be safer than lithium because there is a bigger range between its therapeutic and toxic blood levels. In adults with bipolar disorder, it's clear that both lithium and Depakote are effective mood-stabilizing agents. Similarly, physicians who treat bipolar children find these agents can be quite effective in their young patients. (Future studies will give us much more information on the comparative effectiveness and limitations of lithium versus Depakote in the treatment of manic-depressive disorder in youth.)

On the minus side of the ledger, Depakote has weak antidepressant properties, making lithium preferable to Depakote as a treatment for bipolar depression. I tell parents that they should also be aware that Depakote's more common side effects include headache, nausea, vomiting, sedation, weight gain, agitation, tremor, and confusion. On occasion, Depakote may also cause hair loss (though vitamins with selenium and zinc can help with this side effect) and also a drop in a child's platelet count (platelets are needed for blood clotting to occur). Very infrequent but serious side effects also may include lowered blood counts, hepatitis, and, rarely, pancreatitis (an inflammation of the pancreas). There is some concern that Depakote may cause polycystic ovary syndrome, a hormonal disorder in females associated with ovarian cysts and menstrual irregularities, but the jury is still out on this matter.

At other times, Depakote may cause overwhelming fatigue in children, but the fatigue can also be due to elevated ammonia levels. Ammonia is a normal by-product of protein metabolism and is generally eliminated by a normally functioning liver. Elevated ammonia levels may result in irritability, sedation, and other central nervous system problems. So, if a child experiences extreme exhaustion while on Depakote, she should have her ammonia levels checked.

In general, a child taking Depakote should have his blood levels tested as the dose is increased. Once a clinically therapeutic level is reached, I'd recommend repeating testing in two to four weeks and then, if levels prove clinically stable, once every few months.

Parents should be especially aware that some serious side effects can result if Depakote and Lamictal (lamotrigene), another anticonvulsant, are combined. If the two are used at the same time, the child's Lamictal dose should be lowered. (See the section on Lamictal.)

Depakote is available as sprinkle capsules (beads that can be sprinkled on food) and in tablet, capsule, liquid (Depakene), and extended-release forms.

Tegretol (Carbamazepine)
Extended-release carbamazepine: Tegretol-XR, Carbitrol, or Equetro

Tegretol is discussed here as an example of the carbamazepine group. Tegretol has been used to treat patients with epilepsy since 1974. Some evidence exists that Tegretol works well for adults who have problems with lithium (especially those with mixed episodes, rapid cycling, or psychotic manias). Tegretol is not FDA approved for treatment of adult bipolar disorder. Equetro is the only carbamazepine product that has received approval for use in the treatment of acute manic and mixed episodes associated with Bipolar I Disorder in adults.

Still, some psychiatrists prescribe Tegretol for their children with bipolar disorder. Blood levels of Tegretol should be obtained eight to twelve hours after the previous dose. (The therapeutic range for those with seizure disorders is 4 to 12 µg/ml [micrograms per milliliter].) The safe therapeutic blood level for treatment of bipolar disorder is unclear, so this seizure treatment range is generally used as a fairly safe guideline.

Parents should be mindful that the most common side effects in a child taking Tegretol include dizziness, drowsiness, nausea, vomiting, and unsteadiness. On occasion, a child may develop rashes and/or liver abnormalities (either mild or severe). An important downside of

Tegretol and the related compounds discussed here is that they can, rarely, cause agranulocytosis, a serious drop in a child's white blood cell count that can hinder the body's ability to fight infection. Another very rare but dangerous side effect is aplastic anemia, a disorder in which the bone marrow fails to produce blood cells. It is important for your doctor to know if your child has a fever while taking Tegretol or if he develops mouth sores, an infection, or a rash or begins to bruise or bleed easily. Given the concern about the possible side effects of a decrease in blood count and liver problems, it is very important for your child to get blood tests done as the medication dosage is raised (every one to two weeks) and then, if levels are stable, every few months (two to four).

Tegratol is available in liquid suspension, chewable tablet, tablet, capsule, and slow-release forms.

Trileptal (Oxcarbazepine)

Trileptal was FDA approved in 2000 for the treatment of seizures in children four to sixteen years old as well as in adults. The drug is a chemical cousin of Tegretol and has a somewhat similar structure. Compared to Tegretol, Trileptal has the advantage of having fewer side effects, and it does not require frequent blood tests, a distinct plus when treating children.

Initially, many of us who treat bipolar kids were excited about Trileptal's possibilities. Since then, though, some of my colleagues and I have observed in our practices that it is not as effective as we had hoped. How much this applies to bipolar children in the general population or in other practices is unclear. Until appropriate drug trials are done, the role of Trileptal in the treatment of bipolar children is still unclear. Potential side effects include a drop in sodium level, liver problems, dizziness, double vision, rash, nausea, and vomiting. Of particular interest, Trileptal, unlike the carbamazepine, is presumed *not* to have the tendency to cause significant drops in blood cell counts.

Tileptal is available in liquid suspension and tablet forms.

How Medication Made the Difference

Finding the right medication for your child can be a long, painstaking process. But as this parent can attest, persistence can pay off:

My husband and I went through several highly stressful years of trying to find the best treatment for our son. Brian is a wonderful, alert child. But in his early years, he had multiple challenges. He had frequent episodes of impulsivity, all-consuming cravings for new toys, snacks, or whatever else caught his gaze. He had difficulty with academics and paying attention in school. He was a nonstop talker, and on one occasion—a trip from New Jersey to Boston—he talked nonstop for four hours, even between bites of lunch.

Brian was diagnosed as hypomanic in first grade and later placed on an anticonvulsant. He started to show signs of improvement soon thereafter. He was better able to focus and concentrate. He was able to verbally describe the changes he could discern, calling his medicine his "thinking pills." He told us that his mind was not as "busy" as before. Brian even told us that he didn't need to tease his little brother as often.

He began to make progress in school, and his teachers noticed an improvement in his attentiveness. Brian's dosage of medication has increased to keep pace with his growth. Recently, at age ten, he began having some difficulties again, and his doctor added a very low dose of an antipsychotic medication. This balance has been successful in helping to stabilize his mood, and though he still has occasional episodes of impulsivity and "busyness," he is a happy child.

We now have our son in full, out from behind the curtain of bipolar disorder that kept his true self hidden. We feel truly fortunate that Brian has had the care he's had, and we count our blessings that we live in this age when the mysteries of bipolar disorder, especially for children, are becoming better understood.

Neurontin (Gabapentin)

Neurontin has been approved since the 1990s for use in the treatment of certain types of seizures, and it is approved for this use in children ages three and over. Neurontin was initially viewed as promising in the treatment of bipolar disorder, especially given its relatively benign side effect profile. But this promise has not been borne out by recent, more scientifically controlled research.[3] I have, on occasion, found Neurontin to be helpful in the treatment of mood instability in some bipolar children, and some clinicians have observed that it can act as a mild antidepressant in adult bipolar depression. It has often been used as an add-on to other medications, and it may also be helpful in treating anxiety. (The therapeutic range of blood neurontin levels in the treatment of seizures is 4.0 to 16.0 µg/ml [micrograms per milliliter]. Blood testing should be done before a child is given her morning dose of the medication on the day of testing.) When Neurontin is used for psychiatric disorders, blood levels are typically not done unless there is a concern that the level is too high or a question about whether it's safe to increase the dose. Side effects of Neurontin may include gastrointestinal upset, sleepiness, nausea and vomiting, and irritability.

Neurontin is available in capsule, tablet, and oral solution forms.

Topamax (Topiramate)

This anticonvulsant has been available since the 1990s and is FDA approved for use in certain seizure disorders in children as young as age two. Topamax has been used as an add-on to other medications in the treatment of bipolar adults (though it is not FDA approved for this use). As with Neurontin, blood Topamax levels are not routinely checked but are done if there is concern about toxicity. (The therapeutic range of Topamax in blood levels for treatment of seizures is 2 to 25 µg/ml [micrograms per millileter]; blood levels must be taken prior to the morning dose on the day of testing.) One potentially useful side effect of Topamax is appetite suppression. It is sometimes added to a treatment regimen to help with weight loss or at least decrease the likelihood of weight gain, given the significant increase in body weight often seen with many of the other medications used for treating bipolar patients.

Topamax may have negative effects on a child's cognition, especially if the dose is increased rapidly. Parents may observe that their child can't seem to get his thoughts together or process information properly. A variety of physicians (psychiatrists and neurologists alike) have told me that they've observed these cognitive effects in children, and I have seen the same in my practice. Sedation is a fairly common side effect of Topamax. Less frequent side effects include a predisposition to kidney stones, eye problems, and metabolic problems. Be aware that combining Depakote and Topamax may result in an elevated ammonia level for your child, which, in turn, can cause confusion and disorientation. It's best to check your child's ammonia level if such symptoms occur.

Topamax is available in sprinkle capsules and in tablet form.

Lamictal (Lamotrigine)

Lamictal, available since the 1990s, is approved for the treatment of certain seizure disorders in children as young as age two. Lamictal was FDA approved in 2003 for use in the maintenance treatment of adults with Bipolar I Disorder (that is, the form of bipolar disorder that includes mania or mixed states), indicating that it may lengthen the time to recurrence of a mood episode (hypomanic, mania, depression, or mixed episodes). The FDA has noted that Lamictal maintenance had a stronger effect in delaying the onset of bipolar depression rather than bipolar mania. Over time, evidence continues to mount that it can be quite helpful in an individual with bipolar depression. Because Lamictal is available in a chewable form, children who cannot swallow pills often find it very easy to take.

A nice upside to this medication is that no routine blood monitoring is necessary in the treatment of mood disorders, though testing should be done intermittently to check for side effects. (The therapeutic range of Lamictal in blood levels for the treatment of seizures is 2 to 20 µg/ml [micrograms per milliliter], drawn before the morning dose.) A child may experience some common side effects, including sleepiness, tremor, nausea, vomiting, weakness, dizziness, and negative cognitive effects. In my practice, I have also seen it induce tics, or "sudden rapid recurrent, nonrhythmic stereotyped movements or vocalizations," in children with a history of a tic disorder or Tourette's disorder.

It should be noted that clinicians are exercising a great deal of caution about Lamictal's off-label use in those under sixteen years of age because it is associated with an increased incidence of serious rash (in approximately 1 percent of young patients). This rate is close to three times the frequency seen in adults. Benign rashes may occur in addition to rare but severe and potentially fatal skin reactions. Any patient on Lamictal should be cautioned to report any signs of a skin rash to his doctor immediately. To decrease the risk of side effects, Lamictal should be started at a very low dose and increased gradually.

As noted earlier, caution needs to be applied when mixing Lamictal and Depakote. Depakote decreases the body's clearance of Lamictal and therefore can more than double Lamictal levels. This is important to know given the concern about Lamictal levels becoming too high too rapidly, which, in turn, can increase your child's risk of side effects. If Depakote and Lamictal are used together, the dose of Lamictal should be less than half of what is needed when it is the only medication used.

Lamictal is available in tablet and chewable tablet forms.

Antipsychotic Medications

When you hear the term *antipsychotics*, you probably think of medications that are used to control psychosis—a condition in which a person has breaks with reality and hallucinations or delusions or disorganized thought processes. But just as aspirin can be a painkiller, a heart attack preventative, and a fever reducer, antipsychotic medications also serve a variety of functions in addition to treating psychoses. These include treatment of aggression, acute mania, tic disorder, and poor impulse control as well as maintenance treatment of bipolar disorder.

The first generation of antipsychotics, which began with Thorazine (chlorpromazine) in the 1950s and then came to include Haldol (haloperidol), Mellaril (thioridazine), and Navane (thiothixene), provided an inroad into treating a variety of disorders but carried a risk of neurologic side effects, among them Parkinson-like symptoms (tremor, drooling, slow movement, expressionless face, and stiffness in arm movements), dystonia (painful muscle spasms most frequent in the face and neck), akathesia (a very uncomfortable sense of internal restlessness), and tardive dyskinesia (an abnormal movement disorder that has the potential to be irreversible).

The newest generation of antipsychotics and the ones most familiar to those reading this book are known as atypical antipsychotics— atypical because they are better tolerated and have fewer side effects than the previous antipsychotics and because similar side effects are less frequent. Unlike the typicals, the atypicals have somewhat different effects on neurotransmitters, making them safer than their predecessors. Any of the antipsychotics are serious medications that should be approached with appropriate caution. That being said, the atypicals can be significantly helpful in a variety of ways. They can help decrease a child's agitation, control aggression, decrease impulsivity, and treat psychosis. In adults, they are an FDA-approved treatment for bipolar disorder. As of this writing, the only atypical antipsychotic approved for use in children and adolescents is Risperdal. In late 2006, it received FDA approval for use in the treatment of irritability in autistic youngsters. However, the following atypicals are widely used off label in children.

- **Zyprexa (olanzapine):** Available as tablets or as Zyprexa Zydis (an orally disintegrating form) and Zyprexa IntraMuscular for injection.
- **Risperdal (risperidone):** An older atypical and often used in children. Available as tablets or Risperdal M-Tabs (orally disintegrating tabs), an oral solution, or an intramuscular injection.
- **Seroquel (quetiapine):** Available as tablets.

- **Abilify (aripiprazole):** Available as tablets and an oral solution.
- **Geodon (ziprasidone):** Available as capsules and an injectable form (ziprasidone mesylate), for intramuscular injection only.
- **Clozaril (clozapine):** A seldom-used medication, it carries a significant risk of serious side effects, including agranulocytosis (lack of a certain type of white blood cells), seizures, and serious heart problems. Available as tablets.

Although the atypicals are free of many of the dangers of their earlier counterparts, they have their own set of side effects, chief among them weight gain. This is especially a problem with Zyprexa, Risperdal, and Clozaril, but other atypicals, such as Seroquel, can and often do have a similar effect. Abilify, a relatively newer antipsychotic, has been touted as "weight neutral," in other words, not causing weight gain. But many of my colleagues and I have seen kids gain weight even on this medication. Geodon so far does appear to be weight neutral.

Another important concern associated with these antipsychotics is what's known as metabolic syndrome. This refers to a group of metabolic risk factors—including abdominal obesity, elevated triglyceride levels, abnormal cholesterol levels, high blood pressure, insulin resistance, and evidence of a predisposition to clotting or inflammation on blood testing. Taken together, these factors can place a person at increased risk for heart disease, stroke, other vascular disease, and Type II Diabetes.

When parents know about the possibility of metabolic syndrome, they can take precautions to protect their child against it. One way is to begin steering bipolar kids away from high-fat, high-carbohydrate foods and toward healthier choices that will keep weight in check as their appetites begin to increase. Granted, this is easier said than done with a group of kids who typically crave carbohydrates, but it's a goal for which to strive. Given the concern about the possibility of developing metabolic syndrome, the physician generally monitors baseline and subsequent fasting blood sugar, fasting triglycerides, and cholesterol levels. If your child's levels are too far off the mark, the medication regimen may need to be discontinued or modified.

Antipsychotics can sometimes cause a problem with electrical conduction within the heart. Geodon has received considerable press about this issue, but no atypical antipsychotic is free of cardiac risk. Conduction problems are infrequent, however, and having a baseline electrocardiogram will help you learn about any abnormalities that would dictate that your child should not be given antipsychotics. Intermittent ECGs are another safeguard that can be implemented as the dosage is raised or when your child reaches an effective dose of the medication.

Stimulants and Antidepressants

As noted earlier, stimulants and antidepressants, given without an accompanying mood stabilizer, can throw a bipolar child into a tailspin. Their use is controversial in bipolar children, but physicians sometimes turn to them to treat disorders that co-occur with bipolar disorder.

The stimulants, (generally the compounds containing methylphenidate or dexedrine) such as Ritalin, Dexedrine, and Adderall, are used to treat ADHD symptoms. Though it may seem counterintuitive, stimulants can have a calming and focusing effect on individuals. It's akin to the alertness adults feel after having caffeine.

Some evidence suggests that stimulants may be beneficial in the bipolar population.[4] But many of us who treat bipolar children would recommend stabilizing the mood before even considering treating attention-deficit/hyperactivity disorder.

Stimulant treatment can also cause some children to experience a phenomenon called rebound. This effect begins about four to five hours after the last stimulant dose (for short-acting stimulants). The child appears overactive, excitable, impulsive, and hypertalkative and basically seems to have the same symptoms that you treated him for in the first place—sometimes even more than he started out with. Parents are often good at recognizing the time period that rebound begins and ends. In a child with bipolar disorder, it is very important to be able to tease out which symptoms are related to the mood disorder and which are manifestations of rebound. Remember, this phenomenon occurs after the medication has been taken and is wearing off, not during the time it is supposed to be effective. Generally, parents tell me that the rebound effects last one to two hours.

Antidepressants are also the subject of intense debate, for the treatment of both bipolar children and those with major depression.[5] The most commonly used antidepressants are the selective serotonin reuptake inhibitors (SSRIs): Prozac (fluoxetine), Zoloft (sertraline), Paxil (paroxetine), Celexa (citalopram), Lexapro (escitalopram), and Luvox (fluvoxamine). Older antidepressants such as Tofranil (imipramine), Norpramin (desipramine), Pamelor (nortriptylene), Elavil (amitriptylene), and Anafranil (clomipramine), commonly known as Tricyclic antidepressants, are used less frequently because of their potential side effects. Other antidepressants prescribed include Wellbutrin (bupropion) and Effexor (venlafaxine). Thus far, the only medications that have FDA approval for use in children are Prozac (in ages eight and older for depression; age seven and older for OCD), Zoloft (age six and over for OCD), Luvox (age eight and older for OCD), and Anafranil (age ten and over for OCD).

In 2004, the FDA placed a black box warning, the strongest warning it can require to be placed on a prescription drug, on all antidepressants used in children and adolescents. Named for the border around the warning section on the package insert, the black box indicates there are medical studies showing that the drug can cause serious and potentially life-threatening side effects. The warning indicates that there is some evidence of increased suicidal thinking and behavior in short-term studies in children and adolescents with major depressive disorders and other psychiatric disorders treated with these medications. Keep in mind, however, that there were no actual suicides in any of the children studied (data from 2,400 children and adolescents in antidepressant trials pooled together were reviewed).

Is there ever a time when stimulants and antidepressants should be used for bipolar kids? The answer, in my opinion, is "yes," sometimes. Stimulants may be helpful for a bipolar child with ADHD whose mood is stabilized. Antidepressants, often in very low doses, may benefit depressed children or those with obsessive-compulsive disorder. Given the possibility that either antidepressants or stimulants can cause mood shifts in a bipolar child who was previously stable, these medications should be prescribed with caution in a child who is suspected of having bipolar disorder.

Antianxiety Medication

As we've seen, if a bipolar youngster has an anxiety disorder, it often appears worse during the depressive phase of the illness. Once the mood is stabilized, the remaining anxiety symptoms should be addressed if they are excessive. In some bipolar children, anxiety symptoms disappear completely or almost completely as soon as the depression has been effectively treated. For many youngsters, behavior therapy becomes a much more effective tool once they are stable and can fully make use of it.

Although I usually prescribe a mood stabilizer first for bipolar kids, there are some youngsters who are extremely anxious and can't wait for a mood stabilizer to be fully effective. These kids are almost paralyzed by their anxiety. For them, I might select one of a class of medications known as benzodiazepines—Klonopin (clonazepam), Ativan (lorazepam), Xanax (alprazalam), and Valium (diazepam). Of these, only Valium is approved for use in young children, but this is for treatment of certain seizure disorders and muscle spasms. Buspar, a nonbenzodiazepine antianxiety agent that is sometimes used in bipolar youngsters, is not FDA approved for children, and its effectiveness in this population is unclear. Generally, I prefer not to use most of these medications for a lengthy period, as some benzodiazepines have a potential for physical addiction.

Alternative Therapies

Omega-3 essential fatty acids, naturally occurring substances found in food, have long been known to play a role in brain development. Now, research shows that these long chains of fatty acids may be of use in treating bipolar disorder. A study by Harvard researcher Andrew Stoll, MD, for instance, looked at a group of thirty bipolar adults who were given a four-month trial on either omega-3 fatty acids or a placebo (in this case, olive oil). The study found that the omega-3 group had a longer period of remission of symptoms than the placebo group. Stoll did not recommend omega-3 fatty acids as a first line of treatment. Patients who were already on mood stabilizers continued on them along with the large doses of omega-3 fatty acids that were added to their treatment regimens.[6]

How omega-3 fatty acids can improve mood is still a matter of debate, but some scientists theorize that it has an effect on brain function in ways that are similar to lithium and Depakote. It's been suggested that there may be an association between the increased prevalence of depression and the lower consumption of omega-3 fatty acids in the modern diet. Omega-3 fatty acids are found in fatty fish such as mackerel, halibut, herring, salmon, and tuna and also in plant sources such as canola oil, flaxseed oil, ground flaxseed, leafy greens, soybean oil, tofu, and walnuts.

In my practice, I prescribed omega-3 fatty acids to two siblings (of different bipolar, child patients) who seemed mildly depressed. In both cases, the ingestion of omega-3 fatty acids appeared to normalize their moods. However, one to two years later, one of the children developed clear manic episodes and needed to be treated with a mood stabilizer. The other child became more depressed within a few years after starting omega-3 fatty acid treatment but showed no evidence of bipolarity and did well on an antidepressant

I also decided to try omega-3 fatty acid supplements with two girls who had bipolar disorder and ADHD and had experienced a variety of side effects while on different mood stabilizers and stimulants. To my surprise, both girls appeared much improved with this treatment alone. Recently, I ran into the parents of one of the girls; the family had moved to Pennsylvania, and I had not seen their daughter (who was now eighteen and about to go off to college) in four years. They told me that her new psychiatrist had continued her on the omega-3 fatty acids and that her mood has been relatively stable over the years. She had experienced some intermittent mild mood swings, but they were treated with psychosocial interventions and had resolved without adding medication.

Potential side effects of omega-3 fatty acids treatment include loose stool, increased irritability, elevated mood, a fishy aftertaste, and nosebleeds. One boy I treated, with no known history of allergies, developed a rash all over his body shortly after starting on omega-3. Why this happened is unknown, but the rash definitely ended his treatment with fish oil.

One more caution should be added: As omega-3 fatty acids can potentially interfere with the ability of blood to clot, they should not be taken by people with clotting disorders or by those on anticoagulants (blood thinners), nor should they be taken before surgery. In addition, given the ability of omega-3 fatty acids to act as a medication, I'd recommend checking with your doctor before beginning a therapeutic trial on your own. Dietary supplements are probably a good way to get higher doses of omega-3 fatty acids, as excessive fish consumption can cause a potentially dangerous elevation of mercury levels in the body. It's recommended that vitamin C and E supplements also be taken with the fish oil treatment.

Light Therapy

As mentioned in Chapter 3, bipolar disorder is accompanied by seasonal affective disorder in some children, making them acutely sensitive to seasonal changes. For these kids, the changing of seasons has an overwhelming effect. This disorder is treated by exposure to a specialized type of light box (phototherapy) for a set amount of time daily during the time of year when the individual is depressed.[7] It is hypothesized that phototherapy works by affecting a hormone (melatonin) and a neurotransmitter (serotonin) that affect the brain and mood.

When I heard about light therapy for the first time in the 1980s, I remember being skeptical. It was not until I treated Nicholas, a sixteen-year-old high school junior, that my skepticism went out the window. Nicholas had ADHD, learning disabilities, and what I later realized was bipolar disorder. At fifteen, he had been hospitalized in mid-January for a major depression and a suicide attempt. In the hospital, Nicholas was placed on an antidepressant and given various types of therapy. Within a few weeks, he seemed happier and was discharged to outpatient treatment. He returned to school a more social and serious student, despite ongoing minor issues. Nicholas said he was no longer depressed, and he appeared to be absolutely fine, in retrospect, perhaps a little too fine. I discontinued his antidepressant at the beginning of August, which had no apparent negative effect.

Nicholas began his senior year in high school with mild anxiety. This made sense. Given his learning difficulties and the pressures of school as well as preparation for college, most adolescents in this situation would feel stressed and nervous. By the third week in September, though, he started feeling overwhelmed and was unable to focus in school. He subsequently sank into a depressive cycle, and throughout the winter months, despite resuming treatment with an antidepressant, he was overwhelmed, sad, angry, had many physical complaints, and resisted all efforts to get him to attend school. He once again became suicidal and was hospitalized. His antidepressant was changed, and his condition improved but not to the extent that it had in the past. He was discharged from the hospital and started attending school again.

In May, Nicholas asked to be taken off his medication. He said that he felt "great." He became very social, attended lots of parties, and said he did not want to spend the rest of his life being "dependent" on medication. He seemed the happiest that I had ever seen him, and I wondered if he was almost too happy.

I tapered him off his medications, and he was happy to graduate from high school. He found a job in a local video rental store within two weeks of getting his diploma. His employer was pleased with his work, and fellow employees enjoyed working with him. But over the first few weeks of September, he appeared to grow unhappy with his job. Suddenly, his boss was too demanding, and the guys he went out with after work weren't real friends; he thought they were leaving him out of activities and talking about him behind his back. By the third week in September, he was clearly entering a major depressive episode.

I discussed Nicholas's situation with a senior colleague, who always seemed to be involved with cutting-edge treatments. He asked me if I thought there was a seasonal component to Nicholas's illness, and it was then I realized that the answer was "yes." Every year, Nicholas became depressed by the end of September, just when the amount of daylight was decreasing. I had previously thought his September depressions were due to increased pressures brought about by school. This year, there was no school, but everything still seemed to go downhill for him by the end of September.

Since Nicholas refused to take medication, we decided to try phototherapy. Gradually, he increased the amount of time he spent in front of the light box until he was up to one hour every morning. He began to feel better as the phototherapy time increased, and within a few weeks, he was back to feeling good. In the spring, while still on phototherapy, he began showing clear signs of being on the border between hypomania and mania—characterized by rapid speech, exuberance, and high energy. I tapered his light therapy, and these symptoms lessened. He remained mildly hypomanic but not to a troublesome degree. My experience with Nicholas taught me to have respect for the role of phototherapy in the treatment in bipolar disorder.

Over the years, I have used light treatment with many bipolar youngsters. It's rare that it has been the only modality of treatment; more often, it is in addition to a mood stabilizer. I tell parents the story of Nicholas and how, in his case, this treatment acted like an antidepressant medication. Some kids have told me that after using the light box in the morning, they have more energy and feel better able to deal with the school day.

For children I think may be helped by phototherapy, I generally prescribe a specially designed light box. These can be purchased by mail order through companies such as Apollo Light Systems, Inc., or the Sun Box Company. The amount of light reaching the eyes (the light intensity) is measured in units called lux. Generally, I ask patients to purchase a 10,000-lux light box, which can be used for periods from ten minutes up to an hour or more. (Some insurance companies offer reimbursement for light boxes if they receive a physician's note indicating that it was prescribed for treatment purposes.) I generally recommend that children begin with a ten- to fifteen-minute exposure and work up to an effective dose. In some cases, kids report feeling happier and more energetic after the first treatment, but others may need a few days or weeks to increase the period of exposure and get the full effect. Potential side effects include headache, irritability, hypomania, overactivity, and insomnia.

The timing for using the light box varies from child to child. Some need it around the time school starts for the year, others not until later in the fall or early winter. Increasing the amount of light exposure in the winter months may be helpful.

Just how light boxes work to alter mood is still unclear, but it's thought that the hormone melatonin plays a role. Scientists have postulated that there isn't enough morning light to suppress the melatonin that some children's bodies produce. Exposure to the specialized light may help correct this situation. Although some researchers and light box manufacturers say phototherapy is best done in the morning, using it at other times of the day that are more convenient may also be effective.

Melatonin Supplements

When bipolar disorder proves disruptive to your child's sleep, melatonin supplements may be helpful. Melatonin, a natural substance secreted by the pineal gland in the brain, regulates the sleep/wake cycle as well as many other functions in the body. It is believed that melatonin levels in bipolar kids may be too low at night and too high in the morning hours, prompting the brain to send ambiguous signals about when it's time to sleep and wake up. The idea behind the use of the supplement is to add melatonin to what the body already produces.

Various brands of both natural and synthetic forms are available in health food stores, though the man-made synthetic product is preferable. Melatonin should be given twenty minutes to an hour before bedtime. The proper dose varies from child to child, but I've found that anywhere from 0.5 mg to 4 mg/day can be effective, although some of my colleagues use higher dosages on occasion. So far, it appears that melatonin helps children fall asleep faster, sleep longer, and wake up fairly alert.

Melatonin is well tolerated, though I've found that some bipolar children occasionally experience an increase in depression with this hormone. Cautious use of melatonin is recommended because the hormone has not been subject to FDA review, and studies still need to be done to clarify melatonin's effectiveness and its side effects over the short and long term. Parents should be aware that melatonin supplements can have side effects including a change in sleep patterns, confusion, headaches, transient depression, problems with performing motor tasks early in the morning, fast heartbeat, high blood pressure, and an increase in blood sugar.[8]

What Treatment Will Work for Your Child?

I always tell parents to imprint in their minds what their child is like when his mood disorder is under control. This is who he really is. The goal with treatment is to return to that better place and higher level of functioning. The approach your doctor takes in treating your particular child will depend on a variety of factors, including the child's age, his predominant symptoms (elevated or depressed mood, irritability, oppositionalism, aggression, suicidal tendencies, and so forth), and whether he displays signs of a comorbid disorder.

Far more research needs to be conducted on the use in children of the medications discussed in this chapter, and it needs to be conducted soon. Once again, it must be kept in mind that these medications have not been approved for treatment of bipolar disorder in children, and they, like any other medication, can have side effects. But fear of side effects shouldn't prevent you from getting your child the help he needs. New treatments are in development every day. And there's a good chance that down the line, new and better medications with more favorable side effect profiles will become available.

Until then, vigilance and teamwork on the part of both you and your child's doctor can stop many problems in their tracks and get your child on the path to feeling better. Medication is just one step on that path, but it is often essential to the journey.

8
❦

Why Therapy Matters

One Saturday night, the mother of a patient called me in a panic: Her eight-year-old son, Felix, had announced that he was leaving home to tour the world, and she was very worried. Since Felix had been cycling between mania and depression (and had tried to walk away from his mother in the grocery store earlier that day), his mom feared he might make good on his promise. She had tried reasoning with him, but in his grandiose mood, Felix was convinced that he could travel on his own. "You don't understand. I have to go!" he had screamed to his mother.

His mom put Felix on the phone so that we could talk. When I pointed out the loopholes in his plan—"you need money to travel, eat, and so on"—he began to grow angrier and more agitated, insisting that he would still go. Clearly, a different tack was in order. I acknowledged that his idea seemed interesting and that I could understand why he would want to see the world. Then I asked if he knew that I occasionally see grown-ups as well as children in my office.

"Yes," he said.

"Well, if you were one of my adult patients and said you wanted to go see the world," I continued, "I would say, 'OK, that's a very exciting idea, but it's not something to do on the spur of the moment. We should sit down and talk about it before you decide to take off and leave.' The adults usually say, 'That makes sense,' and then we discuss it at the next session."

I suggested to Felix that we should take the same approach with him, given the importance of his complicated decision. He grudgingly said OK, and we agreed we would continue our conversation when I saw him on Monday. In addition, I increased his mood-stabilizing medication. By the time I saw him, however, Felix was feeling calmer and had forgotten all about touring the world, and neither of us mentioned it again.

This may seem like a curious conversation to have with an eight-year-old, and it was. But it was also a moment that helped reinforce for me the importance of psychotherapy—also called "talk" therapy—for bipolar children. In my experience, medication is rarely, if ever, the only intervention that bipolar kids need; psychotherapy is the second vital component of treatment.

The term *psychotherapy* refers to a variety of techniques that help people deal with psychological problems and function better in day-to-day life. A growing body of scientific research speaks to the long-term benefits of psychotherapy, and even though most of this research has been conducted in bipolar adults, there is much to be learned from it that may apply to children. For example, a study conducted by David Miklowitz, PhD, professor of clinical psychology at the University of Colorado, Boulder, demonstrates that involvement in one type of therapy (Family-Focused Therapy [FFT], as described later in this chapter) may help individuals take their medications more regularly and therefore decrease their rate of relapse. Other evidence suggests that teaching about potential causes, symptoms, medication treatments, and ways of recognizing early signs of recurrence—a process referred to as psychoeducation—also helps decrease relapses.[1]

This psychoeducational component is crucial for bipolar kids and their families. As youngsters grow older and become more independent, the more they know about their problems and how to cope with them, the better equipped they'll be to help their doctors find the treatments that work best for them. As I tell my teenage patients, "either you will learn to control your illness or your illness will control you."

One of the most important elements of talk therapy is the same "listen to the words" approach I used with Felix: hearing what a child says, entering his world of thinking, and making him feel respected and understood (and meaning it). In Felix's case, this included seeing the situation from his point of view, recognizing his grandiosity, and using this knowledge to help him delay action (his plan to travel the world) until his impulsivity lessened.

The same kinds of techniques can work for parents as well. Mothers and fathers can help their children immensely by listening carefully to their words and not letting difficult behavior (the music) drown out their messages. This approach of discussing problems and working out solutions encourages children to develop their own coping strategies.

The story of seven-year-old Shariff and his mother further illustrates how well this approach can work. Shariff, a would-be film director, had created a play in which his younger siblings, all dressed up in costumes, were the stars. But things weren't going so well. Shariff was yelling at his brother and sister, who weren't performing the way he wanted them to, and he told them that they were dumb and not listening to how the story should go.

His mom knew she had to intervene before the situation escalated. She spoke to Shariff gently and said, "Look, you're very smart, we know that. But if you want to be a director one day, you can't just go and boss your actors around and think that they're going to listen to you. If you do, there's a good chance they will quit, and there could be no one who wants to work with you. Film directors know that if you want to get the best performance from your actors, you need to figure out how to make them feel comfortable and also respect you. Yelling at them won't get you what you really want."

Shariff pondered his mother's words for a moment and then replied, tentatively, "OK, I guess I can do that." He went back to his young actors and described how he thought the story should go, but he also asked if they had any other ideas. The arguing stopped, and in the end,

they all had a great time acting out the story line that Shariff had created (but with some modifications by each of them). His mother had
reached him by listening to his ideas and treating him with respect.
Had she gotten angry and begun yelling, the situation could have easily spiraled out of control.

Parents can also employ some of the techniques of talk therapy to
help them distinguish between behaviors that may stem from bipolar
disorder and those that reflect normal adolescent development.
Here's how one mother got to the bottom of her son's angst over
talking to a girl at school.

*My oldest son came home from school teary and exhausted. He declared
that his medicine was no longer working. He confessed that he had been
crying all day and had been frustrated by his lack of control. He asked me
to call the doctor and get some help.*

*I was already going down my mental checklist: Had he gotten his meds
the night before? What time did he get to bed? I couldn't think of anything
that might be causing his biology to be out of kilter.*

*I decided to slow things down a minute and get more details. First, I
asked him when he first started to feel bad. He told me it was the past two
days. I asked him to describe the past two days. He began to recount the
moment when he first realized that something had gone terribly wrong.
One of his best friends had introduced him to a girl. This young girl had
asked him a couple of questions, and my son found that he could not
respond—could not utter a sound. It scared him and then made him angry
with himself. The next day at school, his friends teased him about it. He
was humiliated. "Mom," he told me, "she is the hottest girl in school!!! I
am so stupid!!!"*

*With great relief, I realized that my boy was not unstable—he was growing
up. This was not a failure of medication or the puberty chemical-imbalance
nightmare that we secretly feared. It was a typical preteen experience.*

*By talking with him, I was able to convince him that things would be OK
and that what he had experienced had happened to most of us at one time or*

another. (He later talked to his therapist, who reinforced this message.) It was then that I realized: Sometimes the best medicine is a loving parent.

Which Therapist Is Right for My Child?

You may have decided by now that therapy is a good idea for your youngster. But perhaps the mention of the word *therapy* conjures up the image of a patient on a couch and a bearded male therapist who listens intently for the hidden secrets or long-forgotten traumas that control a person's behavior. In reality, this is the television and film industry's inaccurate portrayal of a specific type of psychotherapy: psychoanalysis. Psychoanalysis focuses on bringing out a person's unconscious struggles to help him or her relieve emotional pain. Psychotherapy, by contrast, has a much broader definition. It refers to the treatment of mental and emotional problems with the goal of relieving disturbing symptoms (such as anxiety) and helping to improve a person's daily functioning.

Just as finding the right psychiatrist for your child may take some hard work and trial and error, so will locating the best therapist for your son or daughter. But certain issues that all bipolar kids share need to be addressed in therapy, and it's important that everyone involved in the therapeutic relationship be aware of the following guidelines.

Therapy Is a No-Blame Zone

All members of the family are affected by the child's unpredictable mood and behavior. By the time they see a therapist, the typical family already has some significant dysfunctional patterns. It's important for the family and the therapist to recognize that these patterns likely did not play a role in causing the child's out-of-control behavior. Instead, they represent the ways in which the family is coping in order to survive life in a chaotic, ever-changing household. The concept of blame is not helpful to parents, the bipolar child, or anyone else in the home.

Biology May Not Be Destiny, but It Is Extremely Important

When the child has a major rage outburst and is out of control, parents and even therapists can lose sight of the fact that the child's biology is out of kilter. This doesn't mean that environment does not play an important role in who we are or who we will become or that kids don't need limits or behavioral supports. But biology and temperament are major forces as well. Though it's not necessary for therapists to be experts in bipolar disorder, they should have a basic understanding of the illness. In addition, they need to be open to learning more about it.

Flexibility Is Critical

When treating a bipolar child, the parents and the clinician need to be flexible and able to adapt to the child's changing needs. I often tell my families that stability is a temporary condition—be it for two hours, two days, two months, two years, or two decades. Medication may work for a while and then stop doing its job. A child's biology may change for unknown reasons or because of an environmental stressor. For example, the death of a loved one may trigger a child's depression. Puberty may also throw a wrench into the works. I tell parents and therapists that the majority of the bipolar kids I've seen sooner or later experience a change in their symptoms and level of functioning.

I recommend what I call an I.V. approach to therapy for children and families—I.V. referring to intensity and variability. The idea is that the symptoms of bipolar disorder will become more intense from time to time and will vary periodically. The therapist must understand that a treatment that worked for a reasonably stable bipolar child may have to be set aside when the child becomes depressed or manic. For example, a child who was doing well with cognitive behavior therapy (CBT), in which a therapist worked with her to challenge her negative thoughts, before she developed a manic episode, may do better with a supportive approach until after she stabilizes. Therapists including psychologists, social workers, family therapists, and psychiatrists must also be prepared to exercise some creativity. Whether that means following a child wherever that may lead when he tells you he's feeling suicidal or talking to a youngster in the office-building parking lot because he refuses to leave the car, a good therapist must approach treatment with the idea that tailoring the method of therapy to a child's current emotional state is part of the job description.

Once you've lined up a flexible, competent therapist, how do you know which approach your child will respond to best? Of the many different therapeutic methods for the treatment of bipolar and other psychiatric disorders, only a few have been subject to scrutiny by scientific studies designed to compare their effectiveness. In my clinical opinion (based on twenty-five years of practice and not a placebo-controlled, rigorous, scientific study, mind you), there's no one "best" therapy for a bipolar child.

A variety of factors must be considered when choosing a therapist. These include your child's age, cognitive ability, symptoms, temperament, and motivation.

Some kids need a therapist who is soft and gentle; others respond to one who is tough and more direct. A shy, frightened child may do better with a low-key and nonthreatening therapist (this in no way means ineffective). An angry adolescent may need a therapist with a strong, no-nonsense approach to treatment, whereas some irritable, tense teenagers may be calmer and feel less challenged by a soft-spoken therapist.

Another factor to take into account when choosing someone to work with you and your child is the therapist's gender. As youngsters approach adolescence and begin to explore issues of sexuality and identity, they may feel more comfortable with a same-sex therapist. Probably the single most important element of successful treatment, however, is trust. If a family does not feel comfortable with and have faith in a therapist, it is difficult for a child to make progress. The youngster senses the parents' doubts, and this colors her approach to treatment.

Psychoeducation Equals Demystification

Psychoeducation—the process of educating children and families about the conditions that affect them—is based on the principle that the more the patient and the family are aware of the different aspects of an illness, the more empowered they will be to deal with it. I believe that psychoeducation is one of the most helpful interventions at a mental health professional's disposal. I try to help my patients' parents learn as much as they can about childhood bipolar disorder by encouraging them to read books, explore Web sites, and participate in chat rooms (the Child and Adolescent Bipolar Foundation has an excellent one at www.bpkids.org). I love it when a parent brings me new information, for just as families learn from me, I learn from them. The news on childhood bipolar disorder is constantly evolving, and the sharing of information benefits both the doctor and the patient and may lead to a child having better control over the course of the disorder.

Here's an example of how psychoeducation can help. Mrs. Helm, a bright woman who cared deeply about her daughter, was fighting with nine-year-old Jenine over almost every part of their morning routine: waking up, getting out of bed, choosing clothes for school, brushing her teeth, eating breakfast, and on and on. She felt that her daughter was being stubborn and argumentative on purpose, just to torture her. When Jenine's mom and I met alone, we went through each of the events from her crazy mornings and explored them in detail. I asked a number of questions: Why did she think her daughter was doing some of these things on purpose? What benefit could she possibly get from this difficult behavior? It sounded to me as though Jenine ended up feeling even more upset than her mother over the morning's chaos.

When Jenine and her mother came in the next week to continue the evaluation, Mrs. Helm said that things at home had gotten a bit calmer. She had begun to realize that perhaps what was happening in the morning was not really a cruel joke that her child was playing on her but pertained instead to Jenine's innate difficulties. Although her mother undoubtedly still struggled with the morning routine, she was able to be more sympathetic and to better help Jenine get ready, rather than becoming furious at her daughter. Her increased understanding helped ease tensions between the two.

Educating themselves about the more subtle signs of bipolar disorder, especially the particular triggers that can set off an affective storm, can also help parents and children to cope. Since many bipolar kids don't routinely have violent and aggressive outbursts, understanding the spectrum of manifestations and their warning signs can be a godsend. Does the child have a change in energy before a swing? Become more irritable? Sleep more? Is there a seasonal component? If so, when does it start? When does it usually end? Poor grades and rejection by peers can also bring on mood swings, as can a lack of sleep.

Mood charts can be very useful tools for parents to employ in recording a child's mood swings and to help them identify patterns that signal a swing is imminent. These charts can be used to track the efficacy of medication treatment as well. The Internet is a valuable resource for locating these materials.

Types of Therapy

Generally, three different types of therapy are used in treating mood-disordered children and their families: individual, family, and group treatment. (Psychoeducation, as detailed earlier, is a common component of many types of therapy.) How frequently a child sees a therapist varies, depending on the therapist's orientation and the child's past history. There may be times when a child is quite ill and the family sees the therapist a few times a week. When the child is well, the therapist may be seen only once a month.

Individual Therapies

Cognitive Behavior Therapy

Cognitive behavior therapy (CBT) refers to a type of treatment in which a therapist works alone with a child to help him learn to challenge his negative thoughts and misperceptions. It is a therapeutic way (if a child's mood is not too unstable) to approach the rigidity we sometimes see in bipolar children—by teaching him the relationship between his thoughts and his behavior. The premise of cognitive behavior therapy is that by mastering particular ways of thinking, a child can learn to help himself function more effectively in the world around him.

Consider the following example. Suppose Frank is walking down the sidewalk and sees his classmate John walking down the other side of the street from the opposite direction. John looks down at his feet instead of making eye contact. Frank decides John isn't looking at him because John doesn't like him. He feels angry that John doesn't like him. Frank then goes home and sends an e-mail message to his friend Greg saying that John is a miserable, stupid kid who didn't even have the decency to look at him and say hello.

A cognitive behavior therapist would work on trying to get Frank to think about the other possible reasons John may have had for looking down and not making eye contact. Was it that he had a bad cramp in his toe? Maybe there was a nail in his shoe? Or was he worried about math class? The fact is, it's possible the reason he looked down had absolutely nothing to do with Frank. If this last explanation was what really was going on, Frank begins to learn that he might have jumped to conclusions and misinterpreted the situation, which led to his bad feelings and subsequent behavior.

Cognitive behavior therapy requires work. Not only does a child have to want to get better, he also has to commit to doing daily or weekly exercises designed to help change his behavior. For example, a bipolar child might be asked to practice deep breathing three times a day as part of his treatment program. Next, he would be instructed to use this technique whenever he feels anxious. Not all kids, and sometimes not even adults, are motivated to put forth this kind of effort. This type of therapy requires that a child have a certain maturity and the willingness to examine his own behavior. As you can imagine, this might not be the most appropriate treatment in young children or in children whose moods are labile.

But CBT can have good results for those who are motivated to give it a try. The Treatment of Adolescent Depression Study, a twelve-week study conducted in 2004 by John March, MD, MPH, director of the Division of Child Psychiatry at Duke University School of Medicine, and his colleagues, compared 439 depressed adolescents who were divided into four treatment groups: those taking Prozac (fluoxetine) alone; those using CBT alone; those taking Prozac with CBT; and a placebo group. Rates of response for Prozac with CBT were 71 percent; Prozac alone, 61 percent; CBT alone, 43 percent; and placebo, 35 percent. Therefore, it was the combined group that used both CBT and medication that experienced the most improvement.[2] Cognitive behavior therapy has also been found to be a useful tool for medicated bipolar adults as compared to a medicated group without CBT. The combined-treatment group had significantly fewer and shorter bipolar episodes and better social functioning.[3]

Cognitive therapy can have a number of variations. One type uses a treatment technique known as contrasting visual imagery. The idea is that if you think of and visualize something positive, you will be unable to focus on something negative at the same time. Ian's mother explains how visual imagery helped in her son's treatment:

A child with significant anxiety and a phenomenal imagination is often his own worst enemy. But one day not long ago, we discovered that it was also my son Ian's own best defense.

As we sat in the doctor's office with Ian, then age eight, we watched him put on a brave face as he explained some of his worst anxieties. He told us how alone he feels when he goes upstairs at night or when he arrives at school on days that he has "worries." It was heartbreaking to listen to him confess his discomfort at falling asleep (even while he was denying that it was so bad) as he blinked back the tears and described the monster that plagues his dreams.

We were at a crossroads of sorts. Then, the doctor came up with an idea. She suggested that he think of the funniest animal he could think of— something that would really make her laugh. Ian immediately thought of a cow in a pink tutu with matching lipstick; the cow was revealed to have clog dancing shoes on and a passion for juggling and riding its unicycle.

After the two of them had a good laugh, the doctor asked my son the cow's name, to which he responded, "Bob." The laughing resumed, only this time, it was almost uncontrollable. When they both calmed down, the doctor asked Ian to try to practice thinking of "Bob" a few times a day and right before he fell asleep. Ian did this for a week and was having an easier time drifting off to sleep. The next week, the doctor asked Ian to bring "Bob" to school with him and picture him anytime thoughts came into his mind that he didn't want.

"Bob" has given my son a way to talk about feelings that he had previously denied. It gave him back a sense of control, and he now feels empowered to banish the bad feelings. It has been several months since "Bob" came into our lives. If you ask Ian about him, he will smile . . . and tell you that this silly-looking cow in clogging shoes helps keep the bad thoughts away.

CBT can be used with children as young as five, if the child is cognitively able to use this approach. Michael Osit, PhD, a psychologist in Warren, New Jersey, describes using this therapeutic technique to help five-year-old Shawn conquer his fear of being kidnapped from his bedroom at night. The doctor showed the little boy a box filled with hundreds of pebbles, but only one of them was gold. He had Shawn close his eyes and pick up one of the stones. Then, he had him repeat the exercise over and over again. Shawn never got the gold pebble. The psychologist used this example to show the youngster that being kidnapped was as unlikely as getting the gold pebble. By working at the youngster's level, he was able to help alleviate Shawn's fears.

Interpersonal and Social Rhythm Therapy
Interpersonal and social rhythm therapy (IPSRT) is an innovative approach that has been used in adult bipolar patients since the 1990s and has great potential to be helpful for youth. Developed by Ellen Frank, PhD, and her colleagues at the University of Pittsburgh, it combines interpersonal therapy—a short-term therapy that has been used for treating depression in adolescents and depression and bipolar disorder in adults—and social rhythm therapy, an intervention aimed at regulating patterns of sleeping, eating, and light exposure (also known as circadian rhythms).[4]

How do these two therapeutic components work together? Interpersonal therapy aims to educate a person about the relationship between her mood and behavior and the ways in which one can affect the other. The thinking goes that by improving a person's interpersonal skills and working on any problems in her relationships, her mood disorder symptoms should lessen.[5]

The guiding principle of IPSRT is that bipolar disorder stems from a mixture of psychosocial and biologic causes. Stressful life events, especially interpersonal ones, and disruptions in an individual's biologic clock (that is, social rhythms) play an important role in bipolar disorder. In their research, Frank and her colleagues compared adults with Bipolar I (manic or mixed episode) who underwent this type of treatment with adults who had intensive clinical management treatment (ICM), a form of talk therapy that addresses the causes, symptoms, and treatments of bipolar disorder without an emphasis on social rhythms. Those in the social rhythm therapy group received education about the disorder, as well as assistance in improving and regulating sleep times and having predictable hours for meals and sunlight exposure. The study concluded that adults who received IPSRT during their acute illness went for a longer time without a recurrence of symptoms in the maintenance phase (the period after the acute illness, when the goal is to maintain the improvement after the episode) than did those without IPSRT.

Here's an example of how IPSRT might work in an adult. Let's say a worker changes from a day job to a night job. His sleep is disrupted, which, in turn, affects his mood. He can't see his friends because he is working when they are at home. The biologic and interpersonal changes interact, and he becomes even more depressed. Changing back to a day job corrects both his circadian rhythms and his social relationships—which should then improve his depression. How this therapy might be useful in kids is now under investigation. At this writing, Stefanie A. Hlastala, PhD, at the University of Washington School of Medicine is studying the use of IPSRT—with some developmental modifications—in adolescents with bipolar disorder.[6]

In my own practice, the importance of regulating biorhythms is borne out everyday; I find that children who have consistent sleeping and eating patterns as well as structured daily routines tend to do better at managing their bipolar disorder than kids with more erratic patterns.

Play Therapy

Some children who struggle with talking directly about their feelings can be virtuosos at using toys to communicate. In fact, play therapy can be an effective way for getting at the issues with which children, especially young ones, struggle. The goal of this treatment is to help these children work out emotional and/or behavioral issues that are causing problems in their lives.

Four-year-old Cathy, for example, had been having more tantrums at home since her brother was born five months ago. According to her mother, she was extremely caring with the new baby and very gentle and loving toward him. But when Cathy and I played with a family and a dollhouse, it wasn't until she made the baby doll go live with another family that she began to calm down. If she was even aware of her anger at her new sibling (and I'm not sure that she was), she wasn't comfortable talking about these feelings. Play therapy gave her a way of working on and overcoming her angry feelings.

Play therapy can also be helpful for prepubertal or early adolescents who are somewhat nonverbal about their feelings. Forest, a creative seven-year-old, was much more comfortable playing with puppets than he was talking about major issues in his life. His mother confided to me that she was struggling financially but hadn't let her son know. In play, Forest repeatedly pretended that his puppet was trying to buy a new car or some other item but didn't have the money to do so. It was clear that, on some level, he was aware of what was going on in his household.

One downside of play therapy, as with many therapies, is that it's very difficult to use if a child is too rigid or unimaginative or if his mood and behavior are too out of control. Kids need to be able to play and talk and become involved with (and focus on) a story, skills that can come and go with different mood states when a child has bipolar disorder.

It's important to note that parents should not adopt the role of a psychotherapist with their own child. But they can use the skills of observation and careful listening to better understand and assist the child with his struggles. Using elements from the cognitive therapy approach, they may help their youngster learn how to keep from misinterpreting certain situations, and by employing their own form of social rhythm therapy, they can help their child maintain a fairly structured and predictable daily program.

Family Therapy

Family therapy can take a variety of forms. It may include all family members or different combinations—parents and the child, the bipolar child and siblings, and extended family. In family therapy, one goal is to change dysfunctional patterns that have developed over the years (in part because of raising a bipolar child). Treatment can support the family in dealing with the difficult situation of raising such an unpredictable youngster; it may also provide education about bipolar disorder and ways of using behavioral interventions at home. Before this change can occur, however, it's important to address parents' questions and to deal with the pain and sense of loss they may have in accepting that their child has difficulties. A child's individual therapist will frequently recommend family therapy to help parents deal with these and other feelings, learn about the disorder, and come up with ways to help their child manage his illness. The importance of family therapy should not be underestimated: After all, the child lives within a family, not by himself. Parents should be involved with their child's treatment, as they are primary partners in the therapy process. Here are a few types of family therapy that seem most relevant to pediatric bipolar disorder.

Collaborative Problem Solving

Developed by Ross Greene, PhD, a Harvard-affiliated psychologist and author of *The Explosive Child*, the collaborative problem solving (CPS) approach operates on Greene's mantra that "children do well if they can." Collaborative problem solving revolves around the idea that a child's rigidity and inflexibility can be thought of in the same vein as a learning disability, or, as Greene puts it, a "flexibility disability." He proposes that difficult children and adolescents "lack important cognitive skills essential to handling frustration and mastering situations requiring flexibility and adaptability."[7]

The idea behind CPS, says Greene, is to ask not "What's it going to take to motivate this kid to behave differently?" but "Why is this so hard for this child? What's getting in his way? How can I help?" and to go from there.[8] The effectiveness of this method has been explored and demonstrated in studies conducted by Greene.

Greene calls on parents to prioritize their expectations for their child into Plans A, B, and C: Plan A contains behaviors that the child absolutely must follow (for example, not running with a knife); Plan C refers to situations in which parents consciously decide not to impose their will on the child (for example, whether he wears gloves to school in the winter).

But most conflicts eventually fall under Plan B, the main skill-teaching plan in CPS. This is the plan designed to help caregivers work through problems with kids to find mutually agreeable resolutions.

Let's look at the following scenario: Solomon wants to see his friend Lance for a playdate. His parents remind him for the third time that week that they are going on a family trip to the art museum.

In CPS, Plan B consists of three steps. The first is "Empathy (plus Reassurance)." Here, the goal is to identify and understand how a child feels about a given issue and to let the child know that the adult won't insist on his own way in resolving the issue. This is to indicate to the child that his parent respects and recognizes the importance of this issue to the youngster. The parent says, "I know that you want to play with Lance today. You guys are good buddies."

Next comes the "Define the Problem" step (under the CPS model, a problem is described as "two concerns that have yet to be reconciled"). This step is to identify the adult's concerns on an issue. The parent then says, "We made a commitment to both you and Griffen that today is to be family day. So it's important that you come with us." If this step came first, it would definitely create a frictional situation between the parent and child.

The last step is the "Invitation," where the child and adult are asked to brainstorm solutions together, with the goal of figuring out an answer that is realistic and acceptable to both the parent and the child. The parent says, "I know you haven't see Lance in a few weeks. However, we all have been looking forward to going to the museum as a family, and you're a very important member of our family. What do you think we can do to work this out?" After five minutes of discussion, Solomon comes up with the idea that "maybe Lance could come with us to the museum." Since everyone in the family likes Lance, this becomes the accepted resolution.

CPS is a wonderful model for many children; once a child is stable, this approach has the potential to be quite effective. But as any parent of a bipolar child knows, attempting to reason with a manic child can be an exercise in futility. When dealing with a child in this phase, picking and choosing your battles may not be totally under your control. If a bipolar child wants to fight, even if there's nothing to fight about, attempts at reason are typically ineffective. That's why stabilizing the biology is so important.

Collaborative problem solving is another type of therapy that incorporates a "listen to the words" approach. Part of its beauty is that it teaches the importance of flexibility on the part of both the child and the parent or clinician. Mutual respect is a crucial underlying component of this treatment.

Family-Focused Therapy
This therapy (FFT), developed by David Miklowitz, PhD, and colleagues, consists of an intensive, nine-month psychoeducational treatment that is conducted with patients and their family members. After three months of weekly sessions, therapy is biweekly for three months and is then continued on a monthly basis. In the sessions, family participants are educated about the disorder and the different medical treatments available, and they work on developing more positive family communication, improved problem-solving skills, and a relapse prevention plan.[9] Studies show that medicated bipolar adults who participated in FFT with their families had fewer relapses, longer intervals of being well, and less severe depressive and manic symptoms. Research on this treatment has been conducted mainly with bipolar adults, although there have been some positive results from a preliminary study using family-focused treatment in adolescents.[10] Miklowitz and his colleagues at the University of Colorado and researchers at the University of Pittsburgh are studying the therapy's effectiveness in bipolar adolescents and their families.

In 2004, Mani N. Pavuluri, MD, PhD, FRANZCP, and colleagues at the University of Chicago reported on another potentially significant intervention for bipolar youth and their families. This new approach, called child- and family-focused cognitive-behavioral therapy (CFF-CBT), combines family-focused therapy in children with cognitive behavior treatment. As with many of the other treatments mentioned here, more studies need to be done to determine the full effectiveness of this intervention.[11]

Group Therapy

Group therapy can be educational, problem-solving, or supportive, and it can serve a variety of other functions as well. When I was working on an inpatient adolescent unit years ago, I learned that adolescents often listen to their peers better than they listen to adults (even the therapist at times). The old phrase "misery loves company" is often true. There's an element of destigmatization in knowing that others have problems and that you're not alone. By working together in groups, young kids and adolescents get to discover that they are not the only ones in the world who are sometimes held hostage by their mood fluctuations. They also learn that these mood swings don't define who they are. This type of treatment is frequently used in inpatient programs, day programs, and outpatient settings. It can be extremely helpful for children and adolescents who have the verbal and cognitive skills to benefit from it, but its efficacy depends on the match between the group's leader and the individual patients, as well as the compatibility between the patients.

Multifamily Groups

Some clinicians have applied the principles of group therapy to what are called multifamily groups. Mary Fristad, PhD, and her colleagues at Ohio State University first published their results on the effectiveness of multifamily psychoeducation groups (MFPG) specifically for children with bipolar and depressive disorders and their caretakers, in 1998.[12] The current model of this treatment approach consists of eight sessions in which family members (including the child) meet together to learn about mood disorders and better ways of communicating with each other. After the joint meeting at the beginning of the session, the families are divided into two groups, one for parents and one for children. The children receive information about their disorder that helps to demystify the condition, as well as symptom-management skills and social skills training. For example, a youngster who attributes her depressive irritability to "being bad" might be told instead that her short temper and sadness are to some degree innate—in the same way that a tendency to nearsightedness is part of some kids' biologic makeup. But just as you can wear glasses to correct nearsightedness, you can take medicine and have therapy to alleviate the symptoms of bipolar disorder. While the children are in their session, the adults are learning about their children's illness and developing symptom-management strategies, too. At the conclusion of each session, families are given projects to work on together at home.

So far, Fristad's research indicates that both parents and children who participate in the groups feel happier about their relationships, more knowledgeable about the mood disorders present in family members, and empowered to use the new coping skills they've learned.[13] As this book was going to press, a comprehensive study on the effectiveness of multifamily therapy was close to completion. Families may soon be able to avail themselves of this type of therapy outside a group setting. Fristad is now adapting her treatment approach for use with individual families.[14]

Social Skills Groups

These groups are useful for bipolar children and other kids who have difficulty getting along with peers, making and maintaining friendships, and knowing how to act in social settings such as restaurants, family functions, or the grocery store. Often, this type of therapy is recommended by a therapist or the child's teacher, or it is sought out by a parent.

In social skills groups, which are led by trained therapists, children practice such things as how to join in a conversation and take turns in games. They practice socially appropriate behaviors such as how to accept a present graciously or how to ask for help in a store.

One of the goals of social skills groups is to address the misperceptions bipolar kids often have about their world. When these kids are depressed, they often experience paranoia and feel that others don't like them or are saying mean things about them. When they act on these incorrect assumptions, it creates problems. Social skills groups can also help bipolar kids to better "read" facial expressions and emotions, a skill they often find difficult.

How Well Does Therapy Really Work?

Parents sometimes worry when they don't see immediate results in their child's progress during therapy; they wonder if they are wasting their money and their time. But it's important to be patient: Psychotherapy is a long-term investment. Although it may seem that a child is not internalizing what he's learning and that therapy is not producing any immediate returns, a youngster may be banking away for future use the coping skills he's learning now. The benefits can take years to surface, as it can take time for children to begin to transfer what they learn in therapy to the outside world. As the child gets older, develops more self-control, and becomes more mature, he will draw on the tools he's been given for years to come.

I've had many parents tell me that they initially did not believe that therapy had helped their child but later realized that it had made a huge difference over time. Here's what the the mother of Herman, age eleven, had to say about his psychotherapy experience:

I believe it was at Herman's four-year physical when I broke down in tears asking for help. I explained to Herman's pediatrician that I could not handle this child's behavior; we needed further help. My pediatrician referred me to a psychotherapist, and for years, the therapist and I worked on how to handle Herman's dangerous, defiant, and often destructive behavior.

I began reading books on positive discipline and learned everything I could about parenting. Herman began seeing a behaviorist for individual therapy, and we all became involved in family therapy.

Meanwhile, we began to see a child psychiatrist who worked tirelessly with us for several years trying to get Herman's medications adjusted. The medications seemed to help for a while but never were perfect. No matter what kind of therapy we provided, it didn't seem to help. We felt as though nothing could help until his biology changed. We began to feel he would never be any better no matter what type of help was provided. We decided at one point to discontinue behavior therapy. What was the point of spending the time and the money? We were on a roller-coaster ride with no signs of stopping.

At one point, we had Herman get neuropsychological testing to help determine the presence of cognitive and/or neurologic deficits. These tests were helpful in understanding what specifically was difficult for him. I do believe the information we gained was helpful in showing Herman that we understood what his difficulties were. I think he felt he could trust us completely with the unbearable pain and unrest that lay within him. I gradually began to realize that the psychotherapy was helping more than we thought.

During the past year, Herman's medication combination finally seemed to really work. He has been the most stable he has ever been, with a few bumps in the road. He has a very clear understanding of how he feels and can now verbalize his feelings, which is very helpful. During the summer, Herman has been going to sleep-away camp. I can see changes in him positively ever since he started camp. I can see him implementing the skills he has absorbed. I know the roller-coaster ride is not over. There will be many more chapters to follow, but I can see the light. There is some normalcy in his life and in ours.

The neuropsychological testing to which Herman's parent refers is a battery of cognitive tests that examine brain function and attempt to identify problem areas. By using this type of testing to clarify a child's deficits, teachers and parents can learn how to help him compensate for areas of difficulty.

Once Herman's medication helped him achieve biologic stability, all those years of hard work in a variety of therapies proved to have been most valuable. After Herman's mood was stabilized, his life changed. He and his family have been much happier, and Herman has become far more successful in his involvement with the outside world.

Stories such as Herman's should be kept in mind when you feel as though therapy serves no purpose. Sometimes, you discover that psychotherapy really does help, even if its effects are somewhat delayed. In many cases, it's the combination of therapy and medication that, in the end, turns a child's life around. And the earlier the intervention, the more profound its effect will likely be.

9

❀

Hospitalization:
When Therapy and
Medication Aren't Enough

No parent likes to think that his child may need hospitalization, but sometimes, therapy and medication are not enough to help the child get better. Hospitalization may be required for any number of reasons: There may be safety concerns, a child may refuse to take medication and have breaks with reality, or he may be unable to attend school and function in the world.

When I talk with parents about psychiatric hospitalization for their child, they often look at me with tremendous sadness, fear, and anxiety. Their reaction is perfectly understandable. Their child may have severe separation anxiety. She is unable to sleep in her own bed or go to school because she's too scared to leave her home and family, yet here I am suggesting that this child be placed in a hospital. To add to the tension, the thought of a psychiatric hospital conjures up images from *One Flew over the Cuckoo's Nest* for many people. It is a scary picture, indeed.

But psychiatric units are far different places these days, and though it may seem better to try to keep your child at home, hospitalization may be the most humane course of action in the long run. In a good inpatient setting, a child can be evaluated by a variety of trained clinicians. Being in a hospital also allows a physician to make significant medication changes much more quickly than can be done when the child is at home. The youngster is in a safe, controlled setting, monitored by trained nurses and staff who are able to deal with any sudden psychiatric or medical problems that could arise.

Monitoring a child's mood is also less complicated in the hospital. The pressures of daily life are gone, making it easier for clinicians to observe the child's behavioral styles. The youngster may also be more apt to share some of his feelings in an inpatient setting. I've known hospitalized children to admit to having experiences with hearing voices or with suicidal thoughts, revelations that they hadn't shared with anyone until they were in that setting. The hospital can also be a good place for children to start to recognize self-defeating behaviors and to begin to take responsibility for helping themselves.

Stays at psychiatric hospitals are much shorter than they were years ago. And that can be both good and bad. Children come home quicker. But because of insurance constraints, the stays may be so short that medication and therapy don't have time to fully work. Years ago, when psychiatric hospitalizations could potentially run as long as three to six months, I was amazed by the changes that inpatient treatment could accomplish in some children's lives. Did it work for everyone? No. But did it help make a difference for some kids? Absolutely. Many times, kids were able to return to the outside world and transfer the gains they had made in the hospital to real life. For others, a brief period of a few days or weeks in an inpatient unit was all that was needed to help them feel and function better.

Today, longer, more intensive treatment is much harder to find. It can be difficult to get a child or adolescent into the inpatient unit of a hospital (depending on the hospital, the child might be placed on a children's ward or a ward with both children and adolescents), and insurance coverage is often limited.

Under some insurance programs, in fact, the doctor or a staff member has to call the insurance company almost daily to get approval for the child to stay another day or two. If the company declines to approve the stay, the parents can be left with a very large bill. Meanwhile, the hospital is called on to stabilize the child's condition in a couple of days, even though it may have taken months or years to develop.

Take the case of eleven-year-old Justin, a child who had been depressed even while on two mood stabilizers and who had intermittent thoughts of ending his life. He didn't tell anyone initially, but the violent drawings in his notebook, which pictured people being knifed or shot, should have been a clue. He had tried to kill himself once before by ingesting fifteen over-the-counter cold pills from the bathroom cabinet, but he told no one. When he couldn't get up for school the next morning and stayed home because he felt nauseated and weak, his family assumed he had a virus.

It wasn't until he wrote beautiful poetry about the serenity of being dead that his teacher and family realized something was terribly wrong. He was admitted to the hospital, where he finally told the doctor about his suicide attempt. The doctor there started adding a low-dose antidepressant to Justin's existing medication. He also discussed with the family the risks of the new medication bringing out mood shifts as he was diagnosed with bipolar disorder. Over the next few days, Justin said he wasn't feeling suicidal anymore. Instead, he appeared cheery—almost too cheery. After hearing of Justin's improvement, the insurance company refused to pay for continued inpatient hospitalization. Since Justin was no longer deemed acutely suicidal, he was discharged the next day and treated on an outpatient basis.

It didn't matter that both the doctor and his parents knew that putting Justin on a low dose of antidepressant (in addition to his previous medications) increased the risk that he could have unpredictable mood swings. There was a good chance that he didn't exhibit (and the doctor wouldn't see) any worrisome signs within just four days, and the insurance company wasn't concerned that a somewhat too cheerful mood might be a sign of impending hypomania. As it turned out, within a week of leaving the hospital, Justin became manic. It took weeks to stabilize him by lowering his dose of antidepressant and adding an antipsychotic medication.

The moral of this story is that inpatient psychiatric hospitalization is often Band-Aid care these days, sometimes at the whim of insurance companies and what they deem to be necessary treatment, which makes it all the more important that parents, doctors, and therapists alike be vocal advocates for their young patients. But I don't share this story to frighten parents away from hospital care; on the contrary, I believe inpatient hospitalization can be extremely helpful for children who are dangerous to themselves or others, psychotic, nonfunctional, or in need of medication adjustment under close medical supervision.

Different Forms of Hospitalization

Inpatient Hospitalization

A variety of inpatient psychiatric hospital programs exist for children. These include:

- A psychiatric unit for children in a medical hospital
- A state psychiatric hospital
- A private psychiatric hospital program

If there is an acute emergency, police generally take the youngster to the nearest psychiatric emergency screening center or to the local emergency room. Each state has its own regulations and procedures for psychiatric hospitalization. These days, patients' choices of hospital programs are limited by their insurance plans. If possible, parents should learn which programs their insurance covers if it appears hospitalization might be needed in the near future. Parents can also talk to their child's therapist, in advance, to learn more about the various programs available to get some guidance in this process.

Contrary to what people might think, psychiatric hospitalization is not available only for the wealthy. Each state has its own approach to providing help for those who cannot afford it. Keep in mind that when a child needs hospitalization, he is usually in tremendous pain and needs more help than even the world's best parents can provide at home.

Partial Hospitalization Programs

These programs, sometimes called day programs, offer an alternative to full hospitalization. They allow children to live at home but attend a therapeutic program on weekdays. In partial hospitalization programs, children are grouped with other youngsters who have psychiatric problems and who are not yet ready to return to their regular school and full social functioning. A psychiatrist oversees medication issues, and the programs are typically staffed by trained counselors. Individual therapy, family therapy, group therapy, and a school component, as well as transition services, help ease the child back into a normal life. In theory, partial hospitalization is a good option. It can be an opportunity for therapists to observe what the youngster is like in a setting that is closer to real life, and it can help the child focus on examining the issues he needs to confront. It also presents a chance to adjust the child's medication in a somewhat controlled environment.

The effectiveness of this type of treatment, however, depends on a host of variables: the quality of the therapists, the frequency of their interaction with the children (individually or in groups), the ages and diagnoses of the other children in the program, the types of daily activities offered, the involvement of knowledgeable psychiatrists, and the motivation of both the child and the family. As noted earlier, one of the goals of a partial-day program is to help ease kids back into life in the real world. But if a child is highly unstable, suicidal, homicidal, dangerously out of touch with reality, or worsening in part secondary to extreme tensions within the home, full inpatient treatment may be needed.

To most parents, either form of psychiatric hospitalization represents the great unknown. To make matters worse, the consideration of whether to hospitalize a child often must be made during a time of crisis. One parent described the experience this way:

The toughest part was the decision to hospitalize. As parents, we tried everything before doing so . . . the best doctors . . . best therapists . . . a variety of meds . . . working with the school. When we finally did hospitalize Luke, it was the hardest decision of our lives. He was ten years old. We felt we had failed him in some way and lost control over the situation. But we felt we had little choice. His depression was not responding to medication, and he had started having suicidal thoughts.

Telling Luke he was going to the hospital was very hard and emotional for us as parents. Giving him up to a hospital was difficult, too. We drove about fifty miles on a Wednesday night. He fell asleep in the car from crying so much. We then met the hospital greeter (in our case, we used the child unit of a private psychiatric hospital) who took a history and then admitted him. We could not even see his room.

Luke later told us that a stuffed animal (not his very favorite one but a special one from his room) was a very important tie to his family, and he hugged it while crying through most of his first night. We went the next day to see him, and we were surprised that he looked as good as he did. We felt that he let us off the hook for putting him there. He actually wanted us to leave after a while so he could be with his group.

Luke had a good doctor who kept in close contact with our psychiatrist. This was key to our sanity as parents. The doctor was able to change all his meds in a fairly short period of time. We felt that we had a team working together and that Luke would be better as a result. We also received support from Luke's school and our friends.

After ten days or so, the hospital indicated he was improving and that his discharge was imminent, so we made the choice to take him out on a

Friday. Luke had reported that many of the activities that helped pass the day were not scheduled on weekends, so we thought that taking him out and his being with both parents for the weekend was a good decision.

The hospital put Luke onto a path that allows him to function normally. It worked out better than we could have imagined. Luke wants to avoid hospitalization again, however, and he now takes his medication religiously. We hope this lasts through his adolescence.

Although most parents don't have the opportunity to ask a lot of questions before admitting their child to the hospital in an emergency, here are some of the most common questions mothers and fathers ask me before deciding to hospitalize their child:

Q. Before we decide to go ahead, can I visit the unit where my child will be staying?

A. Not usually. With privacy concerns paramount these days, hospitals typically do not allow visits to inpatient units because it might violate patients' rights to confidentiality. The next best thing to visiting is asking questions of the doctors and administrators. Find out how the unit is set up and how the program is structured. What kind of treatment do the children receive, by whom, and how often? Are there separate units or groups for children and adolescents? What is the rooming set-up, and how is it determined? What do the kids do all day in the hospital?

Many times, parents are worried (appropriately so) that their kids will have therapy once a day and spend the rest of the day doing nothing, except maybe watching television and talking to kids much more ill than they are. Can you imagine the chaos and trouble that might arise if you had a group of kids just sitting around all day without structure and supervision? The goal isn't to bore them to death and cause an uprising—it's to help them. Generally, child and adolescent psychiatric programs have a schedule that includes individual, family, and group psychotherapy; a school component (so that the kids don't fall too far behind in their education); and recreational activities. There may be art therapy; dance therapy; and a quiet hour, during which the kids have some time to rest, read, and write letters. Frequent group therapy sessions that include the kids and trained therapists are often a major part of the therapeutic program.

You might think that group therapy is a waste of time. What benefit is your child going to get from listening to a bunch of other kids with problems? I have been amazed, however, at how honest and insightful youngsters can be about other kids' behavior. Peers can make incredibly on-target observations about each other and offer helpful recommendations.

Q. **Who staffs the unit?**

A. Generally, psychiatric nurses, psychologists, social workers, and mental health assistants. A psychiatrist—full- or part-time—is always part of the treatment team. During your child's stay, it is the hospital's psychiatrist, rather than his private psychiatrist, who will determine what medication will be given. Although some parents find this worrisome, assessment by the hospital's psychiatrist actually allows for a second opinion. It also allows for adjusting the child's treatment with closer observation than would be possible if the child were an outpatient. Given the amount of information your private psychiatrist has about your youngster's past treatment, however, an exchange of information between the two physicians can benefit your child.

In the hospital, your child will have regular contact with a psychiatrist and the therapist(s) assigned to him, and the nursing staff will administer his medications. The psychiatrist and staff will review your child's progress and follow a treatment plan that is created specifically for him. The staff will monitor him carefully for any side effects or other health problems.

Q. **Can I stay in the hospital with my child?**

A. No. One of the significant advantages of a child being in the hospital and away from his normal environment (and that includes parents) is that it provides the opportunity to see how he functions on his own. This gives staff members more clues as to what issues he is struggling with and which ones may be contributing to his illness.

Q. **But if my child was having his appendix out, I could stay with him—why isn't that possible here?**

A. This situation is different. The appendix will not react differently if the parent is around. Many times, these children are completely dependent on their families and extremely fearful of separation. Sending kids the message that they can survive in the hospital, that they possess strength on their own and are not fragile, is important. Children and their parents may also fall into dysfunctional patterns that interfere with a professional's learning about the child's strengths, weaknesses, and coping skills. Also, children are better able to become involved with the treatment program if parents are around only during visiting hours.

Q. **Can I visit him every day?**

A. Most psychiatric inpatient units have a few hours of visitation for family members on weekdays, with additional visiting hours on weekends. Inpatient psychiatric units located within children's medical hospitals tend to have the most liberal visiting arrangements. There can be certain hours when phone calls to family members may be made and received. In some programs, this may be a privilege that the child has to earn. The goal is to keep children and adolescents focused on the program and not distracted by the outside world.

Q. **Will being in the hospital make a difference in how my child feels and behaves?**

A. One hopes so. The first goal of hospitalization is to protect your child from dangerous behavior—either toward himself or others. Maybe he's confused, hearing voices, extremely anxious, not eating, paranoid, or nonfunctional in some other way. Acceptance of an illness is difficult for anyone and especially a mental illness in a child. But the adult needs to take charge. If a child is agitated, out of control, or unable to function (doesn't go to school, has no friends, has major destructive tantrums, refuses medication, and so on), then something has to happen to help get the child on the right track. Hospitalization is a start. It is not a cure.

Q. Will he ever forgive me for putting him in an inpatient unit?

A. A better question may be, "Will he ever forgive you if you don't help him get his life together or if he ends up in jail or chronically institutionalized?" As parents, we are often forced to make tough decisions. The hardest but most rewarding job for a mother or father is to help your child grow up to be a healthy, stable, productive, and self-sufficient human being. Sometimes, sadly, hospitalizing a child is part of that process.

Q. Won't he learn bad things from the other kids there?

A. Again, you need to find out as much as you can about the treatment units, including the ages and general types of diagnoses of the patients there. Do not be afraid to ask questions. If there is time before the hospitalization, check out the different inpatient and day programs that are available to determine which one is the best fit for your child. Discuss the treatment options with your child's doctor and therapist.

The mix of patients and the focus of the program are important. For example, I wouldn't recommend that a mildly antisocial child be placed with adolescents who have been involved with a great deal of illegal behavior.

Q. Why can't a child take a hair dryer, sweatpants with pullcords, or paper clips?

A. Many children who are in the hospital are there because they are in a heightened, impulsive, and potentially dangerous state. A child can electrocute or injure herself or someone else with a hair dryer. The pullcord in pants can be used to harm oneself or others. A child can cut herself with paper clips or even cause serious physical harm to someone else. You may think your child would never do that, but remember that she isn't the only person on the unit. To control the environment for everyone's well-being, there are limits as to what can be brought and left with a youngster in an inpatient setting.

Q. **What's the difference between putting my child in a child psychiatric unit of a medical hospital and putting him in a psychiatric hospital?**

A. If a child has both an active psychiatric problem and a medical problem, being in a medical hospital definitely has its advantages. But if this is not the case, one can argue for either type of setting, depending on what is available in your area. A child unit in a psychiatric hospital has the advantage of a staff and facility that is more focused on youngsters with emotional problems.

Q. **Why does the unit not look as nice as the pediatric unit on *General Hospital*?**

A. There is no question that treatment units should be clean. But in psychiatric units, everything the patient has access to must be safe and mustn't have the potential to inflict harm. So, furnishings tend to be sparse. If there's a pool table, for example, it's often in a locked room, as pool sticks can be dangerous.

Q. **How will they keep my child under control? Are they going to load him up with medicine?**

A. Most units for children and adolescents work on a behavioral point system. Once youngsters are on the unit for a while (and learn that they will not be leaving or getting privileges unless they earn them), they usually become more accepting of the program. A quiet room, for times when they are out of control and need time to calm down, is available. Medications for agitation are much less likely to be necessary when the child is in the hospital, but of course, they may be used to stop out-of-control or potentially dangerous behavior.

Q. **My child's only problem is that he refuses to take his medicine. How can I justify to myself resorting to such a drastic measure as hospitalization?**

A. If your child doesn't take medicine and he's really fine, then there's no issue here. He shouldn't be hospitalized and maybe doesn't need the medicine. But what if he's not fine, doesn't go to school, has no peer relationships, and can be unpredictably violent to others or himself? What if medicine can put a dent in all of this? Hospitalization may be part of the answer.

Q. **My doctor says I should put my daughter in the hospital because she's on several medicines at once but not getting better. At this point, it's even hard to know if any of her medicines could be making her worse. Why not try this as an outpatient? I'll stay with her all the time and watch her carefully.**

A. A few of the medications used in bipolar children should not be stopped without someone watching the patient carefully for adverse effects or major and possibly dangerous mood swings. In some cases, the hospital is the best place for accomplishing this. There's a trained nursing staff whose job it is to monitor your child's behavior and vital signs twenty-four hours a day, and again, hospitalization allows doctors to increase and decrease medications much more quickly than they could if your child were at home.

Hospitalization for your child, under any circumstances, can be a bewildering and upsetting experience for the entire family. But even though the hospital corridors are foreign places to many parents, you shouldn't be shy about asking the questions you want to have answered. After all, you're only asking for what every parent would want: to rest assured that your child is getting the care that he needs in order to get better.

10

Going to School:
Easier Said Than Done

Time and time again, parents describe how frustrating it can be to try to help their children be successful and happy at school. Many parents are at their wits' end—and understandably so. Given the difficulties that bipolar children can have with getting up in the mornings, separation anxiety, quick transitions, controlling their emotions, and in many cases learning disabilities, it can be particularly hard for them to feel comfortable at school.

But there's plenty that can be done to make your youngster's school day happier and more productive. Where to start? In talking with parents about the subject, I inevitably return to my favorite mantra: Listen to the words, not just the music. If you and the teachers listen to your child's words ("I hate handwriting"; "I have to cover my ears when we eat lunch in the school cafeteria") and not just his music (throwing a tantrum during writing assignments; refusing to go to the lunchroom), it will be far easier to help him deal with the daily demands placed on him.

Some youngsters will be able to make their way in a mainstream classroom with few supports other than outside therapy (and perhaps earplugs for lunchtime), but others may need a classroom aide, tutoring, more time on standardized tests, a resource room, a special school, or a computer for writing assignments. Still others will require a combination of educational supports. Federal and state laws mandate that these types of accommodations be available for children with learning, emotional, or behavioral disabilities that interfere with learning. So, if you believe your youngster could benefit, don't hesitate to talk with school personnel about evaluating his needs.

I'm not suggesting, however, that we offer kids a free pass because of their special needs. The message should not be, "You have a handicap, and the world should change to meet your needs." To the contrary, we should be saying, "You have some difficulties—all people do—and you need to work to overcome them as best as possible, while simultaneously maximizing your strengths to live a happy and productive life." The goal is to empower, not to pity, our kids.

Granted, your child's school struggles may seem like uphill battles on some days. But take comfort in the fact that school is one of the most difficult jobs your child may have during his lifetime. As adults, we have a tremendous choice in how we spend our days, whether we decide to be salespeople, plumbers, journalists, electricians, doctors, teachers, or something else entirely. Kids have no such option. As noted pediatrician and learning expert Mel Levine writes in his book *A Mind at a Time*,

> It's taken for granted in adult society that we cannot all be generalists skilled in every area of learning and mastery. Nevertheless, we apply tremendous pressure on our children to be good at everything. Everyday, they are expected to shine in math, reading, writing, speaking, spelling, memorization, comprehension, problem solving, socialization, athletics, and following verbal directions. Few if any children can master all these trades. And none of us adults can.[1]

Our job as parents and clinicians is to help kids find their place, while at the same time helping them to learn the academic and social skills needed in life. What follows are some of the common concerns parents share with me about their children's school experiences, accompanied by a "listen-to-the-words" guide—sample language that shows how bipolar kids sometimes express the challenges school presents. Included in each section are various creative ways for helping you help your child get the most out of school.

"We Can't Get Out the Door in the Morning"

The child: "All I wanna do is sleep. I can't move any faster. Stop pressuring me! If I go to school, I'll explode. I almost had my [socks straightened, hair combed, shoelaces even] and you bothered me. Now I have to start all over."

As many parents know, perhaps the most daunting educational obstacle many bipolar children face is just getting out of bed in time for school. Because of their disorder, they may have a hard time falling asleep, staying asleep, and/or waking up. In addition, they may feel sedated by the medication they are taking, making it even harder to get up in the morning. Once awake—which may not occur until long after the school bus has pulled away—they are both tired and annoyed at being forced to get up.

But getting your youngster awake in the morning is only half the battle; getting him dressed and out the door is the second leg of the morning marathon. A number of factors may make this easier said than done. Crankiness, anxiety, sensory integration difficulties, separation anxiety, and obsessive-compulsive behaviors often stand between your youngster and the schoolhouse door. Your child may not want to leave you, his home, or his younger brothers and sisters who get to stay home with Mom and play, or he might want to remain at home with a sibling who is sick and does not have to go to school. He may not like the way his socks feel on his feet. He may have compulsions that include tying his shoes over and over again, adjusting his pants, combing his hair in a particular way, or any number of other time-consuming tasks that, in his mind, must be done. In most cases, logic and reasoning ("If we don't leave for school in five minutes, you'll be counted late") or threats ("If you don't get to school on time, there'll be no TV") are not enough to break the cycle.

The child may become so anxious and overwrought and, perhaps, embarrassed by his difficulties that he refuses to go to school—period. We clinicians call this behavior school refusal. The term does not imply any cause but is a descriptive term used when a child declines to attend school. This behavior could have any number of causes in addition to the ones already mentioned: maybe a child doesn't like the teacher, the other students pick on him, or he perceives the work as being too hard. One form of school refusal is school phobia. In other words, there is something specific about the school environment or the school itself that induces fear in the child. Just as people with fears of elevators and dogs do their best to avoid those anxiety-producing triggers, children with school phobia avoid school.

Usually, the behavior of a bipolar child is *not* a phobia but, for a variety of reasons, a manifestation of intense anxiety. Parents and teachers may mistakenly assume that their youngster is reluctant to attend school because he is lazy, manipulative, or has an aversion to academics. Most often, this is not really the case. When their moods are fine, most bipolar kids *want* to go to school. They know school is their job. Yet they are also aware that showing their bipolar symptoms in a classroom can be dangerous and self-defeating. I've known kids to say, "Mom, I can't go to school today, I'm afraid I'll get in trouble." Sure, this can be manipulative, but often, it's because the child recognizes that, at this particular time, he has very limited self-control. He knows that his bad mood may cause him to talk back to the teacher or fight with friends—behavior that he's aware is unacceptable but he's not sure he can control.

Sometimes, these children don't get enough credit for their self-awareness and skill at self-protection. In the end, parents struggle every day with deciding whether they are being too harsh or too lenient. Many times, they compromise by trying to get their child into school even if it's for just a few hours. This often works better for the child, but it can set parents up for criticism. The school may interpret the parents' actions as indulgent and criticize them for letting the child be in charge of what happens at home. Sometimes (because of lack of understanding), the message from the school is that if the parents were firm enough, the child would be on time every day.

Some teachers and school psychologists tell the parents they must *push* their child to go. The difficulty arises when those giving the advice don't fully understand the reasons for the school refusal in a bipolar child—and what a can of worms they may open. I have seen wonderful children get angry and physically assaultive when their parents attempted to force them to go to school. These kids were not trying to be difficult; they were terrified. And in a more practical vein, a child may simply be too big to force out of the house and into the car. If he is well and refusing school simply because he's manipulative, the approach clearly should be different. Working with a skilled therapist can help a parent better determine when this is the case.

Unfortunately, if you are the parent of a bipolar child, you may find yourself being considered a "bad" mother or father by your child and not forceful enough by school personnel. Keep in mind, though, that no one knows what you *really* live with. You may start each day with an expectation that things will be better and that your child will go to school without a major outburst, only to find that this may not be the case. Your heart sinks on the days he's too depressed to go, and you're incredibly joyful on days he does go.

Ways to Help

As with many issues surrounding bipolar disorder, stability is crucial. It's going to be difficult, if not close to impossible, for your youngster to get up and get going if he's too immobilized by depression. It's important to let the school personnel who are involved with your child know that when his biology is "off," there are limits as to what can be accomplished. I can't stress this enough: *You have to tame the biology first.*

It's also important to educate school personnel that stability is a fluid concept. Your child may be stable on a medication for a few months and then lapse into periods of illness. At these times, he may experience symptoms that require modifications in his educational program. For example, if he can't wake up in time to get the school bus and is depressed, he may need a later start time. When his mood improves, efforts should be made to return him to his regular schedule. Other changes that may be helpful include having the child attend school for only part of the school day and/or (if possible) rearranging his schedule so that he has more challenging academic subjects in the afternoon when he is more awake and alert.

Many kids can benefit from a semistructured daily agenda. By this, I mean a plan that keeps your youngster's internal body clock ticking on a regular schedule. This is best accomplished when a child's sleeping, eating, physical activity, medicine taking, and exposure to sunlight follow a regular, predictable pattern.

As mentioned, children with seasonal affective disorder can help keep their body rhythms regular by using light therapy, which can regulate their sleep/wake cycles and help them get to school earlier. If your child needs light therapy but won't tolerate sitting in front of a light box at home, consider asking the school to help figure out a way to incorporate it into his early morning schedule.

Eight-year-old Carter, for instance, was a handful of trouble when his mood was off. His parents had always known there was a seasonal component to his depression, but one winter not long ago, his low was severe. He frequently talked of wishing he was dead, had severe separation anxiety, and had trouble getting to school in the morning. I suggested he start light therapy at home, and after ten days, it was clear that Carter was feeling better. But within two weeks, he began fighting with his mother again and telling her that he felt better and no longer wanted the lights. His mom reported that the arguments at home in the morning were escalating.

When it became clear that the situation was getting out of hand, we worked out a plan with the principal at Carter's special-education school to use the light box in the morning soon after he arrived. The next day, his mother brought the box into school, and the staff figured out how to position it without causing a major disruption in Carter's schedule. Since his first class was math, in which each child did individual work, he was able to sit and do light therapy in class easily. Not only did this solution help stabilize his mood, it also eliminated a major morning battle with his mother.

When morning tiredness is the result of medication, giving the dosage earlier in the evening—perhaps around dinnertime—rather than just before bedtime may make your child less groggy in the morning hours. (Be sure to check with your doctor before making a change in the time of dosing.) Sometimes, medications that facilitate sleep or compounds of the hormone melatonin can help kids who have trouble falling asleep at night (see Chapter 7). It's also important that there's no caffeine consumption in the evening hours. This includes caffeinated sodas and, for some children, chocolate (which typically has a small amount of caffeine), both potential dietary causes of insomnia.

Despite your best efforts at regulating your child's mood and sleep routines, there may still be periods when school is simply not in the cards if your bipolar youngster is not yet stable. On a morning when you feel that your child's instincts to stay home are good ones, then it's probably best to keep him home for the full day or at least part of the day, until he feels better. Or if the situation is not too tense, you could send him to school but with the understanding that if he doesn't feel well, he can ask the school nurse to call a parent.

Occasionally, staying at home under the careful observation of a parent can help a child who is quite ill—but not in acute danger—to avoid hospitalization. A few years ago, one nine-year-old, Mark, had expressed thoughts of killing himself and said he wished he could blow up his school and destroy all the children and teachers. It was clear that he was in a mixed state and was close to hospitalization. I wasn't worried that he'd harm someone else, but I was concerned that with his impulsivity and his intermittent uncontrollable anger, he would put himself in danger. His mother and I kept in close phone contact, and I saw Mark at least twice a week. I told the school that he was under tenuous control and that he would be better off staying home until his mood and behavior were more stable. The directors of his special school were supportive. They did not want Mark to suffer the humiliation of losing control in front of the other kids and the teachers. By taking an almost month-long break—with close observation on his mother's part and frequent contact between his mother and me—Mark was able to avoid hospitalization and maintain his dignity with his peers and himself.

Eventually, of course, all bipolar kids have to get back on the learning bus. Though not a cure-all, one universally helpful strategy is to supply your child with a predictable morning routine. The mother of ten-year-old Joey, for instance, found that a high degree of structure upped the odds of getting him out the door in the morning. "He has a lot of the same clothes in different colors—pants and T-shirts, so he always knows what he will wear. We bought special comfortable socks without seams. His backpack is always by the door in the exact same place. We try to wake him up at the exact time every day—and it is always his father who does the morning routine," she explained.

It's crucial to communicate with the school when helping your child make the transition back to the classroom. Parents, patients, teachers, and doctors can all learn from one another to find the approach that works best. Here's the story of how a team effort helped one eight-year-old boy diagnosed with Bipolar II:

Michael had mood swings that included brief hypomanic periods, but he was mainly depressed. He had a hard time getting out of bed in the morning and cried when his mother told him he had to go to school. He said that he was too uncomfortable to go; the other kids didn't like him, he said, and the work was too hard.

Even though he was a good student and knew that his teacher was supportive, Michael would cry if he made a mistake on his classwork. "I hate myself, I can't do anything right," he'd say. "Why was I born? What's the matter with my brain?" After careful questioning, he acknowledged that he felt safer and more comfortable being at home with his mother. After baseline testing, I started him on lithium for his depression. In the meantime, his therapist, parents, principal, teacher, school psychologist, and I tried to work out a plan for getting him back into school once he seemed adequately stable.

His mother remembered that Michael had had a difficult time with school refusal in first grade. This occurred after he missed school for three weeks because of severe asthma and bronchitis. All of us reminded him of how successful he had been in the past when he was faced with returning to school. Together, we came up with a plan that initially had him return for half days until he was able to do so without too much anxiety. His teacher recommended that he have a tutor at home for a few weeks to help him catch up on any work he missed. She didn't want him to feel he was behind other students, as this would demoralize him even further.

It was decided that his father would drive him to school and that the principal would come out to meet him and help him to separate from his father. Because Michael was much more clingy with his mother, his father did the drop-off. Michael carried a picture of his mom in his folder so that he could look at it when he missed her. He and the teacher worked out a way for him to signal her when he needed help in dealing with his anxiety: If he was too overwhelmed, he would rub his forehead as if he had a headache. The teacher would then ask him to run an errand or inquire if he felt ill and needed to go to the nurse. The goal here was to make him feel more at home in the school building and not embarrass him in front of his classmates.

Michael had a hard time getting out of the car on the first day we implemented the plan, even though he was with his father and the principal. But after three days spent in the nurse's office, he went to his class. The psychologist met with him once or twice a week to touch base and troubleshoot *problems. Gradually, as he became more and more stable, we increased the amount of time he was supposed to spend in school. It took a major team effort, with frequent revising of the medication and the treatment plan, but Michael eventually felt better and returned to the classroom full-time.*

Some schools even provide "curb service" to help anxious or mood-disordered children get back into the classroom. Such is the case at the Newmark School, a wonderful special-education school in Plainfield, New Jersey, designed to help children with learning and/or behavioral difficulties. After meeting the kids at the curb, staff members provide counseling and an incentive system to help youngsters get to school every day. "We always have to remember that our students are kids first and have a mood disorder second," says the cofounder and director of the school, Regina M. Peter, EdD. "As they become more stable, we try to help them see that a mood disorder can't run their lives—they must. We help them to develop coping skills because when they are twenty-five years old and working, the boss may not care that they are bipolar. It's important to develop these skills early so they don't adopt bad habits for life."[2]

"My Son Can't Shift Gears"

The child: "I'm not going to speech therapy. I don't like the new teacher. What do you mean you're canceling art class for the assembly? Not fair!"

Many bipolar kids have trouble making transitions—from home to school, from lunch to reading, from the spelling workbook to the math workbook—as well as trouble dealing with even the smallest change in routine. It's harder for them to "go with the flow" than it is for most kids. When asked to move from one activity to another, they may act out, refuse to make the transition, or have meltdowns that, to the casual onlooker, seem nonsensical. It's unclear exactly why bipolar kids have problems with "shifting set," as we call it, but their difficulties appear to be, to some degree, related to their biology and not simply to being stubborn.

The rigidity we see in bipolar children in real life can actually be demonstrated by a neuropsychological test known as the Wisconsin Card Sort Test.[3] The test is somewhat like a card game with no instructions. An examiner presents a child with a series of cards of various colors, shapes, and numbers of images, and the child is then asked to sort a deck of pictures by identifying a rule that applies to all of them. Is it sorting by color, number of items, or shape? If sorting by similar color is the rule, the youngster has to realize this on her own, without being told the rule. Given the choice between an orange circle and a green square, the correct answer would be to match an orange card with another orange card. After a certain number of trials, the examiner shifts the category rule without telling the youngster. Then the child must transition to a new rule (sort by shape, not color, for example) and figure out which pictures belong to the new category and which do not. After each try, the examiner tells the child if her answer was correct or incorrect. The better a child's ability to abandon an old rule and begin responding according to a new strategy, the better her performance on the test.

Children with bipolar disorder often have a decreased ability to shift set, and frequently, they perform more poorly on this test than members of the general population. Why is this? It may be that they have trouble letting go of the old rule and replacing it with a new one. They continue to pick the orange object even though they are repeatedly told that choice is wrong. The Wisconsin Card Sort Test may help us to better understand the curious inflexibility of bipolar children. Although they appear to be nothing but stubborn, the truth is that they simply may not get the "rules" of change; consequently, it takes some time for them to adjust to new requirements, whether in the form of a shift in the class schedule, a new kind of math homework, or a surprise guest in the classroom. The test's results are consistent with what we see in real life. How we think (our cognition) determines how we feel (our affective/emotional state), which then affects how we act (our behavior).

Ways to Help

When we look at bipolar children, we often focus on their behavior. But according to psychologist Michael Osit, who works with bipolar patients, we would do better to address their cognitive styles first. That's because a bipolar child's cognitive style translates into his emotional style, which, in turn, is displayed as behavior.

"The child's behavior is what is on the surface and what the adults respond to. But it's important to understand how thinking influences the feelings behind the behavior. Using an educational approach rather than a punitive one teaches the child alternative ways to think about a situation that will help him to avoid getting stuck," says Osit. For example, when a child refuses to open his math book to do his homework, it's best to avoid arguing about his stubbornness and telling him what privileges he's losing and focus instead on brainstorming about possible ways of solving the problem. Instead, why not tell him, "OK, if you don't want to start with math homework, fine, then which homework are you going to begin instead?" By taking this approach, Osit explains, you're giving the child some power, which is frequently what these arguments are really about—that is, who's in charge here?[4]

But let's say the child does not go with the choice presented and replies, "I don't want to do any homework, I want to watch TV." Then the parent may say, "Well then, how can we work out the situation so that we can both get some of what we want?" If he responds, "I just want to watch TV!" the parent's next suggestion is, "How about you work for twenty minutes and then you can watch half an hour of TV?" Basically, Osit explains, what the parent is attempting to do is to give the child some power and choice within the parent's parameters. Rather than being told what he has to do, the child is asked to get involved in the solution. This approach treats him with respect and allows him to be a partner in determining how to best accomplish the task with which he is presented.

Bipolar children are also better able to switch gears if they have a predictable, structured school environment. At the Newmark School, for example, staff members are positioned in the same area during transition times—when the children enter school, go to recess, go to lunch, change classes, board the bus, and so forth. The teachers set the same morning and afternoon transition routines and stick to them— every day. Schedules are posted in the classroom and on students' desks as needed so they can anticipate what will come next. Says the school director, "Most of the kids know the schedules better than the adults and keep us to task!"[5]

The school also has a plan in place for kids who may have had a bad start to the day. "If I have a student whose parent calls and tells us he had a difficult morning, we can address his needs even before he gets into the classroom. The student sees a minimum of ten staff members (including three counselors) before he even enters his classroom. The same is true at dismissal time."

But what if a child is not in a special school? It's very important that parents and school personnel work together to develop a plan for difficult times. It may be that a child will have regular weekly meetings with the school social worker or psychologist to touch base and troubleshoot any potential problems. A child could also benefit from having an adult such as the school nurse or vice principal to turn to if she becomes very upset. It is important that the child's teacher be apprised of the situation so that she and the parents can strategize how best to help the child in the classroom.

"My Youngster Has Trouble Concentrating"

The child: "It's useless. I try to read, but I can't get past the first page. This math book is boring (stupid, hard to understand). When did you say that? I didn't hear you. It's hard to look at what the teacher's doing when I can see them practicing football on the field outside my class window."

Many children who are used to being high achievers in the early years in school may later find themselves unable to concentrate because of their mood disorder. Their depression may slow them down to the point where they feel as if they are moving and thinking at the speed of a turtle. Or they may become so agitated that just sitting still at a desk requires a major effort. They may be unable to tend to homework, remember assignments, or even read a book. Eleven-year-old Juan, for instance, had been the class geography bee champ in third grade before being diagnosed with bipolar disorder and OCD. Juan's recall of geographic information was astounding, and his teachers expected him to go on to the regional championship for students his age. But when depression set in, he dissolved into tears every time he tried to focus on the geography study sheets his teacher supplied. Similarly, children can lose their ability to concentrate because they're in a manic state, are highly distractible, and/or have racing thoughts.

Ways to Help

Ask your child's teacher to seat your youngster in the front of the room. If you have a child with concentration problems who is also very distractible and you put him in the back of the classroom or near the door, you might as well consider putting him in the parking lot. For some children, music can block out the distracting noises that interfere with concentration. Letting the child do class work while listening to soothing music through a headset (if it's allowed) or having music in the background while he's working at home can be a good way for some kids to filter out distracting, extraneous noise. Children with concentration difficulties may do best with an aide who can guide them to work, stay on task, and control negative behavior. If a child's concentration is extremely poor because of his unstable mood, discuss with the teacher ways to modify schoolwork and homework until his condition has improved.

"My Child Has Trouble
Doing Schoolwork—Sometimes"

The child: "I guess I'm just dumb. Do I have to write it down? I hate math. I remembered eight times nine yesterday, but now I forgot."

Bipolar children are often very bright, but they can have learning difficulties that make certain kinds of academic tasks especially challenging for them. Learning problems can include:

- **Executive function deficits:** This term refers to a child's ability to work with, organize, sort, and manage incoming information. Thomas E. Brown, PhD, a nationally renowned specialist in ADHD, likens executive functioning to what happens in an orchestra when it performs a symphony.[6] You have a variety of instruments, each one very important in determining the quality of the music produced. With executive function, instruments in the cognitive "orchestra" (verbal memory, attentional skills, delayed recall) join together to determine how a person functions in day-to-day life. Children with poor executive function have difficulty planning, managing, and estimating the time it takes to complete a task, and they cannot easily differentiate the essential from the nonessential actions involved in doing so. They may be unable to retain the plans and steps required in their working memory long enough to execute them. A child with executive function deficits may seem disorganized and a bit spacey, unable to "get it together" long enough to complete a sequence of tasks—for example, taking notes about a homework assignment, collecting the materials needed to complete it, transferring his papers to a backpack, and then organizing his notes once he gets home.
- **Problems with written communication:** Kids with this type of difficulty will do anything to avoid a writing assignment. (By contrast, they are often more adept verbally unless their moods are very unstable.) A depressed youngster can take what seems

like years to write a paragraph. A child with mania may write all over the page rapidly because her mind is moving faster than her hands. And some children have learning disabilities that can affect not only the quality of their handwriting but also their ability to write a cogent story.

- **Math difficulties:** Not infrequently, bipolar kids have difficulties with mathematical skills.[7] These may be problems in computation, with number reversal, and with the application of mathematical concepts. Many of the kids in my practice have a hard time memorizing basic multiplication tables. They may appear to know them in the evening but forget them before the test the next day.

- **Memory problems:** Bipolar children often have difficulty with what psychologists call working memory. As defined by Michael Osit, "Working memory is the child's ability to retain, mentally manipulate, use short-term memory, and be able to retrieve and express the information, usually without a visual cue."[8] The Woodcock Johnson Test, a diagnostic instrument educators use to detect learning disabilities in children, contains an assessment for working memory that goes something like this. The examiner says, "I am going to say some numbers and some words. I want you to first repeat the numbers—in the order that I give them—and then say the words." For example, when the examiner says, "3–5–horse–2–man–4," the child must say, "3–5–2–4–horse-man." "The task requires a child to mentally manipulate information while retaining and sorting the same information," explains Osit. Kids with bipolar disorder often find tasks such as this difficult.

Ways to Help

Faye Brady, a social worker in private practice and a member of a Child Study Team in Warren, New Jersey, offers the following examples of approaches that might be options for your child (though it's best to consult with your child's teacher about shaping individual strategies that will be effective for your son or daughter):

- Placing the child in a structured classroom, that is, one with predictable routines and systems.
- Using color folders for homework and for organizing papers.
- Maintaining an uncluttered workspace, free of visual distractions.
- Using simple, concise language when giving oral instructions.
- Showing students what the end product of an assignment can look like. This can serve as an instructional guide, especially for children who are visually oriented.
- Writing all assignments on the board, and arranging for them to be copied at the same time every day.
- Assigning "homework buddies." (It's best to do this for all the kids in the class so that the bipolar child does not stand out.) If a child misses writing down the assignment, is out for the day, or just has questions about what was given for homework, he can contact his "buddy" to catch up on what he's missed.
- Teaching basic math concepts such as multiplication, division, and fractions by using flash cards, drawings, blocks, or other manipulatives to bring home the point. Demonstrating the concepts and reinforcing them in a variety of ways can help the child master them. However, some bipolar kids can't hold on to multiplication facts for a week or even for a day, no matter how hard their parents, teachers, and tutors work with them. For these youngsters, a calculator may become a necessity and best friend.
- Allowing children who struggle with writing to expand orally on written answers. This approach lets kids know that they need to try to get their thoughts down on paper, but it also gives them a chance to complete the assignment successfully if their handwriting or attention is poor. For a paper or project that was to have been completed in written form, some teachers allow students to include a shortened written portion in conjunction with a creative component, such as telling a story, drawing a

picture, or writing a song. Teachers may not think of this idea on their own, but if you discuss it in a respectful way, most are willing to consider giving it a try, especially if you approach the subject by asking, "Can we talk and brainstorm some options that will satisfy the class requirements and still enable my child to accomplish the task?"

"My Son Has Meltdowns in School"

The child: "I felt like I could explode inside. I don't know what made me do it. He did it to me on purpose."

It's every parent's dreaded moment. The cell phone rings. You recognize the school's number on the screen. They've called to say that Tom had an "episode" in the lunchroom. He thought that another child deliberately spilled milk on him. Tom responded by hurling his lunch tray across the room—with the food still on it. You'll need to come pick him up—now. As we've seen before, bipolar children seem to have what are known as "affective storms," reactions that are out of proportion to the factors that precipitated them. These may be brought on by stress, anxiety, problems with medication, hearing the word "no," or any number of real or imagined stressors.

Ways to Help

Perhaps the most important remedy for such episodes at school begins with identifying the triggers that cause them. For example, if you know that your child is upset by the noise and commotion of the school lunchroom, you may want to ask the teacher to seat him in a quiet place or to allow him to eat in a quiet room with a teacher present. Of course, frustrating situations are inevitable in life, and your child needs to learn in advance how to prepare for them—and prevent his behavior from getting out of control. Many therapeutic schools, that is, schools that focus on helping children with emotional and/or behavioral issues, employ what they call a "level system," based on positive reinforcement for good behavior.

Through a system of points awarded during each period of the day on the basis of good behavior and academic standards, students can earn recess time, items from the school store, and other privileges. The point system can be a powerful tool for preventing or curtailing meltdowns. Kids learn to identify what is happening in their minds and bodies when a "storm" overtakes them and to come up with strategies, such as deep breathing and talking themselves through it, that can help them defuse their anger and maintain their self-control.

When the inevitable happens and a child blows a gasket, it's important to talk to him about what happened and how such outbursts can be prevented in the future. At the Newmark School, Regina Peter has instituted a schoolwide "debriefing" system to deal with students when they lose control. Rather than focusing on what the child wants or has done, the debriefing focuses on the child's reaction to the situation that has just occurred and on what can be done if the same thing happens in the future. "*Keep calm* is the first message we send," says the school's director. "Then, without judgment, we walk the child to a quiet debriefing room and ask him to work with us to fill out a form that describes what happened, how he felt, and what strategies he can use to prevent the same sort of thing from happening again. We try to send kids back to the classroom with coping skills—and a resolve that they can do better next time."

"My Son Is Struggling in the Classroom"

The child: "Can I go to the nurse's office? I don't feel so good. My teacher doesn't like me. She's always yelling at me. What did you say? I don't get it."

Mainstream classroom demands overwhelm some kids. They may ask to go to the school nurse or complain of a headache if they feel unable to do what is asked of them. They may not work as quickly as the other kids and feel academically inadequate compared to their classmates. Often, they require more attention than others in their class, and they may feel that the teacher is picking on them when she tries to help.

Ways to Help

Any number of solutions may be right for your child. In general, the law calls for children to be educated in the *least restrictive environment*, that is, the setting in which a child can receive the educational services he needs but at the same time participate in a regular education program and with nondisabled peers to the maximum extent appropriate. The educational options for accommodating kids with bipolar disorder vary from state to state, but they generally fall into one of four categories:

- **Mainstream class (with the support of a special-education teacher or a paraprofessional):** A classroom aide or other support personnel may be assigned to more than one child, but in most cases, they are available to help any youngster in the class who needs assistance. The beauty in this is that children who have been assigned the support don't have to feel embarrassed or singled out.
- **Resource Room:** When a child needs more individual attention, help can come in the form of a learning disabilities resource room class where a special-education teacher instructs a small group of students. A child might be mainstreamed in certain subjects, say, social studies and science, with an aide or special-education teacher but go to the resource room for math, reading, and writing. The child may be able to have recess, lunch, art, music, and/or gym with the other children in his grade.
- **Self-contained classroom:** This is a small class where the child will generally spend most of the day with a few others students, a teacher, and one or two aides, depending on the class size.

Kids may go into mainstream classes for special events or some subjects, depending on the grade. An aide or teacher usually accompanies them to their mainstream classes from their special-education class. This may be the best level of support for children who require help in a number of different areas.

- **Therapeutic/special-education schools:** These special placements, such as the Newmark School, provide academic, therapeutic, and emotional support for students with special needs. They offer soup-to-nuts programs and may specialize in serving children with emotional issues. Some of these schools are public, and others are part of the private sector. If the school district feels it is the appropriate setting for your child, it will pay for the program.

Of course, the hope is that bipolar kids can stay in mainstream schools with modifications as often as possible. I strongly feel that every child should reach up rather than down. But the reality is that many kids with bipolar disorder are seriously ill. They need a placement in which their academic and emotional needs are met and their self-esteem is not assaulted on a daily basis. It's not in the best interest of these kids to expect them to fit into a mainstream placement that isn't right for them. Many bipolar students start off in the mainstream, but as they get into the upper elementary and middle school grades, they begin to struggle. That's when a specialized setting may become the best option. The decision to place a child outside the mainstream classroom is sometimes a difficult one for parents. But when they see their child in an appropriate setting, doing well academically and blossoming socially, they become more confident that they've made the right decision. Here's one mother's story:

Escaping from "Jail"

My daughter Elissa began to experience difficulty in the first grade, in a class of twenty-two children. Notes came flying home reporting negative behaviors. Her teacher, who was an older woman and was nicknamed "The General" for the way she ran her class, had little tolerance for Elissa and would frequently take away privileges. My daughter often came home crying, saying things like "The teacher told me to sit still in my chair but my body wouldn't stop moving," or "The teacher told me to stop touching other kids but my hands can't stop."

In second grade, things got even worse. The teacher's solution to Elissa's difficulties was to send her out of the room. She was usually taken to a small stark white room with one desk and a chair that Elissa called "the jail." The more she was sent to this room, the more she rebelled— by stamping her feet on the floor, yelling, and crying. The Child Study Team recommended that Elissa might be better off if she was placed in an out-of-district school that specializes in teaching children with bipolar disorder.

Elissa started in her new school this school year. What a difference a year makes! She is now thriving in a place where she receives occupational therapy and small group and individual counseling. She has a shortened school day and has eleven students, a teacher, and an aide in her class. Homework is minimal, which helps to reduce stress levels and outbursts. There is a behavior and academic point system (positive reinforcement), which allows the students to earn points on a daily basis to be used toward recess time and the purchase of items at the school store. The school is all about modifying the school day to help meet the student's individual needs.

Elissa is learning appropriate social and decision-making skills that have helped her to get along better with family and friends. Elissa now gets on the school bus with a smile and gets off with a smile. She is eager to tell me all about her school day and will sometimes even go to sleep early "so that tomorrow will get here faster!"

And here's a story from another mom who also struggled, though triumphantly in the end, to find the right school for her child:

Finding the Perfect Placement

From the time my son was tiny, I've had big dreams of what he might become. As a toddler, he loved being read to, and by the time he was in preschool, his favorite channel was the History Channel. He had a true love of learning, and everyone remarked on how brilliant he seemed.

When first grade came around, he had already been diagnosed with a learning disability and a significant dysfluency of speech that was not responding to intervention. The other students in my son's class were already starting to read. His teachers assured us he was one of the smartest children they had ever had the pleasure of teaching. However, pleasure was not what he was experiencing. The pressure of all the worries squeezing his head had created a thick cover that made his mind almost unreachable. I would explain the simplest concepts, and confusion would spread across his face, followed by intense anger. This gave way to heartbreaking sorrow over how "stupid" he felt.

Homework became something we all hated. In his mind, the memories of every negative thing that ever happened to him in school replayed over and over with the same intensity as when they first occurred. This intense picture show in his head played all day and haunted him at night, but teachers, not to mention his loving family, expected him to explore new concepts and come to conclusions when his brain was screaming "Turn off the cameras! Leave me alone!!!" It took a bipolar friend to help me understand what he must have been feeling. My friend likened the situation to being stuck in a media room with ten different films playing at high volume and trying to balance your checkbook at the same time.

Meanwhile, my son interpreted the teacher's frustration and sorrow at not being able to reach him as disappointment. ("I'm sorry" is a part of his everyday vocabulary even now.) He became more solitary and laughed less and less. His magical mind became confused and inaccessible. The storytime that he loved became a taunting reminder that he was not able to read. He was too tired to play after school. His pain was palpable.

By second grade, our boy, who has a smile that can light up the world, had not had one day of his life that he did not cry tears of true sorrow. He came to hate school. He felt stupid; he could not stop crying. I was forbidden to read at bedtime because he was so bitter that this world of learning was hidden from him.

Our daughter reported that at recess, he would sit by himself on the hill and stare at the sky. We asked him why, and he told us that he wanted to go to heaven and see his grandmother. Things at school began to get worse, and he had debilitating headaches. Getting him to school was painful for *everyone. One morning, he looked at me through tears of despair and cried, "Can't you see I am drowning in darkness?"*

Everyone became increasingly concerned as his behaviors were becoming more and more isolating, and he was very fragile. On the recommendation of his doctor and therapist, my husband and I removed our son from public school. This broke our hearts; I had graduated from this school, and we had built wonderful relationships with many families and staff members. We have three children, and our daughter was having a tremendous experience at this school and our youngest son was just starting his school years. Separating the children and sending him so far away on a bus was daunting. As parents, we endured a lot of well-meaning criticism and unsolicited advice.

Almost immediately, we realized that we had made the right choice. He was welcomed into a small classroom with professionals who are trained in his learning and emotional disabilities. They developed an educational program for him and set up lines of communication between the doctor, therapist, and private professionals. The team approach was crucial. Our son began to relax enough in this environment to ask for help and to learn. This new school addressed him as a whole person. The caring staff knew when to challenge him and when to give him space. His new program gave him the confidence and skill building that he needed to begin to recognize his intelligence. His dysfluency has all but disappeared.

Our son laughs now; he has friends. He has regained his love for learning and is no longer trapped in his own mind. His school and the excellent medical care he has received have given us our son back. The dreams that morphed from "Will he be a famous historian?" into "Let him be comfortable in his own skin" once again have life . . . possibilities, choices . . . dreams to be re-invented by my son.

"I Need Help with Medication Monitoring"

The child: "I feel sleepy. I have to go to the bathroom—again. I missed my medication this morning, and I can't concentrate. It's yucky, and I'm *not* taking it."

Medication can have a number of side effects on a child's ability to behave and concentrate at school. Although privacy issues may be a concern, it's important to let someone (teachers or at least the school nurse) know what medications your child takes and to advise them anytime there's a change in the medication regimen. The nurse may become your new best friend, so it's best not to wait until there's a crisis to forge a relationship. Given the go-ahead from your child's doctor, the nurse can administer medications during school hours. This may also prove useful when your child refuses to take medication at home and you need a helping hand. Here are some side effects that may disrupt your child's school day, as well as suggestions to minimize their effect on the school day.

- **Frequent trips to the bathroom:** Certain medications, such as lithium, may cause your child to urinate more frequently.
- **Thirst/dehydration:** Some medications can cause increased thirst. They may also leave your child more vulnerable to the effects of heat or intense physical activity.
- **Excess fatigue:** A bipolar student may fall asleep in class, raising the question of whether his depression, his medication, or something else could be causing his fatigue.
- **Changes in handwriting:** Lithium can cause hand tremors in children. Also, changes in mood state and attention can result in changes in the neatness and flow of a child's handwriting.

Ways to Help

If a morning medication is causing sleepiness, it may need to be given later in the day. Because many bipolar kids are heat intolerant, it may be necessary for your youngster to avoid outdoor activities on especially hot days. If there's a concern about dehydration, she may need to have access to or be given liquids—water and sports drinks (the latter contains sodium, which can be lost in sweat and, if not replaced, can raise lithium levels)—during the day, especially at recess or gym time. It's also important to let the teacher know if your child needs to use the bathroom frequently, so that she doesn't feel humiliated. Here again, a nonverbal signal between child and teacher can come in handy. A tug on the earlobe, for example, might indicate that your youngster needs to heed the call of nature. She can then leave the classroom with no questions asked. At times when medication interferes with handwriting, limiting the amount of written work or allowing the child to use a computer for her work can help.

"The Teacher Says My Kid Has Ants in His Pants"

The child: "I don't need to sleep. I don't like sitting still."

Some bipolar children have so much energy, they seem to bounce off the wall, especially during the evening hours in their hypomanic or manic states. During the daytime in class, they can have a hard time sitting still in their seats, as they may be incredibly restless. They may ask the teacher to go to the bathroom several times a day just to be able to release some of their excess energy.

Ways to Help

Here's how we helped one child manage her excess energy: Rebecca was in the midst of a hypomanic—almost manic—episode. She seemed to be flying high and had too much energy to burn. Her mother tried taking her to the park after school so she could let out some of that incredible energy. But in school, Rebecca continued to have "ants in her pants," according to her teachers.

It was time to strategize. The principal at her special school worked out a plan whereby Rebecca could take a break every hour if necessary and use the treadmill in the gym. After one of these exercise sessions, she was usually able to return to class with somewhat less energy. If the school had not been so creative, I don't know that Rebecca would have been able to attend school; she was just too energetic. In addition, small adjustments in her nighttime dose of medication helped her to fall asleep more easily.

"His Scores/Grades Are Inconsistent"

The child: "I know a lot of stuff, but when I have to write it down, I lose it. I must be stupid. My brother Martin, who's two years younger than me, is a better learner. I hate math!"

There is evidence that bipolar children and adolescents (as well as children of bipolar parents, who are at high risk for developing bipolar disorder) show particular patterns on IQ testing. Specifically, discrepancies often exist between their verbal IQs (how well they comprehend and use language) and their performance IQs (how well they perform in the areas of perceptual organization and nonverbal learning). Though the verbal IQ test measures such skills as vocabulary, abstract reasoning, and long-term memory, the performance IQ test assesses nonverbal learning skills such as spatial problem solving, visual analysis, and fine-motor skills. Pertinent to this issue is a study published in 1983 by Paolo Decina, MD, and Clarice J. Kestenbaum, MD (and others from Columbia University–affiliated programs and New York University), who looked at verbal and performance IQs in a sample of children who were at high risk for bipolar disorder because they were offspring of bipolar parents. Full-scale (that is, overall IQ) and verbal IQ scores did not differ between the control group and the high-risk children, but performance IQs were significantly lower in the latter group.[9] This finding of a discrepancy between the two scores in children of parents with bipolar disorder has received additional support in the psychiatric literature.[10]

How does this transfer to real life? What I see in my practice is that many bipolar children are verbally quite skilled. If you have a conversation with them, you cannot help but be impressed by the sophistication of their words and ideas. But a red flag pops up when they go to school and their grades are not consistent with their apparent level of intelligence. Many of my children have the potential to be straight-A students if their skills weren't measured by paper-and-pencil tasks. When they can express their knowledge verbally, they do much better gradewise. In addition, their ability to think differently does not always fit neatly into the goals of elementary and secondary school education. Sometimes, their blessings of creativity, intelligence, and individuality can interfere with their ability to get the necessary foundation in their education. Unfortunately, they may need to wait until adulthood to fully use and appreciate their special gifts.

Another pattern often emerges in IQ testing with bipolar children: Kids with depression and anxiety sometimes have periods when their verbal IQs and performance IQs are temporarily reduced—largely because their emotions interfere with their ability to reason, concentrate, and think through language-based problems. In children with either ADHD or bipolar disorder, performance IQ and working memory scores are often lower than might be expected. These are timed tests, and the lower scores may be attributable to the kids' impulsivity, low frustration tolerance, and/or slow motor processing on the day they were administered.

Ways to Help

One option is to allow the child to do some reports and assignments orally instead of requiring that they be written. Another option, if your child's teacher agrees, is for the child to dictate the homework or report to the parent, who then acts as a scribe. Using a tape recorder in class is another option, allowing the child to get the information he needs without taking notes. Some children will also require extra time on tests, so that they have enough time to show what they know.

"My Kid Doesn't Have Any Friends"

The child: "All the kids hate me. Stacey was staring at me in social studies. I ran right up and tried to join the basketball game, but they wouldn't let me play."

Anyone who has or works with a bipolar child or adolescent knows that they often misread other people's actions or reactions, especially if they are depressed. This inability to read emotions may interfere with their ability to make and keep friends. Some studies even suggest that bipolar kids often incorrectly label facial expressions, which may explain some of their social difficulties. Interestingly, studies show that bipolar kids are likely to misidentify faces as showing anger or anxiety even when this is not the case.[11]

Ways to Help

Bipolar kids, like many other children with peer problems, may benefit from social skills training (see Chapter 8). This training takes an educational approach to learning how to overcome thinking patterns and behavior that interfere with a child's social functioning.

How to Be Your Child's Best Advocate

Probably the most effective form of advocacy is establishing lines of communication with the important people in your child's life. This may include teachers, counselors, occupational therapists, and speech therapists; all of these people can work with you to build an environment that will foster learning and emotional growth for your child. It's up to you to determine how much you want to share with each individual, but if your child tends to have difficulties at school, I'd strongly suggest meeting with the appropriate teachers or therapists before or during the first week of school, if at all possible. Your goal is to familiarize the team with the child's academic and emotional problems and the way in which they affect his educational functioning.

If you do nothing more than request that the teachers let you know if your child is struggling in any area (and remember to provide your e-mail address so that they can contact you), you're off to the right start. Don't wait until a crisis occurs or the first report card comes home to discuss your child's needs. It's a lot easier to make demands of the school when you've already earned a reputation as a respectful, concerned parent. Seize the chance to connect with your child's teachers early on, and together, you can keep small issues from becoming big academic problems down the road.

I also strongly recommend that parents familiarize themselves with their educational rights and the support services potentially available for their child. If you believe your child needs special academic services or another placement, it's critical to ask in writing for an evaluation by the school district's Child Study Team (some states may have different names for this group of evaluators). I cannot stress enough the importance of keeping a paper trail of your interaction with the school. Many parents tell me that they've discussed getting their child tested with the district team, but because the request was only verbal, it was put on the back burner or considered nonexistent. Once a request is put in writing, *state law mandates* the time period in which the evaluation must be conducted. (In New Jersey, for example, a parent's written request must be acted on within ninety days.)

The district evaluation is likely to consist of a social and developmental history, a psychological assessment, and an educational evaluation. Depending on your child's needs, other assessments may also be considered, including a speech and language evaluation and an occupational therapy assessment. As part of the evaluation, if you feel it helpful, you may choose to provide the Child Study Team with a psychiatric evaluation, neuropsychological assessment, and educational testing results done by private evaluators; alternatively, your child's assessment team can conduct any of the evaluations just mentioned.

The goal of this testing is to help identify your child's strengths and weaknesses and his learning style. The findings will also help to determine his eligibility for services as well as the programs, strategies, and modifications that are indicated to meet his needs. Once the evaluation is complete and if a determination of eligibility is made, the team will develop an individual education program (IEP). This document includes statements on the child's present level of functioning; measurable annual goals for her educational progress; and the services, supports, and program modifications that will be provided to him.[12]

Being diagnosed with bipolar disorder itself does not determine the educational needs and modifications that your child will receive, but it is one part of the picture. Having a diagnosis—any diagnosis (for example, juvenile onset diabetes)—does not automatically entitle a child to classification and special assistance in school. It is the *impact* of the diagnosis on your child's ability to learn that will be considered.*

There's little doubt that it takes a great deal of thought, resolve, trial-and-error effort, and creativity to make sure that a bipolar child

---

*It's important to learn your legal rights before you seek educational help for your child. In the United States, every school-age youngster is entitled to a Free and Appropriate Public Education (FAPE). Two federal laws mandate these educational entitlements: Section 504 of the Rehabilitation Act of 1973, as amended, and the Individuals with Disabilities Education Improvement Act of 2004 (IDEA). As a civil rights law, Section 504 ensures that individuals with disabilities have the same access to education that individuals without disabilities have, whereas IDEA, an educational benefit law, offers additional services and protections for those with disabilities that are not offered to those without disabilities. To learn more about these laws and what help may be available for your child at school, check out the Resources section in the back of this book.

is present and available to learn each day. But by *listening* to your child's words, knowing his rights, communicating with his teachers, and adopting an appropriate educational plan, you greatly increase the likelihood that, over time, his school days will be happier and more successful.

11

Real Life, Real Answers

When your child has leukemia, people bring casseroles to your house; when your child has bipolar disorder, people avoid your house.
—MOTHER OF A THIRTEEN-YEAR-OLD

Raising a child with bipolar disorder is a singular, and often isolating, experience. It's difficult for the rest of the world to imagine the enormous amounts of work, energy, attention, and inner strength that a bipolar child requires from a parent. It can also be difficult for others to recognize the unique joy, happiness, and excitement these children can bring to life.

And yet, the rest of the world is full of advice. From the relatives at Thanksgiving dinner to the neighbors down the block to total strangers in the grocery store, everyone seems to have an opinion about getting your child to walk in step with those around him. There are the authoritarians: "What do you expect when you let a kid call all the shots? If you ask me, a good spanking would solve everything." And the social commentators: "Look at the influences. You've got both parents working . . . kids who play video games everyday . . . R-rated movies . . . why, kids wear jeans and T-shirts to school everyday. It's no wonder they have no respect!" Then there are the behaviorists: "I have two words for you: positive reinforcement. If he got more praise for socially appropriate behavior, he'd be better." And the grand inquisitors: "Have you tried getting him involved in team sports? . . . Shutting off the television? . . . Finding him a mentor?" Even friends and relatives who are well meaning and well educated can lack a real understanding of the condition.

In all fairness, their confusion is somewhat understandable. Many of the coping strategies that work best for parents of bipolar kids seem to fly in the face of what all the parenting books teach. Consider an example. A few years ago, a friend mentioned watching a segment on childhood bipolar disorder on a popular talk show. One mother who was interviewed said that she had to trim the crust off her ten-year-old's sandwiches in a certain way or else he would throw a fit. My friend thought this was too much. "Imagine letting your ten-year-old control you so much that you have to cater to his wishes about how to cut a sandwich," she said. "If the kid is really in that much of a position of power, there's got to be a parenting component to the problem. He's the kid and he's got to be less in charge of the family. It's not good for him or them."

I'd submit to her, though, that we need a lot more history before making such a judgment. As any parent of a bipolar child can attest, you have to choose your battles. In fact, if a mother told me that she cut a sandwich in a certain way to help her child avoid a violent rage, I'd say I thought she was a very good mother and that she really had some insight into her youngster. But I wondered: If my friend, who is well educated and sensitive, felt the way she did, what did viewers unfamiliar with bipolar disorder think? How do parents like this sandwich-making mom deal with a world that is less than informed and less than understanding? How on earth do they maintain their sanity?

The answer, according to many parents I speak with, is support. Not just the support that comes from a therapist, but also support from others as well as self-support—that is, the knowledge and confidence that you, more than anyone else, know your child best. Think of a flight attendant's familiar words of advice: "Place the oxygen mask around your own nose and mouth before securing your child's." Parents have to have a reliable "oxygen supply" in the form of well-informed friends, support groups, doctors, therapists, and educated teachers in order to get the best help possible for their kids. The "listen-to-the-words" approach includes not only listening to your child but also listening to your own voice and the voices of those around you who can offer help and support.

Listening to Your Inner Voice

It's important to be aware of your self-perception as a parent of a bipolar child. If the voice inside your head is constantly saying, "I give up. I'm an inadequate parent. I can't even get my child to (brush his teeth, eat his vegetables, go to school on time, be nice to his sister)," it's less and less likely that you'll be strong enough to do what's necessary for your youngster.

It's important to recognize that your feelings are normal. It's equally important to get past the self-criticism.

Typically, it's not just the difficult situations themselves that cause parents' anxiety and feelings of self-doubt but also the guilt and embarrassment they experience when a child exhibits inappropriate behavior. As parents, we all feel responsible for how our children behave . . . or misbehave. Once, when my oldest son was five years old, a friend and his mother came to our house for a visit. As we mothers were having coffee in the kitchen, the two boys went upstairs to play. After fifteen minutes, the other boy came down crying and said that my son had scratched him. I was shocked, embarrassed, upset with my son, and puzzled. The other mother, understandably upset, took her child home. I was mortified. Had I done something wrong as a parent? Was I raising an aggressive human being?

These thoughts were racing through my head as I sat down with my son to discuss what had happened. He explained that the other boy had taken his toy from him and then teased him about it. My son said he had tried to be good, but when the other boy tried to grab the toy, he scratched his arm in the process. He knew it was wrong, and he was sorry for what he did.

Though that was a rare incident, I'm still struck to this day by how guilty I felt about what happened, especially when I initially thought my son was exhibiting unprovoked aggression. I subsequently realized that this was only a very small taste of what parents of bipolar kids feel on multiple occasions, nearly every day.

Listening to Each Other: Support Groups

One of the best ways for parents to learn about pediatric bipolar disorder and network with others is to join one of the many support groups around the country. Here's the story of how one such group helped bring understanding and encouragement to a mother of a bipolar child:

The years leading up to our son's diagnosis were agonizing in a multitude of ways. Our search for answers about his condition brought us to the initial diagnosis of ADD without hyperactivity. A friend referred me to an ADHD support group. It was a welcome relief to finally meet other parents who understood the exceptional behavior issues our children faced. As time went on, however, I began to compare notes with another mother, and we realized that the issues the ADHD children faced were a walk in the park compared to those of our kids. We came to be close friends and a two-person support group for one another. Grateful were we to assist each other at a time when we might have been more inclined to withdraw from the world.

During our children's crises, we read books over the phone together, recorded important television shows for one another, and were eventually guided to a bipolar disorder support group meeting, which we attended together.

I will never forget the warm faces of these strong women who talked about their children and gave me hope. They shared their history and spoke with a sense of calm wisdom and confidence that comes with experience. There was laughter and compassion sprinkled with tears of understanding. My son was not stabilized yet, but finding an entire group of people with common adversities and goals left me with an indescribable sense of relief.

I was driven to become as involved as my time would allow. I began to host a bipolar disorder support group in my area, which continued for four years. We discussed every way that bipolar disorder affected our lives. We talked about our bipolar child's (or children's) symptoms, medications, health conditions, and siblings.

We addressed the strains on our marriages and whether we or our spouses might also be dealing with an underlying condition. We, as a group, worked as a unit who, even at times of despair, searched for options, solutions, and hope.

By the end, my son had stabilized, and I was the experienced parent at these monthly meetings. I was teaching others; but I believe I was the one who gained the most.

I remain always thankful for the gift of my son's stability, for the help I got from others, and for the help I could give back. When I look at my son, I see a wonderful human being, an incredible masterpiece with a beautiful heart.

One of the best ways to battle parental guilt is to replace it with useful coping strategies. Some of the most effective parents of children in my practice have adopted this approach for dealing with their child's known "trigger points" (things that set them off), often with considerable success. That's not to say that a parent can always know what might spark an emotional storm in a bipolar child. (The old saying "Life is what happens when you're making other plans" has never been more apt than in a family with a bipolar child.) But strategies and routines that are in tune with a child's emotional state can turn many potentially angst-filled outings into manageable ones.

It's important to remember that others have survived the trials and tribulations, the tears and the struggles of raising bipolar children. Here are some of the everyday situations that typically challenge bipolar kids and the ways some parents have found to handle them.

On Shopping Trips

Time and time again, I hear some variation of the same story: "Jerome was fine until I took him into the store. Then, all hell broke loose. He ended up fighting with the produce man over whether a fruit was called a honeydew or a cantaloupe, and then he threw a fit because I bought the 'yucky' brand of applesauce. After half an hour of shopping, he said he couldn't take it anymore and ran crying hysterically toward the door."

Whether it's due to the crowds, the noise, or a shifting mood, shopping can be one of the most difficult times for bipolar children. My first piece of advice to parents is this: Never take a bipolar child to the store when he's hungry. This piece of advice may seem like a no-brainer, for any child. But you'd be surprised at the number of parents who confide, "I thought he'd have enough tolerance for me to just run in and grab a loaf of bread and some milk, but I was wrong." A number of bipolar children seem to be unable to tolerate any basic body discomfort, including feeling tired, hungry, or overheated. Many children aren't pleasant under these circumstances, but the bipolar child is even more volatile. Having your child eat before he shops may decrease the likelihood of a tantrum.

A child's behavior in the grocery store will be somewhat mood related as well. The hypomanic/manic kid may want everything in the store because he is so acquisitive. To tell him "no" is to frustrate him (after all, he thinks, who are you to tell him what he can and can't get?). The depressed child may ask for everything, but the satisfaction is brief (if there's any at all), or he may be indecisive and have a hard time choosing which cereal to get, even though he *must* have one. An attempt to help him along by offering a couple of choices (the approach many parents try) results in the child becoming angry. This irrational anger then may translate into, "You don't care what I want. You don't want to help me." It's the child's depressive indecisiveness and insatiability that are the problems here; he's trying to fix the pain inside him, and acquiring things doesn't help. The result is that you both feel tortured.

On a day that your child's mood is particularly unstable or unpredictable, of course, you'll want to try to avoid the store altogether. But the grocery store may be too much even for a child whose mood is under control. If your child does have a meltdown there, try thinking about how you'd react if he had another disabling disease. If he had an asthma attack in the aisle, would you blame yourself? Would you care how people looked at you? Or would you focus your energy on helping your child? It's OK to do the same when your own child's brain is in the midst of a storm. Here's how one parent handles shopping trips:

Before my son, Owen, had bipolar disorder, I never gave much thought to the grocery. Now I analyze every part of the trip—beginning with the time we go. The grocery is a great place to be early Sunday morning when it's not crowded. If I take him on weekends, especially during the afternoons, it's too loud, and he gets frustrated and begins to act out. I used to be embarrassed by this. No more. It's not an opera or a ballet, and if it disturbs people, they can skip the aisle. But taking him at less busy times maximizes the chances that we'll both have a good time.

I have developed a few rules for grocery shopping with Owen: I never take him when he doesn't want to go or when I'm in a real time crunch or having company (which I rarely do anymore); I reward him for buying healthy food and for staying calm by giving him the money we save on coupons at the end of the trip.

Even with all of these strategies, we still have good and bad days. But I've found that following my own rules generally makes shopping a whole lot easier.

Of course, if your child has an emotional storm at the store, it's entirely up to you whether you want to explain that he has bipolar disorder to complete strangers. But bear in mind that your child is with you and that, in the process of educating another person, you don't want to make your youngster feel inadequate or different from other kids.

On Eating Out

Eating in a restaurant offers its own forms of torment. Long waits. Noisy kitchens. Unfamiliar smells. The "wrong" food. And yet, getting your child used to eating out is important, and if carefully planned, it can be a nice break for the whole family. Picking the right restaurant is key; it's helpful to avoid those places that are noisy or overly crowded. And going early in the evening may make all the difference.

Often, one of the biggest hassles in restaurant-land is the menu. Chances are that your bipolar child doesn't like surprises, so when she finds out that Charlie's Diner only serves cheeseburgers after she's geared herself up for grilled cheese, you may have a problem on your hands. One parent I know solves this problem by keeping copies of menus from the family's favorite restaurants at home. Her youngster then has time to read the menu over, make some choices before leaving, and feel prepared. By the time she actually arrives at the restaurant, the problem of "menu surprise" has been eliminated.

In some cases, it may be best for you to ask for special accommodations for a child with sensory integration difficulties, such as needing to have her food cooked in a certain way or being seated at a table away from the kitchen. One parent helps her child by requesting a specific accommodation for herself. For example, she asks, "May we please have a table far away from the kitchen? I'm especially bothered by the noise." One day when her child is older, she'll be able to speak up for her own needs. But in this way, the mother has given her child a model of how to do it politely, and at the same time, she hasn't singled her out as different.

On Holiday Gatherings

No matter what holidays your family celebrates—Thanksgiving, Christmas, Chanukah, Kwanza, Ramadan—they're supposed to be joyful. But holidays are the times many parents of bipolar children dread the most. (Truth be told, so do lots of us.) And who could blame them? For a bipolar kid, many of these festive occasions are filled with ingredients for a recipe for disaster: a disruption of your routine (perhaps even different time zones), surprises, crowded houses, foods with different tastes and textures, and, in some cases, lots of unfamiliar people. A bipolar kid's impulsivity and anxiety seem to go into overdrive. Suddenly, he hasn't got the patience to wait until after dinner to begin opening the presents under the tree. He grabs for one, gets reprimanded by an aunt, tells off the aunt, and calls her an idiot. Many parents say that they want to run and hide because of the embarrassment and criticism that often results from these scenes. They also say that their holidays often end with relatives being annoyed at one another. (This may not, of course, seem unusual in *any* family! But in this case, it's caused by a child's actions or reactions.)

Some mothers and fathers circumvent holiday stresses altogether by writing a letter to their relatives in advance that explains bipolar disorder and the kinds of activities that may be difficult for their child. This strategy can be a good one. Although a few relatives may view your preemptive efforts as nothing more than an indulgence, most hosts will be only too happy to oblige in order to make the visit go smoothly. If not, you might want to consider staying in a hotel rather than butting heads throughout the visit.

In some cases, especially when a child is less than stable, parents may want to stay at home and plan a very low-key celebration with just the immediate family. Families often say that their child enjoys spending the holiday in a setting that's familiar and more predictable. Once the child's mood disorder is under good control for a while, it will once again be possible to travel to Grandma's (or another relative's house) at holiday time. If there is a seasonal component to your child's mood, you may want to visit in the summer when he's feeling happier. Here's how one family reintroduced holiday celebrations into their lives:

Like many families, we wanted all the good things associated with holidays. But the first few holidays we spent with our family and our bipolar child turned into disasters. Our relatives wondered why we didn't put Marisol in a fancy dress for the holiday pictures, like the other parents did. But our daughter doesn't like scratchy fabric, and she wouldn't wear the dress we picked out.

She is also sensitive to noise and touch, and of course, on our arrival, everyone wanted to hug, kiss, and talk at once. Marisol ran the other way. The next obstacle was the meal. Marisol didn't like the turkey, and sitting down for too long was an issue. My in-laws have a policy that kids don't leave the table until they've eaten everything on their plates. You can imagine how that went over with Marisol.

And just when we thought the worst was over, she got into a fight with a cousin who, understandably, did not care that things had to be Marisol's way or else. By the end of the day, Marisol was hot, hungry, and just plain miserable.

We thought we would fix things by having the gatherings at our house, but it was not that simple. The day still lacked the structure that Marisol lives by. All things considered, we decided to take a break from holiday gatherings while we worked to find the right mix of medications for our daughter.

Eventually, we began to ease ourselves back into visiting the relatives on holidays, and as we did so, we became more practical in our approach. We found that the key to making things work was planning and then sharing the plan for the day with our child. These days, we have an extensive talk with Marisol about the day ahead and the help she might need from us to handle the situation if something starts to go wrong.

At the same time, we talk candidly with our relatives about Marisol's needs and some of her unusual behaviors and try to involve the family in our plans. They now call to ask us what Marisol is eating these days; they even remember the ketchup with the microwave hot dogs. Our friends remember that she likes her hamburger grilled on tin foil, without having us remind them. We no longer make Marisol wear certain clothes, and we always pack additional ones. (There's nothing wrong with shorts in the winter inside the house.)

We ask Marisol to stay at the table only until after the blessing. When company comes for holidays, we often have buffets instead of sit-down meals. We bring along Marisol's game cube and DVD player and some new games that help break the ice with her cousins. We've also designated a "quiet" room. If Marisol is feeling overwhelmed, she can go to this room for some peace and quiet—no questions asked.

I'm happy to report that now, five years after our first holiday disaster, we actually look forward to our celebrations with the relatives, but the adjustments we've made have been key in getting us to this point.

On Helping Kids Have Friends

One very important part of a child's education and social development comes not from the home or the classroom but from peer relationships. In childhood friendships, kids have the potential to learn a great deal: how to share, compromise, and work as part of a team. Friendship provides an opportunity for a child to explore his leadership skills and to learn how to mentor and be mentored. As with all human relationships, there are times of joy, pain, discovery, confusion, soul-searching, and growth. If you are unable to experience good peer relationships when you're young, you lag behind others in your age-group.

A bipolar kid can have a wicked sense of humor but may still have traits that destroy friendships. If he must always be the boss, tell other kids the *right* way to do things, be the leader in games, and accuse others of cheating when he loses, it's not going to help him win any popularity contests. Consequently, bipolar kids often need a hand at learning how to be good friends. Here's how one father helped his son to make and keep buddies:

My son, Evan, knows he is different, and he struggles to fit in with other children. He is not athletic or physical, so sports activities are not only unappealing, they are isolating.

Sometimes, I can help maneuver Evan's peers into participating in an activity at which he excels. I'll ask, "Have you ever played chess?" Then I challenge the other kids to play me to see if they can beat me. After they beat me (which they inevitably do), I say, "You should play my son; he's really good." While they're playing, the kids get to know each other, and they develop respect for Evan and his confidence soars.

My wife and I keep a close watch during playdates. If Evan seems overwhelmed or isolated, one of us asks if he wants to go for a short walk or take a drive. Meanwhile, we make sure his guest(s) are kept busy (for example, with video or computer games). When Evan comes back, he's usually calmer and able to rejoin his peers.

Of course, it's not always an option to take a short walk when your child has a meltdown during a playdate. You may need to talk to him in another room or send the other child home. At times when your child is impulsive and reacting in the moment, you may need to step in as his "surrogate brain," serving as his intermediary with the world around him.

The best way to curb meltdowns, though, is to take preemptive action. When first setting up playdates with a new friend, it's wisest to plan short (perhaps hour-long) visits and invite the other mother to stay for coffee. This way, you have one grown-up per kid, much better odds than two kids against one adult! You may decide to meet at a fast food restaurant, just to see if the youngsters are compatible in a neutral setting. If they're both having lunch, it is harder to compete with each other, and everybody gets something. There's less chance that the kids will end up being annoyed with each other.

By slowly increasing the number and length of these outings, you may find one day that your child wants to stay for a few more hours or that he doesn't want his friend to leave. If you think there's a good chance that he'll get tired and begin to lose it, just say "no." You want him to leave the playdate with a sense of success, not failure. If, on another day, you think your child isn't going to make it through a short playdate, even with you around, listen to the voice within you and postpone it. You're better off with him tantruming in the privacy of your own home than in front of a peer. If your child's mood is off, then reasoning with him is of limited effectiveness. And you don't want him to be embarrassed later.

Many parents particularly dread birthday parties, where a youngster will be interacting with many other children all at once. Again, this is a situation in which you may have to serve as your youngster's surrogate brain. That may mean going with him to the party—no matter his age. This has to be done with some finesse, however. When a child is younger, accompanying him to a party is no big deal—all the parents are doing the same thing. But by the time he's seven or eight, you may have to devise a clever reason for why you're around. This may mean calling the other child's mother in advance, discussing the situation, and perhaps planning an excuse for why you'll appear on the scene. ("I'm helping Syd's mom with the refreshments." Or, "Caroline's parents need an extra hand at the bowling alley.") This will keep your youngster from being embarrassed when the other parents drop off their kids and wave goodbye.

Of course, there will always be other mothers who think you're too anxious and treat your child like a baby. So what? Your child needs you, and if your being there will allow him to have a good time and be successful with his peers at the birthday party, then so be it. Many people who don't know any better consider parents of bipolar children to be overprotective. But those people fail to understand that you spend almost every ounce of your available energy focusing on your bipolar child. And believe me, it's likely they'd be doing the same thing if they were in your shoes.

On Family Outings

Playdates and birthday parties only last a couple of hours. But taking a vacation or even going on a trip to a museum with a bipolar child can be more challenging. After a few false starts, one family learned some new techniques with their bipolar child to turn their family outings into fun.

The minute we parked the car and hit the street, I knew something was wrong. Our youngest son, who had been full of questions about that day's trip to the Museum of Natural History, grabbed my hand and stopped talking. I told myself he was just taking it all in. We walked through Central Park, and he clung to me, begging to be picked up.

We pressed on. Arriving at the museum would perk him up, we thought. We went on a whirlwind tour of the museum, which ended with a life-size skeleton of a dinosaur. It so traumatized him that we never spoke of it again. (When fear spread over his face, we realized that it was tied to the nightmares he once had about a skeleton.) We then dragged our weary travelers to a restaurant. All the kids wanted to do was go home.

My husband and I were confused. We thought we had planned this excursion so carefully. First a brisk walk to shake off the car ride, taking in the architecture and people watching along the way. We showed all the children the buildings and points of interest. It wasn't until later that we made the connection between too much sensory input and my son's subsequent meltdown. The uncertainty of our impromptu schedule and the energy of the city thrown at him all at once were too much. He was telling us, "I'm exhausted," and we thought he was saying, "I don't want to walk."

Since then, we've become more skilled at planning trips. We build in time to rest during our journey and provide safe havens within the adventure. We don't expect the children to be able to keep an adult pace. If one is opposed to seeing the IMAX movie, we agree to pick something else or split up for awhile. Maybe our children are in better places emotionally, or maybe we as a family just know each other better. Either way, we have found our pace, and family trips are a blast!

On Life Cycle Events

Weddings, funerals, and religious ceremonies can be particularly difficult times for bipolar children and their families. These occasions are so far from the child's daily routine—with so many unfamiliar people suddenly appearing on the scene—that they make most bipolar kids uncomfortable. There are too many deviations from the usual schedule.

Bipolar kids may have times when they want to be the center of the universe and the life of the party, but they want to be able to decide *when* this occurs. Otherwise, they can feel extremely anxious and easily lose self-control. Here's how one family turned a potentially stressful life cyle event—a child's Bar Mitzvah—into a fulfilling occasion for everyone:

When it came time for my son Mason's Bar Mitzvah, I was totally perplexed and stressed about how to celebrate it. His older brother and sister had traditional parties—large affairs with relatives, many friends, disk jockeys, and dancing. They had stood in the synagogue in front of friends, family, and complete strangers who looked on as they recited prayers in Hebrew and made a speech.

Although my son had taken Hebrew lessons and had a real affinity for the language, he decided a traditional Bar Mitzvah would be too much for him. We couldn't help but wonder: "Would he feel deprived if he had something different? Should he have something at all? Would he have a meltdown?"

But we realized that the most important thing was to have a celebration that would suit him and make him happy to be Jewish—not to put pressure

on him that would make him feel unhappy and resentful of the entire process. It didn't matter what others thought—I have learned to focus on
what is best for my son and what would make him proud.

At first, I thought maybe it was best to have no type of service at all.
But the cantor, who knew my son from birth, encouraged me to have a
service and promised me that it would be something special that my son
would feel really great about. Our synagogue had a brand new rabbi, and
this was to be her first Bar Mitzvah.

I told my son that clothes didn't matter, that how much he did truly
didn't matter—that what mattered was that he wanted to do this. So instead of holding the service in the sanctuary, we decided it would be in a
small, private chapel and at a time when no other people were in the synagogue. My son had a few private Hebrew lessons, learned some prayers
very well, and was ready.

When we first met the rabbi, Mason decided to test her by shooting some
spitballs her way. She was unfazed. She began by asking what was important in his life. He told her it was his computer and video games. At first, I
was embarrassed (I always think that when he says things like this, it's his
"bipolar" talking). But the rabbi assured me that almost every thirteen-year-
old boy she deals with says video games or TV. She told him to think about it
and come next time and tell her. The next time, he told her that the most important thing was something he had learned from his mother. "She taught me
not to judge myself by what other people think about me."

When the day came for the Bar Mitzvah, Mason wanted to wear only a
T-shirt, shorts, and sneakers. The rabbi encouraged him to add a shirt with
a collar out of respect and to feel that the day was special. He wore it over
his T-shirt. I made certain that he was not the only person in shorts—so he
wouldn't feel uncomfortable. When we arrived at the synagogue, he asked
that no one talk to him until after the service, and we respected his wishes.

The service came off without a hitch. Every person who attended was
very close to us and knew how hard it was for my son to make it to that
point. Everyone was crying, including the rabbi and the cantor.

For the dinner afterward, we picked Mason's favorite Spanish restaurant—
one that had a casual atmosphere, served the kind of food he liked, and made

him comfortable. My husband and I checked it out in advance to make sure the place wasn't too noisy and that it didn't have another party booked for that day. We knew that the presence of too many strangers would unsettle him.

On the way to the restaurant, my son took off his collared shirt and proceeded to have a great time. Of my three children's Bar Mitzvahs, I ended up enjoying this one the most.

After the whole thing was done, I realized that the lesson I taught my son had come back to me. As parents, we cannot and must not judge ourselves by what others think about our children or our parenting. But if we listen to our kids and respect their needs, things can turn out beautifully.

On Life with Siblings

No matter what you and your family plan to do, siblings of a bipolar child quickly learn that all can be changed or ruined at the drop of a hat. Everything depends on the bipolar child's mood that day. Having friends over requires great care for the sibling, as it's never certain that the bipolar brother or sister won't say something nasty or embarrassing. In fact, many kids who have grown up with a bipolar sibling describe feeling terrorized by their unpredictable brother or sister. They recall getting hit, bullied, and teased only to have their parents tell them that they needed to understand that "Jerrell has a problem, so he can't help his behavior."

All siblings fight to one degree or another, but the battles between bipolar kids and their siblings add new meaning to the term *sibling rivalry*. Take the case of ten-year-old Joaquin and his bipolar sister, Susannah, age eight. At one time, the daily battles between the two became so pronounced that the parents took to driving the children in separate cars when they were traveling. Here's how the mother describes it:

Weekend activities that we used to do together had to be scrapped in favor of each adult taking the other child away for the day, evening, or whole weekend.

On weekdays, I had to leave work early every day to be home the minute they got off the bus, as they would get in huge fights if they were in the house for twenty minutes by themselves. Once, when I didn't make it home in time, Susannah kicked a huge hole in the bedroom door.

Every transaction that involved a family decision—for example, where to eat or when to head to the beach—triggered a loud chorus of "I never get to choose." To prevent this, we had to carefully ask my daughter's opinion and carefully react to it. My husband and I made many decisions based on what would keep her calmest.

At one point, Susannah started dressing in a dark "gothic" way that freaked out my very straight-laced son (they go to the same school). He was very embarrassed by her appearance. When she came downstairs for breakfast, he would give her a "look" that precipitated a huge blowup. In retaliation, she sometimes tried to embarrass him on the bus, either by criticizing him or by being overly affectionate or greeting him loudly at school.

No matter whether he responded or just looked at her, a fight would break out. Breakfast had to be done in two different sittings to avoid some of the problems. Joaquin rarely had a friend come over, as he was afraid she would lose it when someone was over. He became overly involved in just doing schoolwork, refusing to participate in outside activities.

When Susannah had to go to the emergency room because she was talking about killing herself, my son suffered tremendous guilt for months afterward, as he felt he drove her to it. He went to counseling and was put on medication to help him with depression.

Although some siblings limit their fighting to wars of words, it's not uncommon for me to hear from moms of bipolar kids that their children come to blows. The first rule in these instances is safety—no one is allowed to harm another person, no matter what the situation. I advise parents to console the child who's hurt but also to label any violent behavior as totally unacceptable. Separating the kids and enforcing a cooling-off period is often a good first step. What you do will vary with each child and the seriousness of the situation. It's important to get all the information first and to not always assume that

the bipolar child is at fault. Sometimes, the sibling may have insti-
gated the situation just to get the bipolar child in trouble.

Many nonbipolar siblings experience their family as different from
those of their peers, and they're angry that their parents don't protect them. Such was the case with seven-year-old Mindy, who referred to her parents as "Clark lovers" for the slack they seemed to
cut her bipolar brother. Mindy felt that no one listened to her and
that her older brother was the one her parents really cared for.

Feelings of anger and jealousy such as the ones Mindy and Joaquin
harbored need to be addressed before a sibling begins to seek attention by acting out. It's important to carve out regular time to spend
with the nonbipolar sibling. Again, using the divide-and-conquer
approach, with one parent taking the nonbipolar child on an outing
while the other plans an activity for the bipolar youngster, can be an
effective means of making the nonbipolar child feel special.

Finding an interest or hobby that a bipolar youngster and his sibling
can share may also be helpful. It was man's best friend who brought together the siblings in one family. As the mom recalled:

*It had always been extremely difficult for my nine-year-old daughter, Carrie,
to deal with her brother, Oliver, then seven. There were times that she was
embarrassed to have friends visit. Often, she was angry at him, and they
argued to the point where I had to separate them. In many ways, the first
half of their childhood was a blur; I spent most of my time putting out emotional fires.*

*Our lives began to change when we learned we were getting a golden re-
triever puppy to be a service dog for my bipolar son. We had applied for the
dog from a nonprofit agency, and before he arrived, the kids went to the library together to read up on how to care for our soon-to-be pet. When the
dog finally arrived, so did a trainer.*

*She taught my daughter how to train her brother's service dog, and Carrie
rose to the challenge. She walked the puppy, corrected him, went to group
classes, and came along with her brother on trips to the mall, where we so-
cialized the dog and had him practice his "sit stays." The sibling became the*

teacher, and we moved from a bipolar/PDD NOS—focused home to a dog-focused home.

My son loves his golden. He talks about the dog, talks to the dog, draws pictures of dogs, writes current event articles for school about dogs, and is otherwise obsessed. However, it is my daughter who has been most affected by the experience. In helping the dog learn his "social skills," she's also come to understand her brother better and be closer to him. While I can't say there's never a fight between the two of them, there are far fewer fires to put out these days. I'm very thankful for our canine friend and what he's done to bring my kids closer. Believe me, I'd much rather sit and watch the dog sleep than deal with two children fighting.

Sometimes, a dramatic change can occur in siblings' relationship when the bipolar child's mood is stabilized. When I first saw nine-year-old Max, for instance, he was in a mixed bipolar state and said that one of his three wishes was that his sister Judy, age six, would die. Although he was verbally abusive to her, he never physically tried to injure her. His drawings depicted bad things happening to Judy. Once his mood became stable, however, their relationship started to shift. After a few months of calling a truce, he and his sister began to play together. Now, he even gives her horsey-back rides. In Max's case, medication made a dramatic difference in the sibling relationship.

Sometimes, siblings get help coping with a difficult brother or sister by attending individual, family, or group therapy. The latter, of course, lets brothers and sisters know that they're not alone in their worry, shame, and anger over living with a bipolar sibling. As one sister put it, "It was comforting to know that I wasn't the only one living with a weird brother."

In the end, some adults report that they have only positive memories of growing up with a bipolar sibling. Jenny, who remembers her early years with a bipolar sister, described it in this way:

Growing up, my childhood was filled with adventure. I didn't even know about my sister Veronica's bipolar disorder. She was eighteen months my elder, and we did everything together. From 1966 to 1981, our family moved eleven times. This created a bond between my siblings and me that would lead to many years of friendship and loyalty. We became our own entertainment.

The leader of it all was Veronica. Spurred on by her enthusiasm, we would present fantastic performances at family dinners and parties. We created costumes from nothing, wrote elaborate stories, and choreographed dances. Veronica had magic at her fingertips and the music to accompany any occasion.

We spent summers building fantastic forts and creating worlds of imagination that seemed to us to be natural at the time. My sister would spin a tale, and we would spend days pretending to be the characters that she created. We made Barbie dollhouses from my father's extensive reference book collection and attached bedsheets to fans to create the air-conditioned tunnels that were required for hours of fun in an attic in July.

It was no surprise to me that Veronica grew up to be one of the most talented costume designers in her field. She has an incredible ability to picture designs vividly in her head as well as the flow of the fabric, the play of the light on the colors, and the actors' movements. She designs jewelry as well, and it is spectacular.

Thanks to my sister, my children have the best birthday parties on the block—themes to the max! A ten-foot teepee for the cowboy campout in 2001 blew our guests away. Two pirate ships, a treasure hunt, and fantastic sword fight in 2002 gave my boys the reputation of having the coolest parties of all time. There was also the year when my sister turned my home into the Millennium Falcon and provided the crew from Star Wars—all for budgets that would make you laugh.

I feel blessed that my children have enjoyed the same imagination-filled childhood that I cherished. This is a tall order for practical people. Whenever you need a miracle, you need magical people to get the job done.

Living with a bipolar child is an adventure (to say the least). I know that it often feels as though no one around realizes how almost every bit of daily life requires extra work on your part to help your child make it in the real world. How tiring it is both physically and emotionally! But just as a therapist has to be creative and think of problems and solutions from many different angles, so do parents of bipolar kids—many times each day.

The parents in this chapter and throughout this book have devised their own creative strategies for dealing with their real-life situations. My hope is that their experiences and solutions will be useful to you as you guide your child to adulthood.

It is important to keep in mind that despite the land mines you may avoid by modifying your limit-setting in raising your bipolar child, you are his most important teacher. Your goal is to help your child fit into the world he lives in, as the world won't change to fit him. Part of the way to achieve this goal is by remembering that there are times you must take a stand to help your child learn proper behavior and distinguish betweeen right and wrong. He may not want to hear it, and it may not be easy for you either, but these are some of the battles you may have to tough out in order for your child to learn crucial life skills and socially appropriate behavior.

Although others may not recognize it, raising a spirited bipolar child is an enormous task. Give yourself tremendous credit for rising to the challenge!

Epilogue

Learning that your child has bipolar disorder can be scary and intimidating. But a bipolar diagnosis is also an opportunity—one that can be life-saving for your youngster.

Take some comfort in knowing that you are not alone—that there are many who live with and love these unpredictable yet wonderful children. Also take heart in the increasing public awareness of this complex disorder and the dramatic pace at which pediatric bipolar research is proceeding. Both are factors that can only serve to better your child's life in the years to come.

I urge you to go beyond the pages of this book to learn as much as you can about childhood bipolar disorder because it will be *your* advocacy and *your* knowledge that can help your child grow into an independent, responsible, and loving adult. Keep in mind that helping your bipolar child develop mastery over his condition may be a long journey, one requiring patience, practice, energy, a great support group, and a sense of humor along the way. May you have the courage to keep going—and the wisdom to "listen to the words, not just the music." The rewards can be no less than life-changing for you, your family, and your child.

Notes

Introduction

1. R. M. Hirschfeld, Lydia Lewis, and Lana Vornik, Perceptions and impact of bipolar disorder: How far have we really come? Results of the National Depressive and Manic-Depressive Association 2000 survey of individuals with bipolar disorder, *Journal of Clinical Psychiatry* 64 (2003): 161.

2. Child and Adolescent Bipolar Foundation, www.bpkids.org; Juvenile Bipolar Research Foundation, www.jbrf.org.

3. M. N. Pavuluri, B. Birmaher, and M. W. Naylor, Pediatric bipolar disorder: A review of the past 10 years, *Journal of the American Academy of Child and Adolescent Psychiatry* 44 (2005): 846.

Chapter 1
Listen to the Words, Not Just the Music

1. N. Craddock and I. Jones, Genetics of bipolar disorder, *Journal of Medical Genetics* 36 (1999): 585. N. Craddock and I. Jones, Molecular genetics of bipolar disorder, *British Journal of Psychiatry* 178 (2001): S128–S133.

2. J. Kaufman and H. Blumberg, Neurobiology of early-onset mood disorders, in A. Martin, L. Scahill, D. S. Charney, and J. F. Leckman, eds., *Pediatric Psychopharmacology Principles and Practice* (New York: Oxford University Press, 2003).

3. L. L. Altshuler, G. Bartzokis, T. Grieder, et al., An MRI study of temporal lobe structures in men with bipolar disorder or schizophrenia, *Biological Psychiatry* 48 (2000): 147; S. M. Strakowski, M. P. DelBello, K. W. Sax, et al., Brain magnetic resonance imaging of structural abnormalities in bipolar disorder,

Archives of General Psychiatry 56 (1999): 254; V. W. Swayze II, N. C. Andreason, R. J. Alliger, et al., Subcortical and temporal structures in affective disorders and schizophrenia: A magnetic magnetic resonance imaging study, *Biological Psychiatry* 31 (1992): 221.

4. R. A. Kowatch, M. Fristad, B. Birmaher, et al., Treatment guidelines for children and adolescents with bipolar disorder, (special communication) *Journal of the American Academy of Child and Adolescent Psychiatry* 44 (March 2005): 213.

5. N. Craddock and I. Jones, Genetics of bipolar disorder, *Journal of Medical Genetics* 36 (1999): 585; N. Craddock and I. Jones, Molecular genetics of bipolar disorder, *British Journal of Psychiatry* 178 (2001): S128–S133.

6. R. M. Hirschfeld, Lydia Lewis, and Lana Vornik, Perceptions and impact of bipolar disorder: How far have we really come? Results of the National Depressive and Manic-Depressive Association 2000 survey of individuals with bipolar disorder, *Journal of Clinical Psychiatry* 64 (2003): 161; M. Hyun, S. D. Friedman, and D. L. Dunner, Relationship of childhood physical and sexual abuse to adult bipolar disorder, *Bipolar Disorder* (June 2, 2000) 2: 131; The psychosocial correlates of the recurrence of Bipolar I Disorder from the National Comorbidity Survey, paper presented at the Second International Conference on Bipolar Disorder, poster session, June 1997; S. Malkoff-Schwartz, E. Frank, B. Anderson, et al., Stressful life events and social rhythm disruption in the onset of manic and depressive bipolar episodes, *Archives of General Psychiatry* 55 (1998): 702.

Chapter 2
Depression and Mania: Riding the Mood Pendulum

1. R. M. Hirschfeld, Lydia Lewis, and Lana Vornik, Perceptions and impact of bipolar disorder: How far have we really come? Results of the National Depressive and Manic-Depressive Association 2000 survey of individuals with bipolar disorder, *Journal of Clinical Psychiatry* 64 (2003): 161.

2. J. Luby, A. Heffelfinger, et al., The clinical picture of depression in preschool children, *Journal of the American Academy of Child and Adolescent Psychiatry* 42 (2003): 340.

3. B. Geller and J. Luby, Child and adolescent bipolar disorder: A review of the past 10 years, *Journal of the American Academy of Child and Adolescent Psychiatry* 36 (1997): 1168.

4. R. E. Davis, Manic-depressive variant syndrome of childhood: A preliminary report, *American Journal of Psychiatry* 136 (1979): 702.

5. S. L. McElroy, P. E. Keck, H. G. Pope, et al., Clinical and research implications of the diagnosis of dysphoric or mixed mania or hypomania, *American Journal of Psychiatry* 149 (1992): 1633.

6. Geller and Luby, Child and adolescent bipolar disorder; J. Wozniak, J. Biederman, K. Kiely, et al., Mania-like symptoms suggestive of childhood onset bipolar disorder in clinically referred children, *Journal of the American Academy of Child and Adolescent Psychiatry* 34 (1995): 867.

7. Wozniak et al., Mania-like symptoms.

Chapter 3
The Hidden Aspects of Bipolar Disorder

1. A. G. Harvey, D. A. Schmidt, A. Scarna, et al., Sleep-related functioning in euthymic patients with bipolar disorder, patients with insomnia, and subjects without sleep problems, *American Journal of Psychiatry* 162 (2005): 50.

2. D. Papolos, personal communication, 1998.

3. Ibid.

4. C. Popper, Diagnosing Bipolar vs. ADHD: A pharmacologic point of view, *The Link* 13 (1996).

5. J. Wurtman, Carbohydrate craving, mood changes, and obesity, *Journal of Clinical Psychiatry* 49 (1989): S37; R. J. Wurtman and J. J. Wurtman, Carbohydrates and depression, *Scientific American* (January 1989): 68; R. J. Wurtman et al., Carbohydrate cravings, obesity and brain serotonin, *Appetite* 7 (1986): S99.

6. L. B. Christensen and L. Pettijohn, Mood and carbohydrate cravings, *Appetite* 36 (2001): 137.

7. N. E. Rosenthal, *Winter Blues: Seasonal Affective Disorder—What It Is and How to Overcome It* (New York: Guilford Press, 1993).

Chapter 4
How Bipolar Kids Shine

1. D. I. Simeonova, K. D. Chang, C. Strong, et al., Creativity in familial bipolar disorder, *Journal of Psychiatric Research* 39 (2005): 623.

2. Stanford University School of Medicine, Children of bipolar parents score higher on creativity test, Stanford study finds, press release, November 8, 2005.

3. Ibid.

4. C. M. Strong and T. Ketter, Negative affective traits and openness have differential relationships to creativity, 155th Annual Meeting of the American Psychiatric Association, Philadelphia, 2002.

5. Ibid.

6. N. C. Andreasen, Creativity and mental illness: Prevalence rates in writers and their first degree relatives, *American Journal of Psychiatry* 144 (1987): 1288.

7. A. M. Ludwig, Creative mental illness in female writers, *American Journal of Psychiatry* 151 (1994): 1650.

8. D. J. Hershman and J. Lieb, *Manic Depression and Creativity* (Amherst, NY: Prometheus Books, 1998).

9. Ibid.

10. The Churchill Papers at the Churchill Archives Centre, Cambridge University Reference: CHAR 28/44/04.

11. Hershman and Lieb, *Manic Depression and Creativity;* W. J. Boerst, *Isaac Newton: Organizing the Universe* (Greensboro, NC: Morgan Reynolds, 2004); The Newton Project, www.newtonproject.ic.ac.uk/.

12. Churchill Papers.

13. Ibid.

14. Ibid.

15. Hershman and Lieb, *Manic Depression and Creativity.*

16. Churchill Papers.

17. Hershman and Lieb, *Manic Depression and Creativity.*

18. T. O. Mabbott, ed., *The Collected Works of Edgar Allan Poe*, vol. 1, *Poems* (Cambridge, MA: Belknap Press of Harvard University Press, 1969).

19. J. McManamy, The warped muse, available at www.mcmanweb.com.

Chapter 5
The Psychiatric Evaluation:
Finding a Doctor and Examining Your Child's Symptoms

1. J. A Egeland, J. A. Shaw, J. Endicott, et al., Prospective study of prodromal features for bipolarity in well Amish children, *Journal of the American Academy of Child and Adolescent Psychiatry* 42 (2003): 786; J. A. Shaw, J. A. Egeland, J. Endicott, et al., A 10-year prospective study of prodromal patterns for bipolar disorder among Amish youth, *Journal of the American Academy of Child and Adolescent Psychiatry* 44 (2005): 1104–1111.

2. N. E. Rosenthal, *Winter Blues: Seasonal Affective Disorder—What It Is and How to Overcome It* (New York: Guilford Press, 1993).

Chapter 6
Comorbidity:
Is This Bipolar Disorder or Something Else?

1. J. Biederman, S. V. Faraone, E. Mick, et al., Attention deficit hyperactivity disorder and juvenile mania: An overlooked comorbidity? *Journal of the American Academy of Child and Adolescent Psychiatry* 35 (1996): 997; F. S. Butler, D. E. Arredondo, and V. McCloskey, Affective comorbidity in children and adolescents with attention deficit hyperactivity disorder, *Annals of Clinical Psychiatry* 7 (1995): 51.

2. S. West, S. McElroy, S. Strakowski, et al., Attention deficit hyperactivity disorder in adolescent mania, *American Journal of Psychiatry* 152 (1995): 271; J. Wozniak, J. Biederman, K. Kiely, et al., Mania-like symptoms suggestive of childhood onset bipolar disorder in clinically referred children, *Journal of the American Academy of Child and Adolescent Psychiatry* 34 (1995): 867.

3. C. Popper, Diagnosing Bipolar vs. ADHD: A pharmacologic point of view, *The Link* 13 (1996).

4. Wozniak et al., Mania-like symptoms.

5. Ibid.

6. Popper, Diagnosing Bipolar vs. ADHD.

7. Department of Health and Human Services, Centers for Disease Control and Prevention, Autism: How common are autism spectrum disorders? available at www.cdc.gov/ncbddd/autism/ads_common/htm.

Chapter 7
Medication:
The Art and Science of Treatment

1. L. Tondo, R. J. Baldessarini, R. J. Hennen, et al., Lithium treatment and risk of suicidial behavior in bipolar disorder patients, *Journal of Clinical Psychiatry* 59(1998): 405.

2. M. Strober, W. Morrell, C. Lampert, et al., Relapse following discontinuation of lithium maintenance therapy in adolescents with bipolar I illness: A naturalistic study, *American Journal of Psychiatry* 147 (1990): 457.

3. A. C. Pande, J. G. Crockatt, C. A. Janney, et al., Gabapentin in bipolar disorder: A placebo-controlled trial of adjunctive therapy, Gabapentin bipolar study group, *Bipolar Disorders* (3Pt 2), 2 (2000): 249.

4. J. Biederman, E. Mick, J. Prince, et al., Systematic chart review of the pharmacologic treatment of comorbid attention deficit hyperactivity disorder

272   *Notes*

in use with bipolar disorder, *Journal of Child and Adolescent Psychopharmacology* 9 (1999): 247.

5. A. C. Leon, P. M. Marzuk, K. Tardiff, et al., Antidepressants and youth suicide in New York City, 1999–2002, *Journal of the American Academy of Child and Adolescent Psychiatry* 45 (2006): 1054.

6. A. L. Stoll, W. E. Severus, M. P. Freeman, et al., Omega 3 fatty acids in Bipolar Disorder, *Archives of General Psychiatry* 56 (1999): 407.

7. N. E. Rosenthal, *Winter Blues: Seasonal Affective Disorder—What It Is and How to Overcome It* (New York: Guilford Press, 1993).

8. C. W. Fetrow and J. R. Avila, *Professional's handbook of complimentary & alternative medicines,* 3rd ed. (Springhouse, PA: Lippincott Williams & Wilkins, 2004).

Chapter 8
Why Therapy Matters

1. D. Miklowitz, E. L. George, J. A. Richards, et al., A randomized study of family focused pyschoeducation and pharmachotherapy in the outpatient management of bipolar disorder, *Archives of General Psychiatry* 60 (2003): 904; M. Rea, M. Tompson, D. Miklowitz, et al., Family-focused treatment vs. individual treatment for bipolar disorder: Results of a randomized clinical trial, *Journal of Consulting and Clinical Psychology* 71 (2003): 482.

2. J. March et al., Treatment of Adolescent Depression Study, *Journal of the American Medical Association* 292 (2004): 807.

3. D. H. Lam, E. R. Watkins, and P. Hayward, A randomized controlled study of cognitive therapy for relapse prevention for bipolar affective disorder: Outcome of the first year, *Archives of General Psychiatry* 60: (2003) 145.

4. E. Frank, *Treating Bipolar Disorder: A Clinician's Guide to Interpersonal and Social Rhythm Therapy* (New York: Guilford Press, 2005).

5. E. Frank, D. J. Kupfer, M. E. Thase, et al., Two-year outcomes for interpersonal and social rhythm therapy in individuals with bipolar I disorder, *Archives of General Psychiatry* 62 (2005): 996.

6. S. Hlastala and E. Frank, Adapting interpersonal and social rhythm therapy to the developmental needs of adolescents with bipolar disorder, *Development and Psychopathology* 18 (2006): 1267.

7. R. Greene, *The Explosive Child: A New Approach for Understanding and Parenting Easily Frustrated, Chronically Inflexible Children, 2001,* (New York: HarperCollins, 1998).

8. Ibid.

9. D. Miklowitz, E. L. George, J. A. Richards, et al., A randomized study of family focused pyschoeducation and pharmachotherapy in the outpatient management of bipolar disorder, *Archives of General Psychiatry* 60 (2003): 904; M. Rea, M. Tompson, D. Miklowitz, et al., Family-focused treatment vs. individual treatment for bipolar disorder: Results of a randomized clinical trial, *Journal of Consulting and Clinical Psychology* 71 (2003): 482.

10. D. Miklowitz, E. L. George, D. A. Axelson, et al., Family-focused treatment for adolescents with bipolar disorder, *Journal of Affective Disorders*, 82 (2004), Suppl. 1: S113.

11. M. N. Pavuluri, P. A. Graczyk, D. B. Henry, et al., Child- and family-focused cognitive–behavioral therapy for pediatric bipolar disorder: Development and preliminary results, *Journal of the American Academy of Child and Adolescent Psychiatry* 43 (2004): 528.

12. M. A. Fristad, S. M. Gavazzi, and K. W. Soldano, Multi-family psychoeducation groups for childhood mood disorders: A program description and preliminary efficacy data, *Contemporary Family Therapy* 20 (1998): 385.

13. M. A. Fristad, J. S. Goldberg-Arnold, and S. M. Gavazzi, Multi-family psychoeducation groups (MFPG) for families of children with bipolar disorder, *Bipolar Disorders* 4 (2002) 254.

14. M. A. Fristad, Psychoeducational treatment for school-aged children with bipolar disorder, *Development and Psychopathology* (2006).

Chapter 10
Going to School: Easier Said Than Done

1. M. Levine, *A Mind at a Time* (New York: Simon & Schuster, 2002).

2. Regina Peter, personal communication, 2006.

3. D. A. Grant and E. A. Berg, A behavioral analysis of degree of reinforcement and ease of shifting to new responses in a Weigl-type card-sorting problem, *Journal of Experimental Psychology* 38 (1948): 404.

4. Michael Osit, personal communication, 2006.

5. Regina Peter, personal communication, 2006.

6. Thomas Brown, presentation at the 16th International CHADD Conference, Nashville, TN, October 2004.

7. D. C. Lagace, S. P. Kutcher, and H. A. Robertson, Mathematics deficits in adolescents with bipolar I disorder, *American Journal of Psychiatry* 160 (2003): 100.

8. Michael Osit, personal communication, 2006.

9. P. Decina, C. J. Kestenbaum, S. Farber, et al., Clinical and psychological assessment of children of bipolar probands, *American Journal of Psychiatry* 140 (1983):548.

10. P. McDonough-Ryan, M. DelBello, P. K. Shear, et al., Academic and cognitive abilities in children of parents with bipolar disorder: A test of the nonverbal learning disability model, *Journal of Clinical Experimental Neuropsychology* 24 (2002): 280.

11. E. B. McClure, J. E. Treland, J. Snow, et al., Deficits in social cognition and response flexibility in pediatric bipolar disorder, *American Journal of Psychiatry* 16 (2005): 1644; E. Leibenluft, B. Rich, and D. Pine, Fear circuit flares as bipolar youth misread faces, NIMH mood and anxiety disorders program and colleagues, May 29, 2006, Proceedings of the National Academy of Sciences.

12. Wrightslaw: Information and articles about special-education law, including IDEA and Section 504, and advocacy for children with disabilities, available at www.Wrightslaw.com.

References

Altshuler, L. L., G. Bartzokis, T. Grieder, et al. An MRI study of temporal lobe structures in men with bipolar disorder or schizophrenia. *Biological Psychiatry* 48 (2000): 147–162.

American Psychiatric Association. *Diagnostic and Statistical Manual of Mental Disorders*. IVTR, 2000.

Andreasen, N. C. Creativity and mental illness: Prevalence rates in writers and their first degree relatives. *American Journal of Psychiatry* 144 (1987): 1288–1292.

Autism Society of America. www.autism-society.org.

Biederman, J., S. V. Faraone, E. Mick, et al. Attention deficit hyperactivity disorder and juvenile mania: An overlooked comorbidity? *Journal of the American Academy of Child and Adolescent Psychiatry* 35 (1996): 997–1008.

Biederman, J., E. Mick, J. Prince, et al. Systematic chart review of the pharmacologic treatment of comorbid attention deficit hyperactivity disorder in use with bipolar disorder. *Journal of Child and Adolescent Psychopharmacology* 9 (1999): 247–256.

Boerst, W. J. *Isaac Newton: Organizing the Universe*. Greensboro, NC: Morgan Reynolds, 2004.

Brown, Dr. Thomas. Presentation at the 16th International CHADD Conference, Nashville, TN, October 2004.

Butler, F. S., D. E. Arredondo, and V. McCloskey. Affective comorbidity in children and adolescents with attention deficit hyperactivity disorder. *Annals of Clinical Psychiatry* 7 (1995): 51–55.

Child and Adolescent Bipolar Foundation. www.bpkids.org.

Christensen, L. B., and L. Pettijohn. Mood and carbohydrate cravings. *Appetite* 36 (2001) 137–145.

The Churchill Papers at the Churchill Archives Centre. Cambridge University Reference: CHAR 28/44/04. www.winstonchurchill.org.

Craddock, N., and I. Jones. Genetics of bipolar disorder. *Journal of Medical Genetics* 36 (1999): 585–594.

_____. Molecular genetics of bipolar disorder. *British Journal of Psychiatry* 178 (2001): S128-S133.

Davis, R. E. Manic-depressive variant syndrome of childhood: A preliminary report. *American Journal of Psychiatry* 136 (1979): 702–706.

Decina, P., C. J. Kestenbaum, S. Farber, et al., Clinical and psychological assessment of children of bipolar probands. *American Journal of Psychiatry* 140 (1983): 548–553.

Department of Health and Human Services, Centers for Disease Control & Prevention. Autism: How common are autism spectrum disorders. Available at www.cdc.gov/ncbddd/autism/ads_common/htm.

Egeland, J., A. Shaw, J. Endicott, et al. Prospective study of prodromal features for bipolarity in well Amish children. *Journal of the American Academy of Child and Adolescent Psychiatry* 42 (2003): 786–796.

Fetrow, C. W., and J. R. Avila. *Professional's Handbook of Complimentary & Alternative Medicines*. 3rd ed. Springhouse, PA: Lippincott Williams & Wilkins, 2004.

Frank, E. *Treating Bipolar Disorder: A Clinician's Guide to Interpersonal and Social Rhythm Therapy*. New York: Guilford Press, 2005.

Frank, E., D. J. Kupfer, M. E. Thase, et al. Two-year outcomes for interpersonal and social rhythm therapy in individuals with bipolar I disorder. *Archives of General Psychiatry* 62 (2005): 996–1004.

Fristad, M. A. Psychoeducational treatment for school-aged children with bipolar disorder. *Development and Psychopathology* (2006).

Fristad, M. A., S. M. Gavazzi, and K. W. Soldano. Multi-family psychoeducation groups for childhood mood disorders: A program description and preliminary efficacy data. *Contemporary Family Therapy* 20 (1998): 385–402.

Fristad, M. A., J. S. Goldberg-Arnold, and S. M. Gavazzi. Multi-family psychoeducation groups (MFPG) for families of children with bipolar disorder. *Bipolar Disorders* 4 (2002) 254–262.

Geller, B., and J. Luby. Child and adolescent bipolar disorder: A review of the past 10 years. *Journal of the American Academy of Child and Adolescent Psychiatry* 36 (1997): 1168–1176.

Grant, D. A., and E. A. Berg. A behavioral analysis of degree of reinforcement and ease of shifting to new responses in a Weigl-type card-sorting problem. *Journal of Experimental Psychology* 38 (1948): 404–411.

Greene, R. Center for Creative Problem Solving. Available at www.explosive child.com.

_____. *The Explosive Child: A New Approach for Understanding and Parenting Easily Frustrated, Chronically Inflexible Children*. New York: Harper-Collins, 2001.

Harvey, A. G., D. A. Schmidt, A. Scarna, et al. Sleep-related functioning in euthymic patients with bipolar disorder, patients with insomnia, and subjects without sleep problems. *American Journal of Psychiatry* 162 (2005): 50–57.

Hershman, J., and J. Lieb. *Manic Depression and Creativity*. Amherst, NY: Prometheus Books, 1998.

Hirschfeld, R. M., Lydia Lewis, and Lana Vornik. Perceptions and impact of bipolar disorder: How far have we really come? Results of the National Depressive and Manic-Depressive Association 2000 survey of individuals with bipolar disorder. *Journal of Clinical Psychiatry* 64 (2003): 161–174.

Hlastala, S., and E. Frank. Adapting interpersonal and social rhythm therapy to the developmental needs of adolescents with bipolar disorder. *Development and Psychopathology* 18 (2006): 1267–1288.

Hyun, M., S. D. Friedman, and D. L. Dunner. Relationship of childhood physical and sexual abuse to adult bipolar disorder. *Bipolar Disorder* (June 2, 2000) 2: 131–135.

Juvenile Bipolar Research Foundation. www.jbrf.org.

Kaufman, J., and H. Blumberg. Neurobiology of early-onset mood disorders. In A. Martin, L. Scahill, D. S. Charney, and J. F. Leckman, eds., *Pediatric Psychopharmacology Principles and Practice*. New York: Oxford University Press, 2003.

Kowatch, R. A., M. Fristad, B. Birmaher, et al. Treatment guidelines for children and adolescents with bipolar disorder. (Special communication) *Journal of the American Academy of Child and Adolescent Psychiatry* 44 (March 2005): 213–223.

Lagace, D. C., S. P. Kutcher, and H. A. Robertson. Mathematics deficits in adolescents with bipolar I disorder. *American Journal of Psychiatry* 160 (2003): 100–104.

Lam, D. H., E. R. Watkins, and P. Hayward. A randomized controlled study of cognitive therapy for relapse prevention for bipolar affective disorder: Outcome of the first year. *Archives of General Psychiatry* 60 (2003): 145–152.

Leibenluft, E., B. Rich, and D. Pine. Fear circuit flares as bipolar youth misread faces. NIMH mood and anxiety disorders program and colleagues, May 29, 2006, proceedings of the National Academy of Sciences.

Leon, A. C., P. M. Marzuk, K. Tardiff, et al. Antidepressants and youth suicide in New York City, 1999–2002. *Journal of the American Academy of Child and Adolescent Psychiatry* 45 (2006): 1054–1058.

Luby, J., J. L. Luby, A. Heffelfinger, et al. The clinical picture of depression in preschool children. *Journal of the American Academy of Child and Adolescent Psychiatry* 42 (2003): 340–348.

Ludwig, A. M. Creative mental illness in female writers. *American Journal of Psychiatry* 151 (1994): 1650–1656.

————. *The Price of Greatness: Resolving the Creativity and Madness Controversy.* New York: Guilford Press, 1995.

Mabbott, T. O., ed. *The Collected Works of Edgar Allan Poe,* vol. 1, *Poems.* Cambridge, MA: Belknap Press of Harvard University Press, 1969.

Malkoff-Schwartz, S., E. Frank, B. Anderson, et al. Stressful life events and social rhythm disruption in the onset of manic and depressive bipolar episodes. *Archives of General Psychiatry* 55 (1998): 702–770.

March, J., et al. Treatment of Adolescent Depression Study. *Journal of the American Medical Association* 292 (2004): 807–820.

McClure, E. B., J. E. Treland, J. Snow, et al. Deficits in social cognition and response flexibility in pediatric bipolar disorder. *American Journal of Psychiatry* 16 (2005): 1644–1651.

McDonough-Ryan, P., M. DelBello, P. K. Shear, et al. Academic and cognitive abilities in children of parents with bipolar disorder: A test of the nonverbal learning disability model. *Journal of Clinical Experimental Neuropsychology* 24 (2002): 280–285.

McElroy, S. L., P. E. Keck, H. G. Pope, et al. Clinical and research implications of the diagnosis of dysphoric or mixed mania or hypomania. *American Journal of Psychiatry* 149 (1992): 1633–1644.

McManamy, J. The warped muse. Available at www.mcmanweb.com.

Miklowitz, D., E. L. George, D. A. Axelson, et al. Family-focused treatment for adolescents with bipolar disorder. *Journal of Affective Disorders* 82 (2004): Suppl. 1: S113–S128.

Miklowitz, D., E. L. George, J. A. Richards, et al. A randomized study of family focused pyschoeducation and pharmachotherapy in the outpatient management of bipolar disorder. *Archives of General Psychiatry* 60 (2003): 904–912.

The Newton Project. www.newtonproject.ic.ac.uk/.

Osit, M. Personal communication. 2006.

Pande, A. C., J. G. Crockatt, C. A. Janney, et al. Gabapentin in bipolar disorder: A placebo-controlled trial of adjunctive therapy, Gabapentin bipolar study group. *Bipolar Disorders* (3Pt 2), 2 (2000): 249–255.

Papolos, D. Personal communication. 1998.

Pavuluri, M. N., B. Birmaher, M. W. Naylor. Pediatric bipolar disorder: A review of the past 10 years. *Journal of the American Academy of Child and Adolescent Psychiatry* 44 (2005): 846–871.

Pavuluri, M. N., P. A. Graczyk, D. B. Henry, et al. Child- and family-focused cognitive behavioral therapy for pediatric bipolar disorder: Development and preliminary results. *Journal of the American Academy of Child and Adolescent Psychiatry* 43 (2004): 528.

Peter, R. Personal communication. 2006.

Popper, C. Diagnosing Bipolar vs. ADHD: A pharmacologic point of view. *The Link* 13 (1996): .

Rea, M., M. Tompson, D. Miklowitz, et al. Family-focused treatment vs. individual treatment for bipolar disorder: Results of a randomized clinical trial. *Journal of Consulting and Clinical Psychology* 71 (2003): 482–492.

Rosenthal, N. E. *Winter Blues: Seasonal Affective Disorder—What It Is and How to Overcome It.* New York: Guilford Press, 1993.

Second International Conference on Bipolar Disorder. Poster Session. The psychosocial correlates of the recurrence of bipolar I disorder from the national comorbidity survey, June 1997.

Shaw, J. A., Egeland, J. Endicott, et al. A 10-year prospective study of prodromal patterns for bipolar disorder among Amish youth. *Journal of the American Academy of Child and Adolescent Psychiatry* 44 (2005): 1104–1111.

Simeonova, D. I., K. D. Chang, C. Strong, et al. Creativity in familial bipolar disorder. *Journal of Psychiatric Research* 39 (2005): 623–631.

Stanford University School of Medicine. Children of bipolar parents score higher on creativity test, Stanford study finds. Press release, November 8, 2005.

Stoll, A. L., W. E. Severus, M. P. Freeman, et al. Omega 3 Fatty Acids in Bipolar Disorder. *Archives of General Psychiatry* 56 (1999): 407–412.

Strakowski, S. M., M. P. DelBello, K. W. Sax, et al. Brain magnetic resonance imaging of structural abnormalities in bipolar disorder. *Archives of General Psychiatry* 56 (1999): 254–260.

Strober, M., W. Morrell, C. Lampert, et al. Relapse following discontinuation of lithium maintenance therapy in adolescents with bipolar I illness: A naturalistic study. *American Journal of Psychiatry* 147 (1990): 457–461.

Strong, C. M., and T. Ketter. Negative affective traits and openness have differential relationships to creativity. In 155th annual meeting of the American Psychiatric Association, Philadelphia, 2002.

Swayze II, V. W., N. C. Andreason, R. J. Alliger, et al. Subcortical and temporal structures in affective disorders and schizophrenia: A magnetic resonance imaging study. *Biological Psychiatry* 31 (1992): 221–240.

Tondo, L., R. J. Baldessarini, R. J. Hennen, et al. Lithium treatment and risk of suicidial behavior in bipolar disorder patients. *Journal of Clinical Psychiatry* 59(1998): 405–414.

West, S., S. McElroy, S. Strakowski, et al. Attention deficit hyperactivity disorder in adolescent mania. *American Journal of Psychiatry* 152 (1995): 271–274.

Wozniak, J., J. Biederman, K. Kiely, et al. Mania-like symptoms suggestive of childhood onset bipolar disorder in clinically referred children. *Journal of the American Academy of Child and Adolescent Psychiatry* 34 (1995): 867–876.

Wrightslaw. Information and articles about special education law, including IDEA and Section 504, and advocacy for children with disabilities. Available at www.Wrightslaw.com.

Wurtman, J. Carbohydrate craving, mood changes, and obesity. *Journal of Clinical Psychiatry* 49 (1989): S37–39.

Wurtman, R. J., and J. J. Wurtman. Carbohydrates and depression. *Scientific American* (January 1989): 68–75.

Wurtman, R. J., et al. Carbohydrate cravings, obesity and brain serotonin. *Appetite* 7 (1986): S99–103.

Resources

National Organizations
Focused Specifically on Bipolar Disorder

Child & Adolescent Bipolar Foundation (CABF)
Web site: www.bpkids.org
Phone: (847) 256-8525
Fax: (847) 920-9498
Address: 1000 Skokie Boulevard, Suite 570
Wilmette, IL 60091

Depression and Bipolar Support Alliance (DBSA)
Web site: www.dbsalliance.org
Phone: (800) 826-3632
Fax: (312) 642-7243
Address: 730 N. Franklin Street, Suite 501
Chicago, IL 60610-7224

Juvenile Bipolar Research Foundation (JBRF)
Web site: www.jbrf.org
Phone: (866) 333-JBRF (toll-free)
Fax: (973) 275-0420
Address: 550 Ridgewood Road
Maplewood, NJ 07040

Lithium Information Center
Web sites: www.miminc.org/index.asp
www.miminc.org/aboutlithinfoctr.html
Phone: (608) 827-2470
Fax: (608) 827-2479
Address: 7617 Mineral Point Road, Suite 300
Madison, WI 53717

National Organizations
Focused on Mental Health

American Academy of Child and
Adolescent Psychiatry (AACAP)
Web site: www.aacap.org
Phone: (202) 966-7300
Address: 3615 Wisconsin Avenue, NW
Washington, DC 20016-3007

Federation of Families for Children's Mental Health
Web site: www.ffcmh.org
Phone: (240) 403-1901
Address: 9605 Medical Center Drive
Rockville, MD 20850

NAMI Child and Adolescent Action Center
Web site: www.nami.org/Template.cfm?Section=Child_and_Adolescent_
    Action_Center
Phone: (703) 600-1117

National Alliance on Mental Illness (NAMI)
Web site: www.nami.org
Phone: (703) 524-7600
Address: 2107 Wilson Boulevard, Suite 300
Arlington, VA 22201-3042

National Institute of Mental Health (NIMH)
Web site: www.nimh.nih.gov/healthinformation/bipolarmenu.cfm
Phone: 1 (866) 615-6464 (toll-free)
Fax: (301) 443-4279
Address: Public Information and Communications Branch
6001 Executive Boulevard, Room 8184, MSC 9663
Bethesda, MD 20892-9663

National Mental Health Association (NMHA)
Web site: www.nmha.org
Phone: (703) 684-7722
Fax: (703) 684-5968
Address: 2000 N. Beauregard Street, 6th Floor
Alexandria, VA 22311

Co-occurring Conditions—Organizations and Clinics

Anxiety Disorders Association of America (ADAA)
Web site: www.adaa.org
Phone: (240) 485-1001
Fax: (240) 485-1035
Address: 8730 Georgia Avenue, Suite 600
Silver Spring, MD 20910

Children and Adults with Attention-Deficit/ Hyperactivity Disorder (CHADD)
Web site: www.chadd.org
Phone: (301) 306-7070
Fax: (301) 306-7090
Address: 8181 Professional Place, Suite 150
Landover, MD 20785

Obsessive-Compulsive Foundation (OCF)
Web site: www.ocfoundation.org
Phone: (203) 401-2070
Fax: (203) 401-2076
Address: 676 State Street
New Haven, CT 06511

Yale Developmental Disabilities Clinic
Web site: www.med.yale.edu/chldstdy/autism/index.html
Phone: (203) 785-2874
Fax: (203) 737-4197
Address: 230 South Frontage Road
PO Box 207900
New Haven, CT 06520-7900

Education Organizations

All Kinds of Minds (Dr. Mel Levine)
Web site: www.allkindsofminds.com
Phone: (888) 956-4637
Address (Chapel Hill office):1450 Raleigh Road, Suite 200
Chapel Hill, NC 27517
Address (New York office): 24-32 Union Square East, 6th Floor, Suite A
New York, NY 10003

Council for Exceptional Children (CEC)
Web site: www.cec.sped.org
Phone: (703) 620-3660
Fax: (703) 264-9494
Address: 1110 North Glebe Road, Suite 300
Arlington, VA 22201

Internet Resources

CDC Mental Health Organizations by State—Comprehensive list of state programs from the Centers for Disease Control. www.cdc.gov/mentalhealth/state_orgs.htm.

Child Anxiety Network—Site provides useful information about anxiety disorders in children and adolescents. www.childanxiety.net.

ERIC Clearinghouse on Disabilities and Gifted Education—Short summaries of reports on topics of interest to the education community, including federal education laws. www.hoagiesgifted.org/eric.

Familyeducation.com—Resource on homework, learning disabilities, special education, and other education topics. school.familyeducation.com/learning-disabilities/add-and-adhd/34388.html.

Helpguide. Lots of detailed information on bipolar disorder and co-occurring disorders. www.helpguide.org.

LD Online—Information on learning disabilities and ADHD, serving more than 220,000 parents, teachers, and other professionals each month. www .ldonline.org.

MAAP Services for Autism and Asperger Syndrome—Information, advice, and support for parents of children with Asperger Syndrome and other autistic spectrum disorders. www.asperger.org/.

Mary Sheedy Kurchinka, author of *Raising Your Spirited Child*—Resource information on spirited children. www.parentchildhelp.com.

Mayo Clinic—An introduction to bipolar disorder from one of the world's leading medical institutions. www.mayoclinic.com/health/bipolardisorder/ DS00356.

Medscape Psychiatry and Mental Health—Offers the latest news, mental health resources, and an ask-the-expert section. www.healthcentral.com/ common/frame.html?url=http://www.medscape.com/psychiatry-home.

National Center for Learning Disabilities—Provides information to parents and promotes research on learning disabilities. www.ncld.org.

OASIS (Online Asperger Syndrome Information and Support)—www.udel .edu/bkirby/asperger.

Rosalie Greenberg, MD, author of *Bipolar Kids: Helping Your Child Find Calm in the Mood Storm*—News, information on pediatric bipolar disorder, and author lecture schedule. www.RosalieGreenbergMD.com.

U.S. Department of Education Office of Special Education and Rehabilitative Services—Official government Web site offering information on IDEA, Section 504, and other education laws. www.ed.gov/about/offices/list/ osers/osep/index.html?src=mr.

Wrightslaw—Information and articles about special education law, including IDEA and Section 504, and advocacy for children with disabilities. www.Wrightslaw.com.

Children's Books

Brandon and the Bipolar Bear: A Story for Children with Bipolar Disorder. By Tracy Anglada. 2004. Ages 4 to 8.

Darcy Daisy and the Firefly Festival: Learning About Bipolar Disorder and Community. By Lisa M. Lewandowski, PhD , Shannon Trost, and Kimberly Shaw-Peterson. 2005. Ages 4 to 8.

Matt, the Moody Hermit Crab. By Caroline C. McGee. 2002. Ages 8 to 12 and
  beyond.

*Mind Race: A Firsthand Account of One Teenager's Experience with Bipolar Disor-
  der* (Adolescent Mental Health Initiative). By Patrick E. Jamieson and
  Moira A. Rynn. 2006. Teens and young adults.

My Bipolar Roller Coaster Feelings Book & Workbook. By Bryna Hebert; illustrated by Hannah, Jessica, and Matthew Hebert.

Recovering from Depression: A Workbook for Teens. By Mary Ellen Copeland and
  Stuart Copans. Teens.

The Ride. By Martha Davis. 2002. Available at www.marthadavis@patmedia.net.

Sometimes My Mommy Gets Angry. By Bebe Moore Campbell and E. B. Lewis.
  2003. Ages 4 to 8.

The Storm in My Brain. A free publication from the Child and Adolescent
  Bipolar Foundation and the Depression and Bipolar Support Alliance.

Turbo Max, a Story for Siblings of Bipolar Children. By Tracy Anglada. For siblings ages 8 to 12.

Index